International Guide to Privacy

**American Bar Association
Privacy & Computer Crime Committee
Section of Science & Technology Law**

Jody R. Westby, Project Chair & Editor

Section of Science & Technology Law

Cover design by ABA Publishing.

The materials contained herein represent the opinions and views of the authors and editors, and should not be construed to be the action of either the American Bar Association or the Section of Science & Technology unless adopted pursuant to the bylaws of the Association.

Nothing contained in this book is to be considered as the rendering of legal advice for specific cases, and readers are responsible for obtaining such advice from their own legal counsel. This book and any forms and agreements herein are intended for educational and informational purposes only.

©2004 American Bar Association. All rights reserved. No part of this publication may be reproduced, stored in a retrieval system, or transmitted in any form or by any means, electronic, mechanical, photocopying, recording, or otherwise, without the prior written permission of the publisher. For permission contact the ABA Copyrights & Contracts Department, copyright@abanet.org or via fax at 312-988-6030

Printed in the United States of America.

08 07 06 05 04   5 4 3 2 1

Library of Congress Cataloging-in-Publication Data

International guide to corporate privacy / Jody R. Westby, editor.
    p. cm.
  "Section of Science & Technology Law, American Bar Association."
  Includes bibliographical references and index.
  ISBN 1-59031-333-X
  1. Data protection--Law and legislation--United States. 2. Business enterprises--Law and legislation--United States. 3. Privacy, Right of--United States. 4. Data protection--Law and legislation. I. Westby, Jody R., 1950- II. American Bar Association. Section of Science & Technology Law.

  KF1263.C65I58 2004
  342.7308'58--dc22

2004004646

Discounts are available for books ordered in bulk. Special consideration is given to state bars, CLE programs, and other bar-related organizations. Inquire at Book Publishing, ABA Publishing, American Bar Association, 321 N. Clark, Chicago, IL 60610-4714.

www.ababooks.org

CONTENTS

Preface   vii

Abbreviations   xi

List of Participants   xv
    ABA Committee and Project Leadership   xvii
    Organizations with Participating Personnel   xvii

Executive Summary   xix
    A. Introduction   xix
    B. U.S. Legal Framework   xx
    C. International Legal Framework   xxi
    D. Privacy Programs: Plans, Policies, & Procedures   xxiii
    E. Implementation and Science & Technology   xxiv

Introduction   1
    A. Background   1
    B. Scope of International Guide to Privacy Project   9

CHAPTER 1
U.S. Legal Framework   11
    A. Overview   11
    B. Federal Legal Landscape   11
        1. Constitutional Right to Privacy   11
        2. U.S. Laws and Regulations   15
            a. The Privacy Act of 1974   15
            b. Freedom of Information Act   17
            c. Financial Services Modernization Act of 1999
               (Gramm-Leach-Bliley Act)   18
            d. Fair Credit Reporting Act   34
            e. Health Insurance Portability and Accountability
               Act   38
            f. Children's Online Privacy Protection Act   46
            g. Electronic Communications Privacy Act   50
            h. Economic Espionage Act of 1996   54
            i. Trade Secrets   59
            j. Controlling the Assault of Non-Solicited
               Pornography and Marketing Act of 2003   62

iv   CONTENTS

    3.   U.S. Regulatory Action 63
        a. Federal Trade Commission 63
        b. Federal Communications Commission 69
C. Seal Programs 71
    1.   BBBOnline Privacy Program 72
    2.   TRUSTe Privacy Program 72
D. State Legal Landscape 72
    1.   Electronic Surveillance 73
    2.   Social Security Numbers 74
    3.   Testing in Employment (Including Polygraphs) 74
    4.   Laws Targeted at Specific Industries 76
    5.   Reporting 78
    6.   State Attorneys General Actions and Case Rulings 78
E. Conclusion 80

CHAPTER 2

International Legal Framework 81
A. Overview 81
B. Multinational Laws, Treaties, and Agreements 82
    1.   United Nations 82
    2.   Organization for Economic Co-operation and
        Development 82
    3.   Council of Europe 87
    4.   European Union 89
        a. Data Protection Directive 89
        b. Privacy in Electronic Communications 102
C. Other Non-U.S. Countries 106
    1.   The Americas 106
        a. Canada 106
        b. Mexico 110
        c. Argentina 114
        d. Paraguay 117
    2.   Asia 118
        a. Asian Countries with Little Privacy Protection 118
        b. People's Republic of China and Hong Kong 119
        c. India 120
        d. Japan 121
        e. Republic of Korea (South Korea) 123
        f. Singapore 124
        g. Australia 125
        h. New Zealand 127
    3.   Middle East and Africa 127

Contents v

        a. Israel   127
        b. Republic of South Africa   128
        c. Republic of Turkey   128
  D. Extraterritorial Application of Law   128
     1.   United States   128
     2.   European Union   129
  E. Conclusion   130

CHAPTER 3
Privacy Programs: Plans, Policies, and Procedures   133

  A. Overview   133
     1.   The Privacy Program   135
     2.   The Relationship Between Privacy and Security   136
     3.   The Impact of Laws, Regulations, Principles, Standards, and Guidelines   138
     4.   The Importance of a Comprehensive, Enterprise-Wide Privacy Approach   139
  B. Development of a Privacy Plan   141
     1.   Governance Structure   142
        a. Directors and Senior Management   142
        b. Cross-organizational Privacy Team   148
        c. Personnel   149
     2.   Privacy Risk Assessment and Gap Analysis   149
     3.   Legal Considerations and Risks   152
        a. Compliance Requirements with Laws, Regulations, and Standards   152
        b. Jurisdictional Differences   154
        c. Contracts and Nondisclosure Agreements   155
        d. Confidential and Proprietary Information and Due Diligence   155
        e. Political and Cultural Expectations   156
     4.   Data Classification   157
  C. Privacy Policies and Procedures   160
     1.   Main Policy Elements   161
        a. Internal Policies   161
        b. External Privacy Policies   162
        c. Practical Tips for Policies   164
     2.   Procedures   165
  D. Reviewing and Updating Privacy Plan, Policies, and Procedures   165
     1.   Reviews   166
     2.   Change Management   166
  E. Conclusion   168

CHAPTER 4
Implementation and Science & Technology 171
- A. Overview 171
- B. Implementation: What Is Required 174
  - 1. Training 175
  - 2. Monitoring 180
  - 3. Compliance and Audits 184
    - a. Compliance 184
    - b. Annual Audit 186
    - c. Internal and External Audits 188
  - 4. Enforcement and Reporting 194
- C. Technological Considerations 196
  - 1. Encryption 197
  - 2. Authorization and Access Control 200
  - 3. Digital Signature and Authentication Technologies 203
  - 4. Digital Time Stamps and Audit Technologies 203
  - 5. Logs 204
  - 6. Anonymizing and Sanitizing 205
- D. Conclusion 205

Bibliography 207

Index 241

PREFACE

Privacy has become a priority issue closely linked to civil liberties, democracy, and human rights, as well as free enterprise and globalization. Today, we have 730 million people in nearly 200 countries connected to the Internet and information and communication technologies (ICTs) have permeated virtually every aspect of business operations. Following the September 11 terrorist attacks, increased government funding has spurred technological advances and promoted government use of ICTs in unprecedented ways. As a result, citizens, companies, and governments are faced with some of the most profound—and fundamental—governance issues they have ever had to address.

Citizens, today more than ever, are fearful of what information is being gathered about them and by whom, what information is being shared about them and with whom, how that information is being used, and how long it is being retained. Privacy concerns have sparked debates and provoked legislators to enact laws both protecting and restricting privacy—often without due consideration of international law or the fundamental principles underlying their governments. Not all countries, however, have privacy protections. There remain continents and countries without any privacy or data protection laws at all, leaving these governments free to use or gather information in any manner desired.

All in all, this has resulted in a highly inconsistent global legal framework, creating confusion for corporations and citizens alike and hindering global business. This especially hurts developing countries because corporations are reluctant—or prohibited by law—from sending data to a country that does not have adequate privacy protections. Therefore, countries without strong data protection laws can be deprived of foreign direct investment and outsourcing opportunities.

Privacy is an issue that cannot be stovepiped. The natural nexus between privacy, security, and cybercrime is not widely understood even though it is quite simple: without security there is no privacy, and privacy and security breaches are cybercrimes. Today, organizations must look at privacy holistically and from an international perspective. It must be integrally woven into business operations through the development of an enterprise privacy program that is based on global best practices, is consistent with applicable laws and regulations, and is supported by policies and procedures that are implemented across the organization.

This project was designed to complement the American Bar Association's Privacy and Computer Crime Committee's work in the areas of cybercrime and cyber security. This publication is a sister publication to the *International Guide to Combating Cybercrime* and the *International Guide to Cyber Security*. The three publications are intended to promote the beneficial use of ICTs around the world through a better understanding of privacy, security, and cybercrime. We hope they will facilitate international cooperation and a harmonized legal framework. We also hope they will serve as valuable resource materials to stakeholders in developing countries to help them address these issues and become more involved globally. And to put our money where our mouth is: the Committee and the ABA have made all three books available free of charge to persons from developing countries.

Attorneys, government personnel, non-profit staff, university professors, technical experts, and industry representatives came together from around the world to create the *International Guide to Privacy*. They worked shoulder-to-shoulder in the spirit of public-private sector cooperation and generously gave their time and talent over an intense eight-month period. Many of them also contributed to the development of the *Cybercrime* and *Cyber Security* books. They participated in this fully voluntary effort for one reason: passion. They understand the impact ICTs are having in this and the immediate past century. And they understand that the ability to unleash the full beneficial potential of ICTs is dependent upon an international understanding of privacy, security, and cybercrime. We need more of that kind of passion.

It is with that spirit that I dedicate this book to Barbara Wellbery (1948–2003), a partner at the global firm of Morrison & Foerster LLP and a member of the ABA Privacy & Computer Crime Committee. Barbara was one of the leading experts on international privacy issues. She was the chief architect and principal negotiator of the U.S. Safe Harbor accord with the European Union. She dedicated her professional career to fostering a better understanding of privacy laws around the globe and working to resolve key differences—all within the context of protecting individual privacy. The Committee hopes that this book will encourage others to follow her path.

I owe a debt of gratitude to the members of the American Bar Association Privacy & Computer Crime Committee's International Privacy Project. I especially want to thank David Weitzel, vice chair of the Committee and co-chair of this Project, for his superb leadership and assistance. In addition, I would like to express my deep appreciation to Ken DeJarnette, vice chair of the International Privacy Project, and working group co-chairs Paula Bruening, Joseph Schwerha, Don McGowan, Benjamin Hayes, Scott Forbes, Richard Balough, Kristine Baker, and Andrea White, for their guidance and untiring devotion to this project. A special thank you goes to Don Blumenthal, Dave Cullinane, Marc Menninger, and Dave Yee for their seemingly 24/7 support during the project on matters large and small. But it takes more than will and work to turn words into a book. I am grateful to the ABA Section of Science & Technology Law leadership and staff who generously gave support, encouragement, and resources to the publication of this *Guide*, in particular: Heather Rafter, Ivan Fong, Richard Field, Tom Smedinghoff, Shawn Kaminski, Danyale Vann, Kathleen Welton, Rick Paszkiet, Catherine Kruse, and Maureen Grey.

Jody R. Westby
Chair, Privacy & Computer Crime Committee
ABA Section of Science & Technology Law

ABBREVIATIONS

ACLU	American Civil Liberties Union
AES	Advanced Encryption Standard
AICPA	American Institute of Certified Public Accountants
AOL	America OnLine
APEC	Asia Pacific Economic Cooperation Forum
BHCA	Bank Holding Company Act (U.S.)
BBBOnline	Better Business Bureau Online
CAC	Common Access Card
CAN-SPAM Act	Controlling the Assault of Non-Solicited Pornography and Marketing Act of 2003 (U.S.)
CCIPS	Computer Crime & Intellectual Property Section (U.S. Department of Justice)
CEO	Chief Executive Officer
CERT	Computer Emergency Response Team
CERT/CC	Computer Emergency Response Team Coordinating Center, Carnegie Mellon University (U.S.)
C.F.R.	Code of Federal Regulations (U.S.)
CICA	Canadian Institute of Chartered Accountants
CIC	Credit Information Companies (Mexico)
CobiT	Control Objectives for Information and Related Technology
CoE	Council of Europe
CompTIA	Computing Technology Industry Association
COPPA	Children's Online Privacy Protection Act (U.S.)
CPNI	Customer Proprietary Network Information (U.S.)
CPO	Chief Privacy Officer
CSF	Critical Success Factors
CSIRT	Computer Security Incident Response Team
DoD	Department of Defense (U.S.)
DMA	Direct Marketing Association
EC	European Commission
ECPA	Electronic Communications Privacy Act (U.S.)
EEA	Economic Espionage Act of 1996 (U.S.)
EEA	European Economic Area
ECJ	European Court of Justice
EPIC	Electronic Privacy Information Center
EU	European Union
FACTA	Fair and Accurate Credit Transaction Act of 2003 (U.S.)

xii ABBREVIATIONS

FAQ	Frequently Asked Question
FCC	Federal Communications Commission (U.S.)
FCPA	Federal Consumer Protection Act (Mexico)
FCRA	Fair Credit Reporting Act (U.S.)
FDI	Foreign Direct Investment
FIPS	Federal Information Processing Standard (U.S.)
FISMA	Federal Information Security Management Act (U.S.)
FOIA	Freedom of Information Act (U.S.)
FTC	Federal Trade Commission (U.S.)
GAO	General Accounting Office (U.S.)
GLBA	Gramm-Leach-Bliley Act (U.S.)
HHS	Department of Health and Human Services (U.S.)
HIPAA	Health Insurance Portability and Accountability Act (U.S.)
H.R.	House of Representatives (U.S.)
IASP	Internet Access Service Provider
ICC	International Chamber of Commerce
ICT	Information and Communication Technology
IEC	International Electrotechnical Commission
ISACA	Information Systems Audit and Control Association
ISO	International Organization for Standardization
ISP	Internet Service Provider
IT	Information Technology
KPI	Key Performance Indicators
Law on PPI	Law on the Protection of Personal Information (South Korea)
LRCIC	Law for Regulating Credit Information Companies (Mexico)
MACs	Message Authentication Codes
MIC	Ministry of Information and Communication (South Korea)
NAFTA	North American Free Trade Agreement
NAIC	National Association of Insurance Commissioners (U.S.)
NASACT	National Association of State Auditors, Comptrollers and Treasurers (U.S.)
NCCUSL	National Conference of Commissioners on Uniform State Laws (U.S.)
NIST	National Institute of Standards and Technology (U.S.)
NLRB	National Labor Relations Board (U.S.)
NPI	Nonpublic Personal Information
OCS	HHS Office of Civil Rights (U.S.)
OECD	Organisation for Economic Co-operation and Development

OMB	Office of Management and Budget (U.S.)
PC	Personal Computer
PDA	Personal Digital Assistant
PDPA	Personal Data Protection Act (Argentina)
PHI	Private Health Information (HIPAA)
PII	Personally Identifiable Information
PIP	Personal Information Protection (Japan)
PIPEDA	Personal Information Protection and Electronic Documents Act (Canada)
PKI	Public Key Infrastructure
PRC	People's Republic of China
Pub.	Public
SB	Senate Bill
SEC	Securities and Exchange Commission (U.S.)
SMEs	Small and Medium-Sized Enterprises
SQL	Structured Query Language
SSL	Secure Sockets Layer
TCPA	Telephone Consumer Protection Act (U.S.)
TSR	Telemarketing Sales Rule (U.S.)
UN	United Nations
UNCITRAL	United Nations Commission on International Trade Law
U.K.	United Kingdom
U.S.	United States
USA PATRIOT Act	Uniting and Strengthening America by Providing Appropriate Tools Required to Intercept and Obstruct Terrorism Act of 2001 (U.S.)
U.S.C.	United States Code
UTSA	Uniform Trade Secrets Act (U.S.)
WLAN	Wireless Local Area Network
WTO	World Trade Organization

LIST OF PARTICIPANTS

American Bar Association
Section of Science & Technology Law
Privacy & Computer Crime Committee

INTERNATIONAL GUIDE TO PRIVACY PROJECT

The following participants, although not all members of the ABA, provided information and assistance in the development of the *International Guide to Privacy.* The statements and views contained in this book are not necessarily endorsed by them or their employers or affiliated entities.

Sarah Andrews
Drew C. Arena — Verizon Communications
Susan Axelrod — New York County District Attorney's Office

Kristine M. Baker
Richard C. Balough
John Barlament — Michael Best & Friedrich
William A. Barletta — Lawrence Berkeley National Laboratory
W. Scott Blackmer
Don M. Blumenthal — Federal Trade Commission
Paula J. Bruening — Center for Democracy & Technology
Angeline G. Chen — International Launch Services (Lockheed Martin)

Dave Cullinane — Washington Mutual, Inc.
Kenneth DeJarnette — Deloitte & Touche LLP
Francis H. Dong — DoMo Associates
Keith P. Enright — Virtumundo
Bart Epstein — Latham & Watkins
Richard L. Field — Law Offices of Richard Field
Robert L. Föehl — Target Corporation
Ivan K. Fong — General Electric Vendor Financial Services
Scott C. Forbes — Microsoft Corporation

Steve Ganis	Law Offices of Stephen L. Ganis
Arlan Gates	Baker & McKenzie
Francoise Gilbert	IT Law Group
Edward X. Gilbride	Federal Deposit Insurance Corporation
Sol Glasner	The MITRE Corporation
Richard H. Gordin	Tighe Patton
Fredric P. Greene	Greene Security & Audit
Pam Hassebroek	Georgia Institute of Technology
Benjamin S. Hayes	Kirkpatrick & Lockhart
Janine Hiller	Virginia Tech
Alexander D. Hoehn-Saric	Latham & Watkins
Mark Isham	Law Office of Mark W. Isham
William Karam	Baker & McKenzie
Tom Kellermann	The World Bank
Susan Koeppen	Microsoft Corporation
Jason Krasnove	
Bray Laybourne	
Zachary M. Lewis	Latham & Watkins
Theodore C. Ling	Baker & McKenzie
Magnolia Mansourkia	MCI
Richard D. Marks	Davis Wright Tremaine LLP
Don McGowan	Osler, Hoskin & Harcourt LLP
Marc R. Menninger	Washington Mutual, Inc.
Mark Merrill	CIGNA Systems Division
Michael J. Miasek	Law Offices of Michael J. Miasek
Jessica A. Milano	DoMo Associates
Geoffrey Mitchell	SynXis Corporation
Betty Southard Murphy	Baker & Hostetler LLP
Jorge Navarro	International Legal Telecommunications, e-business & IT Consulting
Milton Olin	Manatt Phelps Phillips
Ronald E. Plesco, Jr.	SRA International, Inc.
Michele J. Rubenstein	solutions4networks
Peter E. Sand	Pennsylvania Office of Attorney General
Nina Santucci	The Windermere Group
Joseph J. Schwerha, IV	Office of the District Attorney for Washington County
Satwiksai Seshasai	Massachusetts Institute of Technology (student)
Daniel A. Silien	Preston Gates Ellis & Rouvelas Meeds
Christopher Sloan	Liberty Mutual Insurance Company
Thomas J. Smedinghoff	Baker & McKenzie

Philip J. Smith	TrustWave Corporation
David Sobel	Electronic Privacy Information Center
Michael T. Spadea	Spadea & Associates
Raj Veeramani	University of Wisconsin-Madison, UW Consortium for Global E-Commerce
Stephen P. Villano	Holland & Hart
Kate Wakefield	Costco Wholesale IS Department
Henning Wegener	
David S. Weitzel	Mitretek Systems
Barbara S. Wellbery	Morrison & Foerster
Jody R. Westby	The Work-IT Group
Andrea White	Toyota Motor Sales, USA, Inc.
Norman Willox	LexisNexis
Amy Worlton	Wiley, Rein & Fielding
David K. Yee	

ABA Committee and Project Leadership

Chair, Privacy & Computer Crime Committee	Jody R. Westby
Vice Chair, Privacy & Computer Crime Committee	David S. Weitzel

Project Co-Chairs	Jody R. Westby & David S. Weitzel
Project Vice Chair	Kenneth DeJarnette
Co-Chair, U.S. Privacy Working Group	Paula J. Bruening
Co-Chair, U.S. Privacy Working Group	Joseph J. Schwerha, IV
Co-Chair, International Privacy Working Group	Don McGowan
Co-Chair, International Privacy Working Group	Benjamin S. Hayes
Co-Chair, Privacy Plans, Policies & Procedures Working Group	Scott Forbes
Co-Chair, Privacy Plans, Policies & Procedures Working Group	Richard Balough
Co Chair, Implementation and Science & Technology Working Group	Kristine M. Baker
Co-Chair, Implementation and Science & Technology Working Group	Andrea White

Organizations with Participating Personnel

The ABA wishes to acknowledge the following organizations that provided assistance to this Project. The statements and views contained in the International Guide to Privacy are not necessarily endorsed by them or their personnel.

American Civil Liberties Union
Center for Democracy & Technology
Costco Wholesale IS Department
Deloitte & Touche LLP
DoMo Associates
Electronic Frontier Foundation
Electronic Privacy Information Center
Georgia Institute of Technology
GW Solutions
Information Systems Security Association
International Legal Telecommunications, e-business & IT Consulting
LexisNexis
Tighe Patton
The World Bank
Toyota Motor Sales, USA, Inc.
University of Wisconsin-Madison, UW Consortium for Global
   E-Commerce
U.S. Department of Commerce
U.S. Federal Deposit Insurance Corporation
U.S. Federal Trade Commission
Washington Mutual, Inc.
World Federation of Scientists, Permanent Monitoring Panel on
   Information Security

Executive Summary

A. Introduction

The Internet and a global communications network are facilitating globalization and making it possible for corporations, including many small and medium-sized enterprises (SMEs), to conduct business around the world. Information and communication technologies (ICTs) are helping all organizations increase their productivity, improve efficiency, and enhance their competitiveness. Today, large corporations are outsourcing much of their "back room" data processing operations, call centers, service centers, and data bank development to lower cost operations in developing countries.   They are also sending manufacturing, production, assembly processes, and related jobs overseas. Organizations are consolidating operations by funneling all data to one central processing location, and businesses of all sizes are using the Internet to dramatically cut operation costs and overhead. The result: enormous amounts of data are flowing over the global communications network with varying degrees of legal protection.

Privacy of information in the digital age has been a concern since computers revolutionized business processes in the 1970s and made the ability to analyze and share information an easy process that could be performed in seconds.   The global legal framework regarding privacy of information has developed slowly, however, over a thirty-year period. Today, international privacy laws are widely inconsistent and present extraordinary challenges for all organizations.   In countries where there are data protection laws, they vary significantly in substance, and there are many areas—indeed, continents—where there are few or no privacy laws at all.

xix

Legal compliance with a myriad of laws can only be achieved through a comprehensive privacy program that consists of a privacy plan and supporting policies and procedures that incorporate guidance and best practices and are implemented across an organization. Numerous scientific and technological considerations also come into play. Thus, privacy today requires a blend of legal, technical, organizational, and managerial expertise that cannot be "stovepiped." *By setting forth (a) the global privacy legal framework and key international initiatives, (b) information on resources, (c) guidance on the development of a complete privacy program, and (d) implementation and technological considerations, this book is intended to serve as a consolidated resource for all organizations in addressing privacy considerations.*

Almost all multinational organizations are involved in privacy, cyber security, and cybercrime in some fashion. Their actions have ranged from treaties to privacy guidelines. There are approximately 40 countries engaged in enacting some form of privacy legislation. All of this activity has resulted in a global legal framework that is quite inconsistent. This array of laws, initiatives, and developments around the globe regarding privacy highlights why an interconnected global network demands that privacy be approached from an international perspective, taking into account (a) national and international initiatives, (b) legal developments, (c) best practices and resources, (d) guidance on developing and implementing effective privacy programs, and (e) technological considerations. Each organization has to evaluate its own unique attributes (such as its system architecture, business operations, culture of the organization, and management policies) with these considerations in mind and develop a privacy program that meets its needs and responsibilities.

The *International Guide to Privacy* is intended to serve as a compendium of information critical to meeting privacy responsibilities and developing an enterprise-wide privacy program. It can be utilized by corporations, governments, academia, policymakers, and legislators.

B. U.S. Legal Framework

Although the U.S. government is subject to omnibus privacy requirements for personal information through the Privacy Act of 1974, the private sector is not subject to any overarching privacy law similar to the European Union's Data Protection Directive or Canada's Personal Information Protection and Electronic Documents Act (PIPEDA). Privacy protections in the United States are a complex patchwork of laws and regulations, administrative decisions, court orders, constitutional rights, and state laws.

Federal privacy laws and their corresponding regulations that affect specific sectors, such as the Health Information Portability and Accountability Act (HIPAA) (health information), the Gramm-Leach-Bliley Act (GLBA) (consumer financial information), and the Fair Credit Reporting Act (FCRA), have a broad reach and significantly affect business operations and privacy plans, policies, and procedures. Laws specific to types of information, such as the Children's Online Privacy Protection Act (COPPA), impose privacy requirements across all industry sectors that collect or handle this type of information. Regulatory agencies, such as the Federal Communications Commission (FCC) and Federal Trade Commission (FTC), also impose privacy requirements on consumer data.

Workplace privacy considerations vary significantly between the United States and the European Union (EU), creating special problems for multinational corporations. Companies must take care to ensure their privacy program meets the legal threshold of economic espionage and trade secret laws to enable them to seek civil damages or criminal penalties. Caution also must be taken in workplace monitoring to ensure the Electronic Communications Privacy Act (EPIC) is not violated. In addition, numerous legal provisions have been added since the September 11 attacks that pose increased burdens on companies and raise thorny and unsettled privacy issues.

Privacy issues are an increasingly hot topic in U.S. state legislatures. Two different and, quite often, conflicting themes are shaping the development of the law at the state level. The first is the ever-increasing impact of the electronic age on personal privacy. The second is the struggle to enhance security, especially following the terrorist attacks on September 11. Clearly, a patchwork of federal and state laws is not the most effective means to address the privacy issues involved, especially from the vantage point of businesses with multi-state or multinational operations.

The U.S. privacy legal framework is far from settled. Recent actions taken by the FTC indicate priority attention will continue to be given to privacy, and state action appears to be increasing. It is important that companies stay abreast of legal developments and ensure that their privacy plans, policies, and procedures meet corporate legal compliance and contractual requirements.

C. International Legal Framework

The U.S. approach to privacy of self-regulation and sectoral legislation is not the universal method for managing privacy issues. Many countries have enacted general, universally applicable laws that govern the collection, use, and dissemination of personal information and have appointed a Privacy Commissioner or similar oversight mechanism to ensure compliance. In other jurisdictions, rules may be developed in conjunction with industry and with Privacy Commissioner oversight. Of course, many countries have chosen not to address privacy legislation at all.

Multinational laws, treaties, and agreements have laid a foundation for privacy rights. The UN *Universal Declaration of Human Rights*, the *International Covenant on Civil and Political Rights*, and *UN Guidelines Concerning Computerized Personal Data Files* each proclaim rights to privacy. The OECD has been a forerunner in the privacy and security arena. Its *Guidelines on the Protection of Privacy and Transborder Flows of Personal Data* and the revised 2002 OECD *Guidelines for the Security of Information Systems and Networks: Toward a Culture of Security*, have been endorsed globally. The Council of Europe's *Convention for the Protection of Human Rights and Fundamental Freedoms* establishes a right to privacy, but its 1981 *Convention for the Protection of Individuals with regard to Automatic Processing of Personal Data* and subsequent Guidelines and Protocols have furthered privacy protections.

The European Union's 1995 Data Protection Directive, however, has had the greatest global impact on privacy. The EU's omnibus approach to the protection of personal information and restrictions on the flow of that data to only countries that provide equivalent, or "adequate," protections has influenced legal frameworks around the world. However, the data retention requirements in the EU's 2002 Directive on Electronic Communications undercut some of the privacy goals of the 1995 Directive.

The international legal framework appears to be leaning toward the omnibus privacy approach taken by the EU Data Protection Directive. The EU approach is consistent with that taken by the OECD and CoE. The EU's "adequate" level of protection requirement for data flowing out of the EU has had a significant global impact. Numerous countries, including those in line for accession into the EU, have drafted laws that are intended to afford equivalent levels of protection to ensure their cross-border data flows will not be interrupted. The Safe Harbor agreement that was negotiated between the United States and the EU has offered participating U.S. companies the same assurance regarding cross-border data transfers. Some developing countries, fearing the loss of outsourcing opportunities from the U.S. if they adopt privacy laws modeled after the EU, are looking to legislation mimicking the U.S. Safe Harbor principles as a compromise position. Even the EU model contractual clauses for data protection are controversial and are indicative of the degree to which the international privacy legal framework remains unsettled.

Even though Canada's PIPEDA is an omnibus privacy law, its deference to provincial laws can make international business difficult. The privacy laws in Latin American countries, such as Mexico and Argentina, are relatively strong, with the EU having recently deemed Argentina's law as "adequate" per the Data Protection Directive. With the exception of Japan and South Korea, Asian countries have few privacy laws.

The extraterritorial application of privacy laws and the looming question of "adequacy" as data moves from country to country highlights the need for increased international agreement regarding privacy of data and cross-border data flows.

D. Privacy Programs: Plans, Policies, and Procedures

Maintaining privacy in today's electronically operated world is much more difficult than in the days when a secretary held the key to the file cabinet and privacy was controlled by one or a few persons. Every company has private information. Some information that is private is protected "personally identifiable information" (PII) or "personal information." Other information must be kept private because of contractual obligations, nondisclosure agreements, or legal/regulatory requirements (such as those required by the Gramm-Leach-Bliley Act (GLBA) and the Health Insurance Portability and Accountability Act (HIPAA)). Additional information that is critical to a business's bottom line, such as supply sources, pricing and customer lists, strategic documents, and intellectual property, must also be kept confidential for business and competitive reasons.

Today, every business should have a privacy program that addresses the collection, use, disclosure, and safeguarding of information, because information is a key corporate asset. Privacy considerations determine what a company can or cannot do with that asset—or should or should not do—without incurring legal liabilities and unwanted risk. Therefore, privacy is a strategic business issue that necessitates the careful attention of the enterprise from the board room to the loading dock. As a consequence, privacy programs must be comprehensive and enterprise-wide, involving all aspects of the extended enterprise, including customer service, sales and marketing, communications, human resources, information technology, security (of information and physical), operations, legal, internal audit, and enterprise partners (for example, agents, contractors, suppliers, etc.).

Privacy programs, consisting of privacy plans, policies, and procedures, are multifaceted and require the full horizontal and vertical involvement of an organization. Most corporate assets today are digital, yet many companies have not developed a comprehensive, enterprise-wide privacy program. In addition, they have not linked their privacy program with their security program. FTC action against Eli Lilly & Co., as well as subsequent cases, clearly links privacy and security and requires an enterprise-wide approach that dovetails administrative, technical, and physical safeguards. In addition, laws like GLBA and HIPAA have imposed privacy and security requirements on corporate and government operations, and these requirements are beginning to be emulated in other regulations and looked to by enforcement agencies, such as the FTC.

The development of a privacy plan requires the involvement of the board of directors and senior management, the line managers, and an active cross-organizational team. It also requires the involvement of the staff that handles the data as part of their job responsibilities. Additionally, the privacy plan must take into consideration the culture of the organization. Privacy risk assessments and gap analysis should be performed, where feasible, as attorney work product to help protect this type of sensitive information from being disclosed in litigation. An analysis of an organization's legal requirements (including compliance with laws/regulations, varying jurisdictional requirements, contractual obligations, and the protection of confidential and proprietary information) is necessary to ensure compliance measures and appropriate safeguards are included in the privacy program. Classification of data is an essential step.

Privacy policies (both internal and external) should be well thought out by senior management. They should be high-level, relatively static statements that set the tone for corporate operations, mandate certain behavior, set levels of measurement, and require compliance. Although brief, privacy policies set the framework laid out in the privacy plan. Procedures guide the daily operational steps. Their effectiveness is dependent upon employee acceptance and "buy-in." Thus, employee involvement throughout the organization is essential. An effective change management system is critical. Regular reviews and updates are an essential component of any privacy program.

E. Implementation and Science & Technology

The goal of any privacy program is to *manage risks* associated with the use of information. This includes managing privacy risks, security breaches, insider and unauthorized activities, theft and sabotage, public relations consequences, employee morale, and *avoiding* liabilities, civil and criminal penalties, loss of market share, drop in stock price, and financial loss. A solid privacy plan with well-designed policies and procedures, however, is of little use and affords little risk protection if the policies are not implemented. The privacy program should be viewed as the foundation upon which business operations can base their use of personal and other protected information.

Risks cannot be managed and institutional assets protected if a privacy plan is implemented only through documentation and privacy management software. A privacy program must be brought to life through the people in an organization and seen as the responsibility of all. In particular, privacy must be viewed as an integral part of the responsibility of all levels of line management, rather than seen as a set of legal or technical requirements emanating from the chief privacy officer or legal counsel.

The FTC actions taken against Eli Lilly & Co, Guess?, and Microsoft clearly indicate that implementation is an important step in an enterprise-wide privacy program that cannot be left as an afterthought. Privacy is dependent upon security. The FTC will look at the security practices and standards employed in a privacy program in determining whether the company has used appropriate levels of protection. The *Microsoft* case demonstrates that even the possibility that private data may not be secure can trigger an FTC investigation. The FTC will also scrutinize training programs and attempt to determine whether policies and procedures were implemented as part of the business operations or were simply pieces of paper in a book. Even if a company trains its personnel, the FTC will look to see if compliance with the policies and procedures was monitored and enforced.

The laws regarding employee monitoring vary significantly from one jurisdiction to another. The EU laws, for example, afford the employee a higher expectation of privacy in the European workplace than that of their counterparts in the United States. Internal and external audits are another avenue for determining compliance with the entire privacy program. Ideally, the external audits are conducted through counsel, with the intention that they be privileged as attorney work product.

Numerous technological considerations affect privacy programs, and there are several useful technology tools that can assist in the implementation of and compliance with an organization's privacy program. The use of encryption, for example, can protect sensitive data but involves administrative overhead and performance considerations. Authorization and access controls (such as passwords, biometric technologies, and common access cards) are in a constant state of innovation but can inject new privacy considerations into an organization. Digital signatures, authentication technologies, and digital time stamps are useful for evidentiary, audit, and security purposes; however, administrative costs and interoperability between technologies must also be considered. System logs are crucial to tracking and tracing attacks and audits. Anonymizing and sanitization technologies also can be useful in protecting privacy.

Overall, privacy of information is dependent upon the effective implementation of the privacy program and the technology tools utilized to help automate the privacy plan and monitor the effectiveness of and compliance with policies and procedures.

Introduction

A. Background

The Internet and an international communications network are facilitating globalization and making it possible for corporations, including many small and medium-sized enterprises (SMEs), to conduct business around the world. Information and communication technologies (ICTs) are helping all organizations increase their productivity, improve efficiency, and enhance their competitiveness. Today, large corporations are outsourcing much of their "back room" data processing operations, call centers, service centers, and data bank development to lower cost operations in developing countries. They are also sending manufacturing, production, assembly processes, and related jobs overseas. Organizations are consolidating operations by funneling all data to one central processing location, and businesses of all sizes are using the Internet to dramatically cut operation costs and overhead. The result: enormous amounts of data are flowing over the global communications network with varying degrees of legal protection.

Privacy of information in the digital age has been a concern since computers revolutionized business processes in the 1970s and made the ability to analyze and share information an easy process that could be performed in seconds. The global legal framework regarding privacy of information has developed slowly, however, over a thirty-year period. Although the United Nations (UN) Commission on International Trade Law[1] (UNCITRAL) has ensured a somewhat consistent legal global

---

[1] *See* United Nations Commission on International Trade Law, http://www.uncitral.org.

2   INTRODUCTION

framework with respect to electronic transactions and digital signatures through its leadership in electronic commerce, no similar guidance has benefited the development of global privacy laws. Today, international privacy laws are widely inconsistent and present extraordinary challenges for all organizations. In countries where there are data protection laws, they vary significantly in substance, and there are many areas—indeed, continents—with few or no privacy laws at all.

Legal compliance with a myriad of laws can only be achieved through a comprehensive privacy program that consists of a privacy plan and supporting policies and procedures that incorporate guidance and best practices and are implemented across an organization. Numerous scientific and technological considerations also come into play. Thus, privacy today requires a blend of legal, technical, organizational, and managerial expertise that cannot be "stovepiped." *By setting forth (a) the global privacy legal framework and key international initiatives, (b) information on resources, (c) guidance on the development of a complete privacy program, and (d) implementation and technological considerations, this book is intended to serve as a consolidated resource for all organizations in addressing privacy considerations.*

Modern views of U.S. privacy law have their roots in the development of tort theories over the last century and include torts such as intrusion on seclusion and false light. Over the last three decades, U.S. privacy laws have developed on a sectoral basis in areas such as government, credit bureaus, financial institutions, and health care entities. The only omnibus privacy laws in the U.S. apply to the federal government. The Privacy Act was enacted in 1974,[2] the Computer Security Act[3] became law in 1987, the Computer Matching and Privacy Protection Act was passed in 1988,[4] the Computer Matching and Privacy Protection Amendments[5] were enacted in 1990, and the Federal Information System Management Act[6] was passed in

---

[2]Privacy Act of 1974, 5 U.S.C. Section 552a, http://www4.law.cornell.edu/uscode/5/552a.html.

[3]Computer Security Act of 1987, Pub. Law 100-235, Jan. 8, 1988, http://csrc.nist.gov/secplcy/csa_87.txt. Section 11332 of the Computer Security Act of 1987, 40 U.S.C. Section 11332, was repealed by the Federal Information Security Management Act (FISMA), and replaced by training provisions in FISMA. *See* 40 U.S.C. Section 11332 as replaced by the E-Government Act of 2002 (FISMA was Title III of the E-Government Act).

[4]Computer Matching and Privacy Protection Act of 1988, Pub. Law 100-503, 5 U.S.C. Section 552a(o) *et seq.*, http://www4.law.cornell.edu/uscode/5/552a.html.

[5]Computer Matching and Privacy Protection Amendments, Pub. Law 101-508, Nov. 1990.

[6]Federal Information Security Management Act, Title III of E-Government Act of 2002, Pub. Law 107-347, http://csrc.nist.gov/policies/FISMA-final.pdf.

2002. The Electronic Communications Privacy Act of 1996 (ECPA) affords privacy protections to individual communications.[7]

In the past few years, there has been a flurry of activity in Congress regarding certain types of information. The recently enacted Health Insurance Portability and Accountability Act (HIPAA),[8] the Financial Modernization Act of 1999 (commonly referred to as the Gramm-Leach-Bliley Act, or GLBA),[9] and the Sarbanes-Oxley Act of 2002[10] have significantly affected corporate operations by imposing privacy and security requirements for health, financial, and accounting data. The Children's Online Privacy Protection Act (COPPA) applies to the online collection of information from children under 13.[11] Other federal laws protect sectoral information.[12] Although several U.S. Supreme Court decisions established constitutional privacy protections from government actors through the Fourth Amendment, these protections are seldom upheld in workplace cyber privacy cases.[13] In addition, the fifty states and the territories and possessions of the U.S. have a wide range of laws protecting specific categories of information and, over the past several years, have become very active in passing privacy laws.

Multinational organizations have also been engaged on the privacy front since the United Nations adopted the *Universal Declaration of Human Rights* in 1948, which explicitly states that "No one shall be subjected to arbitrary interference with his privacy, family,

---

[7]Electronic Communications Privacy Act, 18 U.S.C. 2701 *et seq.*, http://www4.law.cornell.edu/uscode/18/2701.html.

[8]Health Insurance Portability and Accountability Act of 1996, Pub. Law 104-191, http://aspe.hhs.gov/admnsimp/pl104191.htm.

[9]Financial Services Modernization Act of 1999, Pub. Law 106-102, Nov. 12, 1999, 15 U.S.C. Section 6801 *et seq.*, http://www4.law.cornell.edu/uscode/15/6801.html.

[10]Sarbanes-Oxley Act of 2002, Pub. Law 107-204, Sections 302, 404, http://news.findlaw.com/hdocs/docs/gwbush/sarbanesoxley072302.pdf.

[11]Children's Online Privacy Protection Act, Apr. 2000, 15 U.S.C. Sections 6501-6506, http://www4.law.cornell.edu/uscode/15/6501.html; Children's Online Privacy Protection Act; "How to Comply With The Children's Online Privacy Protection Rules, http://www.ftc.gov/bcp/conline/pubs/buspubs/coppa.htm.

[12]*See* "Privacy and Government," http://www.privacilla.org/government.html.

[13]*See Katz v. United States,* 389 U.S. 347 (1967) (outlining the Supreme Court's modern view of technology privacy). Recently, the Supreme Court reviewed the concepts laid out in *Katz* when it examined whether one had a reasonable expectation of privacy from government use of evolving technology to monitor one's home. Workplace privacy issues are raised in *O'Connor v. Ortega,* 480 U.S. 709 (1987). One should be aware that workplace privacy issues may be affected by union issues such as collective bargaining arrangements and the statutory power of government agencies overseeing employment practices.

4   INTRODUCTION

home, or correspondence."[14] The UN issued its *Guidelines concerning computerized personal data files* in 1990.[15] The Organisation for Economic Co-operation and Development (OECD) adopted the *Guidelines on the Protection of Privacy and Transborder Flows of Personal Data* in 1980,[16] the *Declaration on Transborder Data Flows* in 1985,[17] and the *Ministerial Declaration on the Protection of Privacy on Global Networks* in 1998.[18] The OECD issued *Privacy Online: OECD Guidance on Policy and Practical Guidance* in January 2003.[19] The Council of Europe (CoE) got involved in 1981 with its *Convention for the Protection of Individuals with regard to Automatic Processing of Personal Data*[20] and its subsequent 1999 *Amendments to the Convention for the protection of individuals with regard to automatic processing of personal data* (ETS No. 108) *allowing the European Communities to accede.*[21] In 1999, the CoE issued *Guidelines for the Protection of Individuals with Regard to the Collection and Processing of Personal Data on Information Highways*[22] and in 2001 adopted the *Additional Protocol to the Convention for the Protection of Individuals with*

---

[14]*Universal Declaration of Human Rights*, United Nations, General Assembly, Resolution 217 A (III), Dec. 10, 1948, http://www.un.org/Overview/rights.html.

[15]*United Nations guidelines concerning computerized personal data files*, United Nations, General Assembly, Dec. 14, 1990, http://www.europa.eu.int/comm/internal_market/privacy/instruments/un_en.htm.

[16]*Guidelines on the Protection of Privacy and Transborder Flows of Personal Data*, Organisation for Economic Co-operation and Development, Sept. 23, 1980, http://www.uhoh.org/oecd-privacy-personal-data.htm.

[17]*Declaration on Transborder Data Flows*, Organisation for Economic Co-operation and Development, Apr. 11, 1985, http://www.oecd.org/document/25/0,2340,en_2649_34255_1888153_199820_1_1_1,00.html.

[18]*Ministerial Declaration on the Protection of Privacy on Global Networks*, Organisation for Economic Co-operation and Development, DSTI/ICCP/REG(98)10/FINAL, Oct. 7-9, 1998, http://www.oecd.org/dataoecd/39/13/1840065.pdf.

[19]*Privacy Online: OECD Guidance on Policy and Practical Guidance*, Organisation for Economic Co-operation and Development, DSTI/ICCP/REG(2002)3/FINAL, Jan. 21, 2003, http://www.olis.oecd.org/olis/2002doc.nsf/linkTo/dsti-iccp-reg(2002)3-final.

[20]*Convention for the Protection of Individuals with regard to Automatic Processing of Personal Data*, Council of Europe, ETS No. 108, 28.I.1981, 1981, http://conventions.coe.int/Treaty/EN/Treaties/Html/108.htm.

[21]*Amendments to the Convention for the protection of individuals with regard to automatic processing of personal data* (ETS No. 108) *allowing the European Communities to accede*, Council of Europe, 28.I.1981, June 15, 1981, http://www.coe.int/T/E/Legal_affairs/Legal_co-operation/Data_protection/Documents/International_legal_instruments/Amendements%20to%20the%20Convention%20108.asp#TopOfPage.

[22]*Guidelines for the Protection of Individuals with Regard to the Collection and Processing of Personal Data on Information Highways*, Council of Europe, R(99)5, Feb. 23, 1999, http://cm.coe.int/ta/rec/1999/99r5.htm.

regard to Automatic Processing of Personal Data regarding supervisory authorities and transborder data flows.[23]

The privacy issue came alive in Europe in the early 1970s with the enactment of the first privacy law in Germany. To harmonize the privacy laws already in place in most of the EU Member States by the late 1980s, the European Union (EU) adopted the Data Protection Directive in 1995[24] and its 1997 and 2002 Directives concerning the processing of personal data and the protection of privacy in the telecommunications and electronics sector.[25] The EU, however, made privacy a global legal issue through the extraterritorial application of its Data Protection Directive. Its provisions declare that personal data protected under the Directive cannot be sent outside the EU unless the receiving country affords the data "adequate" privacy protections. The EU has made it clear that it will enforce these provisions. Member States also have the authority to enforce their harmonized data privacy laws. This extraterritorial application of the Data Protection Directive has forced governments and organizations around the world to consider the privacy protections that their legal and policy frameworks afford to data. Nation states outside the EU had to determine whether their legal and regulatory framework offered equivalent protection. Multinational corporations had to consider whether their cross-border transfers of EU data were in compliance with the Directive. Significant diplomatic efforts were made between U.S. and EU officials regarding this issue.

Ultimately, the United States and EU agreed on Safe Harbor provisions that U.S. companies could follow and be deemed in compliance with the EU Directive. The Council and the European Parliament have given the European Commission the authority to determine whether a third country affords an "adequate" level of

---

[23]*Additional Protocol to the Convention for the Protection of Individuals with regard to Automatic Processing of Personal Data regarding supervisory authorities and transborder data flows*, Council of Europe, ETS No. 181, 8.XI.2001, Jan. 28, 1991, http://conventions.coe.int/Treaty/EN/Treaties/Html/181.htm.

[24]*Directive 95/46/EC of the European Parliament and of the Council of 24 October 1995 on the protection of individuals with regard to the processing of personal data and on the free movement of such data*, Official Journal L 281/31, Nov. 23, 1995, http://europa.eu.int/smartapi/cgi/sga_doc?smartapi!celexapi!prod!CELEXnumdoc&l g=EN&numdoc=31995L0046&model=guichett.

[25]*Directive 2002/58/EC of the European Parliament and of the Council of 12 July 2002 concerning the processing of personal data and the protection of privacy in the electronic communications sector (Directive on privacy and electronic communications)*, Official Journal L 201/37, July 31, 2002, at 37-47 (replacing EU Directive 97/66/EC), http://europa.eu.int/smartapi/cgi/sga_doc?smartapi!celexapi!prod!CELEXnumdoc&lg= en&numdoc=32002L0058&model=guichett.

protection to data that are transferred from the EU to that country.[26] In 2001, the European Commission issued standard contractual clauses that would offer sufficient safeguards as required by the Data Protection Directive and would permit transfers of data from the EU and three European Economic Association member countries (Norway, Liechtenstein, and Iceland) to third countries.[27]

All of this activity has resulted in a global legal framework regarding privacy that is quite inconsistent. Generally, countries fall into one of three categories: (1) they have an omnibus data protection law, (2) they follow a sectoral approach and often let the private sector resolve these issues, or (3) they have no privacy laws at all. Most developing countries fall into the last category. The United States falls into the middle category, and the EU has the more regulatory approach of the first category. In 1997, the U.S. government's *A Framework for Global Electronic Commerce*[28] declared that government should take a "hands-off" approach toward regulating the Internet, and, for the most part since that time, the United States has taken a back seat to the EU's aggressive, regulatory approach toward online transactions and communications. Today, although the EU approach toward data protection is starting to be followed globally (for example, Canada, Argentina, Australia, and New Zealand),[29] there remain wide inconsistencies in the privacy laws around the world.

On a global level, there are approximately forty countries engaged in enacting some form of privacy legislation.[30] Since the United States does not have an omnibus privacy law similar to the EU's Data Protection Directive, many corporations falsely believe that there is no overarching privacy legal framework in the U.S. that demands compliance. A complex body of privacy law does exist, however, in the United States that comprises federal and state laws, court rulings, administrative decisions, and numerous regulations. In fact, this

---

[26]"Commission decisions on the adequacy of the protection of personal data in third countries," http://europa.eu.int/comm/internal_market/privacy/adequacy_en.htm.
[27]"Model Contracts for the transfer of personal data to third countries," http://europa.eu.int/comm/internal_market/privacy/modelcontracts_en.htm.
[28]William J. Clinton and Albert Gore, Jr., *A Framework for Global Electronic Commerce*, 1997, http://www.open-technology.com/essay541.htm.
[29]"As Data Privacy Laws Evolve Globally Many Nations Consider European Model," *Privacy & Security Law Report*, Bureau of National Affairs, Vol. 2, No. 16, Apr. 21, 2003 at 425-28; "European Data Protection Law Seen as Spilling into Latin America," *Privacy & Security Law Report*, Bureau of National Affairs, Vol. 2, No. 16, Apr. 21, 2003 at 428-30.
[30]David Banisar, "Data Protection Laws Around the World," Apr. 2003, http://www.privacy.org/pi/survey/dpmap.jpg. A map of Data Protection Laws Around the World reveals entire continents (the U.S. and Africa and major portions of Asia) without any laws, compared with areas saturated with protection (Europe, Eurasia, and Canada).

Introduction   7

patchwork of privacy laws poses extraordinary challenges for the corporation whose privacy program must comply with U.S. legal requirements. Moreover, a federal privacy law has been introduced by Senator Dianne Feinstein, the Privacy Act of 2003,[31] and at present at least forty-nine other privacy laws are pending at the federal level.[32]

Organizations around the globe need help in understanding the global legal framework with respect to privacy and developing privacy programs that will fit their business operations and compliance requirements. A couple of truths:

1. Privacy compliance is dependent upon a privacy program that is fully implemented through the organization's personnel and supported by the entity's security program.
2. Privacy compliance is dependent upon security; without security there is no privacy.

Development of a privacy program, which includes a privacy plan and corresponding policies and procedures, is a complex undertaking that requires (a) the involvement and oversight of senior management and the board of directors; (b) a cross-organizational privacy team; (c) an understanding of the legal requirements that apply to corporate operations; (d) a firm grasp of best practices, procedures, and guidance available for privacy protection; and (e) the implementation of the privacy program across the organization, followed by periodic reviews and modifications. In essence, a privacy plan serves as a privacy "business plan" to protect corporate assets and specific types of information. It is supported by policies and procedures. The policies are formal, relatively static, high-level statements regarding how the corporation will handle information in its operations. The procedures are the step-by-step processes performed in daily operations that meet the requirements of the policy and privacy plan.

The U.S. government has issued some guidance for federal systems

---

[31]Roy Mark, "Feinstein Introduces Privacy Act of 2003," *internetnews.com,* Apr. 3, 2003, http://dc.internet.com/news/article.php/2174701; *see also* S. 745, "Privacy Act of 2003, Mar. 31, 2003, http://thomas.loc.gov/cgi-bin/query/z?c108:s:745:.

[32]*See, e.g.,* National Uniform Privacy Standards Act of 2003 (H.R. 1766); Wireless Privacy Protection Act of 2003 (H.R. 71); Student Privacy Protection Act of 2003 (H.R. 1848); Stop Taking Our Health Privacy Act of 2003 (H.R. 1709); Personal Information Privacy Act of 2003 (H.R. 1931); Online Privacy Protection Act of 2003 (H.R. 69); Medical Independence, Privacy, and Innovation Act (H.R. 2196 and H.R. 2544); Consumer Privacy Protection Act of 2003 (H.R. 1636) at http://www.aeanet.org/GovernmentAffairs/gamb_stearnsbill 108th.asp.

that is instructive for all organizations.[33] The U.S. Federal Trade Commission has been the most active regulatory agency in the privacy arena and has issued numerous reports, held workshops, and given testimony to Congress on enforcing privacy policies and promises, consumer privacy issues, online profiling, fair online information practices, self-regulation, and privacy associated with electronic payment systems.[34] Best practices, standards, and guidance of international organizations pertaining to the development of privacy and security plans, policies, procedures, and training also offer excellent guidance. The OECD's *Privacy Online* Guidance and its Privacy Policy Statement Generator[35] are examples. The OECD's Privacy Policy Statement Generator was developed in cooperation with industry, privacy experts, and consumer organizations and has been endorsed by the OECD's 29 member countries.[36] The OECD has also put together an *Inventory of Instruments and Mechanisms Contributing to the Implementation and Enforcement of the OECD Privacy Guidelines on Global Networks*[37] and an *Inventory of Privacy-Enhancing Technologies*[38]

The foregoing listing of laws, initiatives, and developments regarding online privacy highlights why an interconnected global

---

[33]*See* "OMB Guidance for Implementing the Privacy Provisions of the E-Government Act of 2002," Memorandum M-03-22, Office of Management and Budget, Sept. 26, 2003, http://www.whitehouse.gov/omb/memoranda/m03-22.html; "Management of Federal Information Resources," Circular A-130 (Revised), Transmittal Memorandum No. 4, Office of Management and Budget, http://www.whitehouse.gov/omb/circulars/a130/a130trans4.pdf; "Privacy Policies and Data Collection on Federal Web Sites," Memorandum M-00-13, Office of Management and Budget, June 22, 2000, http://www.whitehouse.gov/omb/memoranda/m00-13.html; "Privacy Policies on Federal Web Sites," Memorandum M-99-18, Office of Management and Budget, June 2, 1999, http://www.whitehouse.gov/omb/memoranda/m99-18.html.

[34]"Enforcing Privacy Promises: Reports & Testimony," Federal Trade Commission, Privacy Initiatives, http://www.ftc.gov/privacy/privacyinitiatives/promises_reptest.html.

[35]"What is the OECD Privacy Statement Generator?" Organisation for Economic Co-operation and Development, http://www.oecd.org/document/39/0,2340,en_2649_34255_28863271_119669_1_1_1,00.html.

[36]*Id.*

[37]*Inventory of Instruments and Mechanisms Contributing to the Implementation and Enforcement of the OECD Privacy Guidelines on Global Networks,* Organisation for Economic Co-operation and Development, http://www.olis.oecd.org/olis/1998doc.nsf/linkto/dsti-iccp-reg(98)12-final; *see also* Chapter 6 of *Privacy Online: OECD Guidance on Policy and Practical Guidance* for an updated inventory list, http://www.oecd.org/document/49/0,2340,en_2649_34255_19216241_119699_1_1_1,00.html.

[38]*Inventory of Privacy-Enhancing Technologies,* Organisation for Economic Co-operation and Development, http://www.olis.oecd.org/olis/2001doc.nsf/linkto/dsti-iccp-reg(2001)1-final.

network demands that privacy be approached from an international perspective, taking into account (a) national and international initiatives, (b) legal developments, (c) best practices and resources, (d) guidance on developing and implementing effective privacy programs, and (e) technological considerations. Each organization has to evaluate its own unique attributes (such as its system architecture, business operations, culture of the organization, and management policies) in light of these considerations and develop a privacy program that meets its needs and responsibilities.

B. Scope of International Corporate Guide to Privacy Project

The *International Guide to Privacy* is intended to serve as a compendium of information critical to meeting privacy responsibilities and developing a privacy program. It can be used by governments, corporations of all sizes and industry sectors, by nongovernmental organizations, academia, policymakers, and legislators. The goals of the project are to

- Combine the international legal, technical, managerial, and organizational privacy considerations into one useful publication that will both assist organizations in meeting their privacy obligations and promote privacy globally;
- Foster a better understanding of global privacy laws and regulations;
- Promote the harmonization of privacy laws and regulations globally;
- Facilitate international cooperation in the development of global best practices for privacy programs, policies, and procedures, including technical considerations;
- Help developing countries in the development of privacy laws and regulations and enhance technical assistance in this area.

The *International Guide to Privacy* is organized into chapters devoted to each of the areas critical to privacy:

- Chapter 1 covers the U.S. patchwork of laws and regulations, protected categories of data, regulatory actions, and the state legal landscape.
- Chapter 2 covers privacy laws in other countries and regions around the globe, international agreements, and initiatives in multinational organizations.
- Chapter 3 takes the reader through the development of a privacy program, including privacy plans, policies, and procedures; the

governance structure; assessment and gap analysis; classification of data, owners, and users; risk management considerations; special industry considerations; and reviewing and updating the privacy program.

- Chapter 4 discusses implementation of the privacy program, legal and technical considerations, training, and compliance with and enforcement of privacy policies and procedures.

This guide was written as a cooperative effort between members of the ABA Section of Science & Technology Law's Privacy & Computer Crime Committee and interested persons from outside organizations, including technical experts, who actively participated and contributed to the process. All in all, the project proceeded with the involvement of all stakeholders—lawyers, privacy and security technical experts, government personnel, academia, industry, consumer advocates, and civil libertarians.

CHAPTER ❖ 1

U.S. Legal Framework

A. Overview

Although the U.S. government is subject to omnibus privacy requirements for personal information through the Privacy Act of 1974,[1] the private sector is not subject to any overarching privacy law similar to the European Union's Data Protection Directive (and EU Member State laws) or Canada's Personal Information Protection and Electronic Documents Act.[2] Privacy protections in the United States are a complex patchwork of laws and regulations, administrative decisions, court orders, constitutional rights, and state laws. This chapter will discuss these various privacy elements that make up the U.S. privacy framework and help corporations better understand their compliance requirements and privacy considerations.

B. Federal Legal Landscape

1. CONSTITUTIONAL RIGHT TO PRIVACY

Although a right to privacy is not expressly enumerated in the Bill of Rights, the U.S. Supreme Court has found a right to privacy through its

---

[1]Privacy Act of 1974, 5 U.S.C. Section 552a, http://www4.law.cornell.edu/uscode/5/552a.html.

[2]*Directive 95/46/EC of the European Parliament and of the Council of 24 October 1995 on the protection of individuals with regard to the processing of personal data and on the free movement of such data,* Official Journal L 281/31, Nov. 23, 1995, http://europa.eu.int/smartapi/cgi/sga_doc?smartapi!celexapi!prod!CELEXnumdoc&lg=EN&numdoc=31995L0046&model=guichett.

interpretation of the First, Third, Fourth, Fifth, and Ninth Amendments.[3] The concept of privacy as a legal interest was first enunciated in an article co-authored by Samuel Warren and Louis Brandeis in 1890, who described it as "the right to be let alone."[4] Since the late 1950s, the Supreme Court has upheld a series of privacy interests ("associational privacy," "political privacy," and "right to anonymity in public expression") under the First Amendment and the Due Process Clause. In *Katz v. United States*, the Court recognized Fourth Amendment privacy interests that protected an individual against electronic surveillance.[5] But the Court cautioned that:

> [T]he Fourth Amendment cannot be translated into a general constitutional "right to privacy." That Amendment protects individual privacy against certain kinds of governmental intrusion, but its protections go further and often have nothing to do with privacy at all. Other provisions of the Constitution protect personal privacy from other forms of governmental invasion.[6]

In the 1960s and 1970s, the Supreme Court defined the concept of privacy to include personal decisions concerning reproduction, sex, and marriage. In *Griswold v. Connecticut*, the Court struck down a Connecticut statute that prohibited the prescription or use of contraceptives as an infringement of marital privacy. The majority opinion viewed the case as concerning "a relationship lying within the zone of privacy created by several fundamental constitutional guarantees," that is, the First, Third, Fourth, Fifth and Ninth Amendments, each of which creates "zones" or "penumbras" of privacy.[7]

In *Eisenstadt v. Baird*, the Court extended the right to privacy beyond the marriage relationship to lodge in the individual:

---

[3]"Development of the Right to Privacy in Information," http://www.csu.edu.au/learning/ncgr/gpi/odyssey/privacy/orig_priv.html (from the U.S. Congress, Office of Technology Assessment, *Protecting Privacy in Computerized Medical Information*, OTA-TCT-576, U.S. Government Printing Office, Sept. 1993) (hereinafter "Development of the Right to Privacy in Information"); *see also* Electronic Frontier Foundation, http://www.eff.org/Legal/email_privacy.citations, for a series of citations from U.S. court cases regarding constitutional rights to privacy.

[4]*Id.* The term "the right to be let alone" was borrowed by Warren and Brandeis from the nineteenth century legal scholar and jurist Thomas Cooley. *See* Thomas Cooley, *Law of Torts*, 2nd ed., Vol. 29, 1888.

[5]*Katz v. United States*, 389 U.S. 347 (1967) (hereinafter *Katz*); *see also* S. M. Entwisle, "E-mail and Privacy in the Workplace," http://www.ucalgary.ca/~dabrent/380/webproj/privacy.html.

[6]*Katz* at 350.

[7]*Griswold v. Connecticut*, 381 U.S. 479 (1985); Development of the Right to Privacy in Information at 1.

> If the right of the individual means anything, it is the right of the individual, married or single, to be free from unwarranted governmental intrusion into matters so fundamentally affecting a person as the decision whether to bear or beget a child.[8]

In *Roe v. Wade*, the Court found that the Fourteenth Amendment's concept of personal liberty and restrictions on state action extended the right of privacy "to encompass a woman's decision whether or not to terminate her pregnancy."[9]

In the earliest case that raised privacy issues in the context of computerized medical information systems, the Supreme Court dodged the question of whether the Army's maintenance of such a system for domestic surveillance purposes "chilled" the First Amendment rights of those whose names were contained in the system.[10] A few years later, the Court did not recognize a constitutional right to privacy regarding (1) erroneous information in a circulated listing of active shoplifters[11] or (2) individuals' interests with respect to bank records.[12] In *Whalen v. Roe*, the Supreme Court held that the Fourteenth Amendment protects the privacy of certain information—in that case, sensitive drug data collected by the state.[13]

Since the 1970s, courts have had an ambivalent relationship with privacy. The modern concept of privacy as one's right to control information about oneself has not been fully protected by the courts, but some protections have been added. In *Greidinger v. Davis*, the Fourth Circuit Court declared unconstitutional Virginia's requirement that one's Social Security number be provided before a citizen may register to vote.[14]

The constitutional right to privacy in the cyber context has been applied mostly to workplace privacy issues.[15] Under U.S. law,[16] private sector employees are afforded virtually no expectation of privacy in the

---

[8]*Eisenstadt v. Baird*, 405 U.S. 438 (1972); Development of the Right to Privacy in Information at 2.

[9]*Roe v. Wade*, 410 U.S. 113 (1973); Development of the Right to Privacy in Information at 2.

[10]*Laird v. Tatum*, 408 U.S. 1 (1972); Development of the Right to Privacy in Information at 3-4.

[11]*Paul v. Davis*, 424 U.S. 693 (1976); Development of the Right to Privacy in Information at 3-4.

[12]*United States v. Miller*, 425 U.S. 435 (1976) (no Fourth Amendment reasonable expectation of privacy in records kept by banks "because they are merely copies of personal records that were made available to banks for a limited purpose"); Development of the Right to Privacy in Information at 3.

[13]*Whalen v. Roe*, 429 U.S. 589 (1977).

[14]*Greidinger v. Davis* 988 F.2d 1344 (4th Cir. 1993).

[15]For a discussion of U.S. data privacy rights in the context of the Constitution, *see* Joel R. Reidenberg and Paul M. Schwartz, *Data Privacy Law: A Study of United States Data Protection*, Michie, 1996.

[16]"Workplace Privacy," Electronic Privacy Information Center, http://www.epic.org/privacy/workplace/.

14   CHAPTER 1

workplace[17] and are not protected by the constitutional right to privacy.[18] A few states have laws, including state constitutional provisions, that protect privacy in the workplace. However, a notice to employees that there is no expectation of privacy often removes their effect.[19] Public sector employees, however, may have some constitutional rights to privacy.[20] In *O'Connor v. Ortega*, the U.S. Supreme Court noted:

> Individuals do not lose Fourth Amendment rights [against unreasonable search and seizure] merely because they work for the government instead of a private employer. The operational realities of the workplace, however, may make "some" employees' expectations of privacy unreasonable when an intrusion is by a supervisor rather than a law enforcement official. Public employees' expectations of

---

[17]*See, e.g.*, Patti Waldmeir, "US employees find no right to privacy in cyberspace," *The Financial Times*, Aug. 13, 2001 at 12; Allison R. Michael and Scott M. Lidman, "Monitoring of employees still growing: Employers seek greater productivity and avoidance of harassment liability; most workers have lost on privacy claims," *The National Law Journal*, Jan. 29, 2001 at B9, B15, B17-18. Some U.S. state constitutions do contain express protections of privacy, however, this does not guarantee a right to privacy. *See, e.g.*, "Computer Use Policy, Widespread Monitoring Doom Claim of Privacy in Company Computer," *Electronic Commerce & Law Report*, Bureau of National Affairs, Vol. 7, No. 10, Mar. 6, 2002, at 217.

[18]Cheryl Blackwell Bryson and Michelle Day, "Workplace Surveillance Poses Legal, Ethical Issues," *The National Law Journal*, Jan. 11, 1999 at B8.

[19]A small number of states have statutes that may restrict monitoring of employees. The strength of these protections varies. For example, Connecticut's statute essentially prohibits employers from operating "any electronic surveillance device or system, including but not limited to the recording of sound or voice or a closed circuit television system, or any combination thereof, for the purpose of recording or monitoring the activities of employees in areas designed for the health or personal comfort of the employees or for safeguarding of their possessions, such as rest rooms, locker rooms or lounges." *See* Connecticut General Statutes Annotated Section 31-48b (2003). Delaware laws, by contrast, are largely limited to requiring employers to provide "an electronic notice of such monitoring or intercepting policies or activities to the employee." *See* Delaware Code Title XIX, Section 705 (2003). Also, one must consider labor laws. For instance, the National Labor Relations Board has a requirement that once an election is scheduled in which employees will chose or refrain from choosing a union to represent them, the employer *must* send the union a list of all names and addresses of the employees who will be eligible to vote in the election. This is called the Excelsior List (*see NLRB v. Excelsior Underwear, Inc.* , 156 NLRB 1236 (1966) and *NLRB v. Wyman-Gordon Co.*, 394 U.S. 759 (1969)). Related regulatory implementation is in the *NLRB Field Manual*, 11312.1. *See also* Charles J. Muhl, "Workplace e-mail and Internet use: employees and employers beware," *Monthly Labor Review*, Vol. 126, No. 2, Feb. 2003, http://www.bls.gov/opub/mlr/2003/02/art3abs.htm (describing concerns of employers' lax monitoring of employee e-mail) (hereinafter "Muhl").

[20]"Workplace Privacy," Electronic Privacy Information Center, http://www.epic.org/privacy/workplace/. *See also* Muhl.

privacy in their offices, desks, and file cabinets, like similar expectations of employees in the private sector, may be reduced by virtue of actual office practices and procedures, or by legitimate regulation....Given the great variety of work environments in the public sector, the question of whether an employee has a reasonable expectation of privacy must be addressed on a case-by-case basis.[21]

2. U.S. LAWS AND REGULATIONS

a. The Privacy Act of 1974

The Privacy Act of 1974 serves to "balance the government's need to maintain information about individuals with the rights of the individuals to be protected against unwarranted invasions of their privacy stemming from federal agencies' collection, maintenance, use, and disclosure of personal information about them."[22] It applies to U.S. government agencies and government contractors operating a system of records on behalf of the government.[23] The Privacy Act focuses on four major policy objectives:

1. To restrict disclosure of personally identifiable records maintained by agencies
2. To grant individuals increased rights of access to agency records maintained on them
3. To grant individuals the right to seek amendment of agency records maintained on them upon a showing that the records are not accurate, relevant, timely or complete
4. To establish a code of "fair information practices" that requires agencies to comply with statutory norms for collection, maintenance, and dissemination of records.[24]

The Privacy Act prohibits a government agency from disclosing information to another person or agency except upon written request by, or with the consent of, the person to whom the information pertains.[25] There are, however, twelve exceptions built into the law, under which

---

[21]*O'Connor v. Ortega*, 480 U.S. 709, 718 (1987).
[22]"Overview of the Privacy Act of 1974, 2002 Edition," U.S. Department of Justice, http://www.usdoj.gov/04foia/04foia/04_7_1.html.
[23]Privacy Act of 1974, 5 U.S.C. Section 552a(m)(2), http://www4.law.cornell.edu/uscode/5/552a.html; *see also* "Overview of the Privacy Act of 1974, 2002 Edition," "Government Contractors," U.S. Department of Justice, http://www.usdoj.gov/04foia/04_7_1.html.
[24]*Id.*
[25]Privacy Act of 1974, 5 U.S.C. Section 552a(b), http://www4.law.cornell.edu/uscode/5/552a.html.

16   CHAPTER 1

disclosures are permissive, but not mandatory.[26] These exceptions are (1) "need to know" within the agency, (2) requirement by Freedom of Information Act (FOIA) disclosure, (3) routine uses, (4) information needed to carry out a census, (5) statistical research, (6) information of historical value for National Archives, (7) request by law enforcement, (8) health or safety of an individual, (9) Congressional committee work, (10) information needed for the duties of the General Accounting Office, (11) court order, and (12) information needed for purposes of disclosing bad debt to credit agencies.[27]

The Privacy Act contains provisions that ensure an individual's right of access to his/her own record or information.[28] The access is similar to access guaranteed by FOIA, except that the Privacy Act only permits an individual to seek access to his or her own information, whereas FOIA permits any person to seek access to any agency record (subject to FOIA exceptions).[29] The primary difference between the two laws is the scope of information that can be requested. An individual's request for his or her own information could be processed under either FOIA or the Privacy Act.[30] Exemptions from the individual's right of access include information compiled in anticipation of civil litigation, records maintained by the Central Intelligence Agency, and records maintained by a law enforcement entity.[31]

To ensure that an individual's information is properly safeguarded, the Privacy Act also provides for individuals to pursue civil claims against the government for violations of the Act.[32] Furthermore, the Privacy Act contains provisions for criminal penalties for any officer or employee of a government agency who knowingly discloses protected, individually identifiable information to any person or agency not entitled to receive it.[33] The U.S. Supreme Court, however,

---

[26]"Overview of the Privacy Act of 1974, 2002 Edition," "Conditions of Disclosure to Third Parties: Twelve Exceptions to the 'No Disclosure Without Consent' Rule," U.S. Department of Justice, http://www.usdoj.gov/04foia/1974condis.htm.
[27]*Id.*
[28]Privacy Act of 1974, 5 U.S.C. Section 552a(d)(1), http://www4.law.cornell.edu/uscode/5/552a.html.
[29]"Overview of the Privacy Act of 1974, 2002 Edition," "Individual's Right of Access," U.S. Department of Justice, http://www.usdoj.gov/04foia/1974indrigacc.htm.
[30]*Id.*
[31]Privacy Act of 1974, 5 U.S.C. Section 552a(d)(5), http://www4.law.cornell.edu/uscode/5/552a.html; *see also* "Overview of the Privacy Act of 1974, 2002 Edition," "Ten Exemptions," U.S. Department of Justice, http://www.usdoj.gov/04foia/1974tenexemp.htm.
[32]Privacy Act of 1974, 5 U.S.C. Section 552a(g), http://www4.law.cornell.edu/uscode/5/552a.html; *see also* "Overview of the Privacy Act of 1974, 2002 Edition," "Civil Remedies," U.S. Department of Justice, http://www.usdoj.gov/04foia/1974civrem.htm.
[33]Privacy Act of 1974, 5 U.S.C. Section 552a(i)(1)-(3), http://www4.law.cornell.edu/uscode/5/552a.html; *see also* "Overview of the Privacy Act of 1974, 2002 Edition," "Criminal Penalties," U.S. Department of Justice, http://www.usdoj.gov/04foia/1974crimpen.htm.

recently held that "actual damages" must be suffered in order to be eligible for the minimum $1,000 damage award.[34]

The Computer Matching and Privacy Protection Act of 1988 amended the Privacy Act to add procedural requirements for government agencies to follow when engaging in computer-matching activities, to provide individuals an opportunity to receive notice and refute adverse information before a government benefit was denied or terminated, and require agencies to establish oversight boards to monitor matching activities.[35] The Computer Matching and Privacy Protection Amendments of 1990 further clarified the due process provisions.[36]

b. Freedom of Information Act

Although not a privacy law, the Freedom of Information Act (FOIA)[37] is relevant because it addresses how U.S. government information can be accessed by any individual. FOIA provides the public with the right and the means to access federal agency records. The purpose of FOIA, as stated by the Supreme Court, "is to ensure an informed citizenry, vital to the functioning of a democratic society, needed to check against corruption and to hold the governors accountable to the governed."[38] As the Department of Justice states, however, this goal of openness is balanced against "the public's interests in the effective and efficient operations of government; in the prudent governmental use of limited fiscal resources; and in the preservation of the confidentiality of sensitive personal, commercial, and governmental information."[39]

In furtherance of this balance, FOIA provides for the publication of information concerning agency organization and procedure.[40] Subsection (a)(2) of the Act requires that certain records, such as agency opinions, be made available to the public for review and/or

---

[34]*Doe v. Chao*, U.S., No. 02-1377, Feb. 24, 2004; *see also* "High Court Says 'Actual Damages' Needed to Win $1,000 for DOL's Privacy Act Breach," *Privacy & Security Law Report*, Vol. 3, No. 9, Mar. 1, 2004 at 235-36.

[35]Computer Matching and Privacy Protection Act of 1988, 5 U.S.C. Section 552a(a)(8)-(13), (e)(12), (o), (p), (q), (r), (u), http://www4.law.cornell.edu/uscode/5/552a.html; *see also* "Overview of the Privacy Act of 1974, 2002 Edition," "Computer Matching," U.S. Department of Justice, http://www.usdoj.gov/04foia/1974compmatch.htm.

[36]Computer Matching and Privacy Protection Amendments of 1990, 5 U.S.C. Section 552a(p), http://www4.law.cornell.edu/uscode/5/552a.html; *see also* "Overview of the Privacy Act of 1974, 2002 Edition," "Computer Matching," U.S. Department of Justice, http://www.usdoj.gov/04foia/1974compmatch.htm.

[37]Freedom of Information Act, 5. U.S.C. Section 552 (2003), http://www4.law.cornell.edu/uscode/5/552.html (hereinafter "FOIA").

[38]*NLRB v. Robbins Tire & Rubber Co.* , 437 U.S. 214, 242 (1978).

[39]"Freedom of Information Act Guide, May 2002," "Introduction," U.S. Department of Justice, http://www. usdoj.gov/oip/introduc.htm.

[40]FOIA, 5 U.S.C. Section 552(a)(1), http://www4.law.cornell.edu/uscode/5/552.html.

copying.[41] Subsection (a)(3)—the provision most used by the public[42]—requires disclosure of any records not exempt or excluded if a person makes an appropriate request to the proper agency.[43] FOIA also provides exemptions to disclosure of requested information.[44] Exempt information includes classified documents pertaining to national security, agency personnel rules and practices, trade secrets and privileged or confidential commercial information, inter- and intra-agency memoranda not otherwise available, personnel and medical files, certain law enforcement records,[45] information collected for the regulation of financial institutions, and geological and geophysical data concerning wells.[46] These exemptions are discretionary, however, and do not serve as "mandatory bars to disclosure."[47]

Originally enacted in 1966, FOIA has undergone several changes over the last few decades. In 1974, in the wake of the Watergate scandal, Congress narrowed several exemptions and exclusions while broadening FOIA's procedural provisions.[48] In 1986, however, Congress expanded some of the law enforcement exemptions. Then, in 1996, Congress formally addressed the issue of electronic records and brought them within FOIA's coverage. The 1996 amendments also added requirements for annual reports from federal agencies and the Department of Justice concerning their FOIA operations and FOIA litigation.[49]

c. Financial Services Modernization Act of 1999 (Gramm-Leach-Bliley Act)

After many years of trying to eliminate Depression-era legal restrictions on the ownership and consolidation of banking, securities, and insurance industries in the United States, the Financial Services Modernization Act of 1999 (commonly known as the Gramm-Leach-Bliley Act, for the three Congressmen who sponsored the legislation) was signed into law by President Clinton on November 12, 1999.[50] A

---

[41]FOIA, 5 U.S.C. Section 552(a)(2), http://www4.law.cornell.edu/uscode/5/552.html.
[42]"Freedom of Information Act Guide, May 2002," "Introduction," U.S. Department of Justice, http://www.usdoj.gov/oip/introduc.htm.
[43]FOIA, 5 U.S.C. Section 552(a)(3), http://www4.law.cornell.edu/uscode/5/552.html.
[44]FOIA, 5 U.S.C. Section 552(b), http://www4.law.cornell.edu/uscode/5/552.html.
[45]In 1986, Congress amended FOIA to add three exclusions to Subsection (c) that pertain to the exemption in Subsection (b) relating to law enforcement records.
[46]5. U.S.C. Section 552(b)(1)-(9), http://www4.law.cornell.edu/uscode/5/552.html.
[47]*Chrysler Corp. v. Brown*, 441 U.S. 281, 293 (1979).
[48]"Freedom of Information Act Guide, May 2002," "Introduction," U.S. Department of Justice, http://www.usdoj.gov/oip/introduc.htm.
[49]*Id.*
[50]Financial Services Modernization Act of 1999, Pub. Law 106-102, Nov. 12, 1999, 15 U.S.C. Section 6801 *et seq.*, http://thomas.loc.gov/cgi-bin/bdquery/z?d106:SN00900:| (hereinafter "Gramm-Leach-Bliley Act" or "GLBA").

late addition to this financial modernization legislation was one of the most comprehensive consumer financial privacy statutes in United States history—Subtitle A, of Title V, of the Gramm-Leach-Bliley Act (GLBA or the Act).

The GLBA imposes significant obligations and restrictions on financial institutions with respect to the disclosure of personal financial information of consumer customers to nonaffiliated third parties. These obligations and restrictions became a condition precedent to the passage of the broader financial modernization legislation due to a few highly publicized instances in which financial institutions were sharing consumer customer financial information (primarily for marketing purposes) in a manner that many felt did not respect the sensitive nature of the information. In passing the GLBA, Congress expressly stated its policy that "each financial institution has an affirmative and continuing obligation to respect the privacy of its customers and to protect the security and confidentiality of those customers' nonpublic personal information."[51] This portion of the chapter will outline the entities covered under the GLBA and the substantive requirements of the Act and its implementing regulations.

Entities Covered

The GLBA limits information sharing by financial institutions. The term "financial institution" is defined very broadly in the Act[52] and encompasses any institution the business of which is engaging in the financial activities described in section 4(k) of the Bank Holding Company Act of 1956 (BHCA).[53] The BHCA grants the ability of bank holding companies and their non-bank affiliates to engage in a wide array of financial activities, such as lending money, providing insurance, providing investment advice, underwriting and dealing in securities, leasing certain forms of property, and loan brokering. However, activities also deemed financial in nature include check guaranty, collection agency, consumer reporting agency, tax planning and preparation, management consulting and counseling, courier services for banking instruments, printing and selling checks and related documents, providing financial data processing and transmission services, and activities that are considered "closely related to banking" by the Federal Reserve Board.[54] The term "Financial institution" has

---

[51]GLBA, 15 U.S.C. Section 6801(a), http://www4.law.cornell.edu/uscode/15/6801.html.

[52]GLBA, 15 U.S.C. Section 6809(3)(A), http://www4.law.cornell.edu/uscode/15/6809.html.

[53]Bank Holding Company Act, 12 U.S.C. Section 1843(k), http://www4.law.cornell.edu/uscode/12/1843.html.

[54]*See* Federal Reserve Board Regulation Y at 12 C.F.R. Section 225.28.

20   CHAPTER 1

even been interpreted by the Federal Trade Commission to encompass law firms.[55]

Notwithstanding the broad definition of "financial institution" under the Act, the GLBA exempts some entities that would otherwise be considered financial institutions. Specifically, the Act exempts persons or entities subject to the jurisdiction of the Commodity Futures Trading Commission, the Federal Agricultural Mortgage Corporation, any entity chartered and operating under the Farm Credit Act of 1971, and any institution chartered by Congress to engage in securitizations or secondary market sales as long as such institution does not sell or transfer nonpublic information to a nonaffiliated third party.[56]

The rules and restrictions placed on financial institutions relate to the sharing of nonpublic personal information with nonaffiliated third parties. The Act defines an "affiliate" as any company that controls, is controlled by, or is under common control with another company.[57] As such, the provisions of the GLBA are applicable when a financial institution shares the nonpublic personal information of its consumer customers with any company that it does not control, that does not control the financial institution, or that is not controlled by a company that controls the financial institution. Conversely, the provisions of the GLBA do not apply when a financial institution shares nonpublic personal information with its affiliates. The applicability of the GLBA demonstrates Congress's commitment to protecting the sensitive financial information of consumers, while at the same time recognizing the importance of the free flow of information among corporate affiliates at the heart of financial modernization in the United States.

Interpretation of Requirements

As mentioned previously, the GLBA and its implementing regulations place rules and restrictions on "financial institutions" with respect to the sharing of nonpublic personal information with nonaffiliated third parties. To understand the requirements of the Act and its implementing regulations, a good understanding of some key definitions is critical.

"Nonpublic Personal Information" (NPI) is any personally identifiable financial information that (a) is provided to a financial institution by a consumer, (b) results from any transaction with or

---

[55]*See* Letter to David L. Roll and Warren L. Dennis from William E. Kovacic, General Counsel, Federal Trade Commission, June 30, 2003, http://www.abanet.org/poladv/glbfactsheet/amnestyletter.pdf.

[56]GLBA, 15 U.S.C. Section 6809(3)(B)-(D), http://www4.law.cornell.edu/uscode/15/6809.html.

[57]GLBA, 15 U.S.C. Section 6809(6), http://www4.law.cornell.edu/uscode/15/6809.html.

service performed for the consumer, or (c) that is otherwise obtained by the financial institution.[58] To illustrate these three methods of obtaining NPI, a financial institution may obtain NPI from a consumer when the consumer completes and submits an application for a line of credit, when the consumer draws on or makes a payment to the line of credit, and when the financial institution accesses the consumer's consumer report. Included in the definition of NPI is any list, description, or other grouping of consumers (and publicly available information pertaining to them) that is derived with the use of any NPI.[59] For example, a financial institution uses account numbers to create a list of consumer names and addresses. Since the list was derived with the use of NPI (the account number), the list of names and addresses is NPI.

NPI does not include "publicly available information" as that term is defined in the federal functional regulators' regulations implementing the GLBA.[60] "Publicly Available Information" means any information that a financial institution has a reasonable basis to believe is lawfully made available to the general public from government records (such as real estate records), widely distributed media (such as a telephone directory), or disclosures to the general public required by law (such as political campaign disclosures).[61] To form a reasonable belief that the information is publicly available, the financial institution must take steps to determine that the information is of a type that is available to the general public and that the consumer has not directed that the information not be made available to the general public, if applicable.[62]

The terms "consumer" and "customer" are key definitions in the GLBA and its implementing regulations. A "consumer" is an individual (or his/her legal representative) who obtains financial products and services from a financial institution to be used primarily for personal, family, or household purposes.[63] A "customer" is a consumer who has a continuing relationship with a financial institution whereby the financial institution provides one or more financial products or services to the consumer.[64] It is important to note that under the GLBA and its regulations, a customer is always a consumer, but a consumer is not always a customer.

---

[58]GLBA, 15 U.S.C. Section 6809(4)(A)(i)-(ii), http://www4.law.cornell.edu/uscode/15/6809.html.

[59]GLBA, 15 U.S.C. Section 6809(4)(C)(i), http://www4.law.cornell.edu/uscode/15/6809.html.

[60]GLBA, 15 U.S.C. Section 6809(4)(B), http://www4.law.cornell.edu/uscode/15/6809.html.

[61]16 C.F.R. Section 313.3(p)(1)(i)-(iii).

[62]16 C.F.R. Section 313.3(p)(2)(i)-(ii).

[63]GLBA, 15 U.S.C. Section 6809(9), http://www4.law.cornell.edu/uscode/15/6809.html.

[64]16 C.F.R. Section 313.3(h),(i)(1).

22   CHAPTER 1

Disclosure of NPI

As a general rule, the GLBA prohibits a financial institution, either directly or through an affiliate, from disclosing to a nonaffiliated third party any NPI unless the consumer has been provided with an appropriate notice and an opportunity to direct that such information not be disclosed to the nonaffiliated third party (that is, the consumer may "opt out" of such a disclosure), and the consumer has not exercised his/her right to opt out.[65]

Of course, any general rule invariably comes with exceptions. The GLBA has several important and far-reaching exceptions that should be mentioned. The notice and opt-out requirements do not apply when the disclosure of NPI is necessary to "effect, administer, or enforce a transaction requested or authorized by the consumer."[66] For example, disclosure of NPI by a financial institution to a collections agency for the collection of a delinquent customer loan does not have to be disclosed to the customer in advance of the sharing of NPI. Also, NPI may be shared by a financial institution without providing the consumer with notice and an opportunity to opt out if such sharing is in connection with the servicing or processing of a financial product or service requested or authorized by the consumer, or maintaining or servicing the consumer's account with the financial institution or with another entity as part of a private label credit card program.[67]

Other exceptions to the notice and opt-out requirements include: (a) to protect the confidentiality or security of the financial institution's records;[68] (b) to protect against or prevention of actual or potential fraud;[69] (c) in connection with a proposed or actual sale, merger, transfer, or exchange of all or a portion of the business or operating unit (limited to the information about consumers of such business or unit);[70] and (d) as required by applicable law.[71]

The GLBA and its implementing regulations also place restrictions on the re-disclosure and re-use of already disclosed NPI. The nature of

---

[65]GLBA, 15 U.S.C. Section 6802(a)-(b), http://www4.law.cornell.edu/uscode/15/6802.html.

[66]GLBA, 15 U.S.C. Section 6802(e)(1), http://www4.law.cornell.edu/uscode/15/6802.html.

[67]GLBA, 15 U.S.C. Section 6802(e)(1)(A)-(B), http://www4.law.cornell.edu/uscode/15/6802.html.

[68]GLBA, 15 U.S.C. Section 6802(e)(3)(A), http://www4.law.cornell.edu/uscode/15/6802.html.

[69]GLBA, 15 U.S.C. Section 6802(e)(3)(B), http://www4.law.cornell.edu/uscode/15/6802.html.

[70]GLBA, 15 U.S.C. Section 6802(e)(7), http://www4.law.cornell.edu/uscode/15/6802.html.

[71]GLBA, 15 U.S.C. Section 6802(e)(8), http://www4.law.cornell.edu/uscode/15/6802.html.

the re-disclosure and re-use depend on whether the disclosure of NPI to the nonaffiliated third party is based upon an exception. If a nonaffiliated third party receives NPI from a financial institution *pursuant to* an exception, it may only disclose the NPI to its affiliate or to the affiliate of the disclosing financial institution, and it may only disclose and use the NPI in accordance with one of the Act's exceptions.[72] If a nonaffiliated third party receives NPI from a financial institution *outside* an exception, it, too, may only disclose the NPI to its affiliate or to the affiliate of the disclosing financial institution. However, it may also disclose the NPI if such disclosure would be lawful if made directly to the other party by the disclosing financial institution.[73]

Notice Requirements

As mentioned previously, the general rule of the GLBA is that a financial institution shall not disclose NPI to a nonaffiliated third party without providing notice to the consumer and giving the consumer the opportunity to opt out of the sharing of his/her NPI. In the previous section, exceptions to this general rule allowing for the disclosure of NPI without notice to the consumer were discussed. It is also important to understand the functional requirements that the GLBA and its implementing regulations place on financial institutions that desire to share NPI with nonaffiliated third parties in situations that do *not* fall within the exceptions to the general rule.

To disclose NPI to nonaffiliated third parties in situations in which an exception is *not* applicable, the financial institution must provide notice to the consumer. There are four types of notices outlined in the Act: initial privacy notices, annual privacy notices, revised privacy notices, and opt-out notices.

Initial privacy notices of the financial institution's policies and practices with respect to the disclosure and protection of the NPI of consumers must be provided to customers at the time of the establishment of the customer relationship.[74] The initial privacy notice to *customers* is a requirement of all financial institutions and is not conditioned upon whether the financial institution chooses to disclose NPI. If the financial institution desires to disclose NPI about *consumers* to nonaffiliated third parties, the financial institution must provide the initial privacy notice before such disclosure is made.[75] If the financial institution chooses not to disclose NPI about *consumers* (as opposed to

---

[72] 16 C.F.R. Section 313.11(a)(1)(i)-(iii).
[73] 16 C.F.R. Section 313.11(b)(1)(i)-(iii).
[74] 16 C.F.R. Section 313.4(a)(1).
[75] 16 C.F.R. Section 313.4(a)(2).

24   CHAPTER 1

customers), the initial privacy notice is not required to be provided to the consumer.[76]

Since the initial privacy notice is required upon the establishment of a customer relationship with a consumer, it is critical to understand when such an event takes place. As a general rule, a customer relationship exists when the financial institution and the consumer enter into a continuing relationship. For loans, the customer relationship begins at loan origination (although the customer relationship transfers upon the transfer of loan servicing rights). Examples of establishment of a customer relationship include the following: opening a credit card account, executing an insurance contract, entering into an agreement to obtain financial advisory services for a fee, and providing necessary information to a financial institution for the compilation and provision of access to all of the consumer's on-line financial accounts on the financial institution's website.[77]

There are certain circumstances when the initial privacy notice can be provided subsequent to the establishment of a customer relationship. A financial institution may provide the initial privacy notice within a reasonable time after the customer relationship is established if establishing the customer relationship is not at the customer's election (for example, acquiring the service rights to a loan), or in circumstances in which there would be a substantial delay to the customer's transaction and the customer agrees to receive the initial privacy notice at a later time (for example, agreement by telephone involving the immediate delivery of a financial service).[78]

Under the GLBA and its implementing regulations, financial institutions are required to send an annual notice to their customers of their policies and practices with respect to the disclosure and protection of the NPI of consumers throughout the continuation of the customer relationship.[79] This annual privacy notice must be sent at least once in any twelve consecutive month period during which the customer relationship exists, applied on a consistent basis.[80] Annual privacy notices are not required to be sent to former customers.[81]

For a financial institution to disclose NPI to a nonaffiliated third party in a manner different from that disclosed in an initial or annual notice, the financial institution must provide the consumer a revised

---

[76] 16 C.F.R. Section 313.4(b)(1).
[77] 16 C.F.R. Section 313.4(c).
[78] 16 C.F.R. Section 313.4(e)(1)(i)-(ii).
[79] 16 C.F.R. Section 313.5(a)(1).
[80] *Id.*
[81] 16 C.F.R. Section 313.5(b)(1).

privacy notice—a notice that accurately describes the revised policies and practices—and an opportunity to opt out of such disclosure.[82]

The GLBA and its implementing regulations delineate the information that must be included in the initial, annual, and revised privacy notices. These privacy notices must contain the following, as applicable:

- The categories of NPI that the financial institution collects—information from the consumer, information about the consumer's transactions with the financial institution or its affiliates, information about the consumer's transactions with nonaffiliated third parties, and information from a consumer reporting agency;[83]
- The categories of NPI that the financial institution discloses—categories of NPI that the financial institution does not currently disclose but reserves the right to disclose in the future (along with a few examples) or a reservation of the right to disclose all NPI;[84]
- The categories of affiliates and nonaffiliated third parties to whom the financial institution discloses NPI (other than those parties who are receiving NPI subject to an exception)—financial service providers, nonfinancial companies, and others (along with a few examples of each);[85]
- The categories of NPI about former customers that the financial institution discloses and the categories of affiliates and nonaffiliated third parties to whom the financial institution discloses NPI about former customers (other than those parties who are receiving NPI subject to an exception);[86]
- A separate statement of the categories of information the financial institution discloses and the categories of third party service providers who the financial institution contacted (other than those third party service providers who are receiving NPI subject to an exception);[87]
- An explanation of the consumer's right to opt out of the disclosure of NPI to nonaffiliated third parties, including the method(s) by which the consumer may exercise that right at any

---

[82] 16 C.F.R. Section 313.8(a).
[83] 16 C.F.R. Section 313.6(a)(1), (c)(1)(i)-(iv).
[84] 16 C.F.R. Section 313.6(a)(2), (c)(2)(i)-(ii).
[85] 16 C.F.R. Section313.6(a)(3), (c)(3)(i)-(iii).
[86] 16 C.F.R. Section 313.6(a)(4).
[87] 16 C.F.R. Section 313.6(a)(5).
[88] 16 C.F.R. Section 313.6(a)(6).

time;[88]

- Any disclosures made under the Fair Credit Reporting Act with respect to notices and opting out of disclosures of information among affiliates;[89]
- The financial institution's policies and practices with respect to protecting the confidentiality and security of NPI—a general description of who has access to the information and a statement whether the financial institution has security practices and procedures in place to ensure the confidentiality of the information in accordance with the policy;[90] and
- If the financial institution discloses NPI to nonaffiliated third parties subject to an exception, a statement that the financial institution makes disclosures to other nonaffiliated third parties as permitted by law.[91]

The implementing regulations of the GLBA include the option of using a simplified notice for those financial institutions that do not disclose and are not reserving the right to disclose NPI about customers or former customers to affiliates or nonaffiliated third parties.[92] The option of using a short-form notice and opting out for noncustomers is also available.[93]

Information that must be included in the opt-out notice is also defined by the GLBA and its implementing regulations. If an opt-out notice is required, it must state:

- That the financial institution discloses or reserves the right to disclose NPI about consumers to nonaffiliated third parties— identifying all categories of NPI disclosed or reserved, and identifying all categories of nonaffiliated third parties to which NPI is disclosed;[94]
- That the consumer has the right to opt-out of such disclosure— identifying the financial services to which the opt-out direction would apply;[95] and
- A reasonable means by which the consumer can exercise the opt-out right—such as prominently designating check-off boxes, including a reply form that includes the address to which the

---

[89] 16 C.F.R. Section 313.6(a)(7).
[90] 16 C.F.R. Section 313.6(a)(8), (c)(6)(i)-(ii).
[91] 16 C.F.R. Section 313.6(b).
[92] 16 C.F.R. Section 313.6(c)(5).
[93] 16 C.F.R. Section 313.6(d).
[94] 16 C.F.R. Section 313.7(a)(1)(i), (a)(2)(i)(A).
[95] 16 C.F.R. Section 313.7(a)(1)(ii), (a)(2)(i)(B).

form should be mailed, or providing an electronic means via electronic mail or website process (if the consumer agrees to electronic delivery), or providing a toll-free telephone number.[96]

The initial privacy notice and the opt-out notice may be combined into a single form and provided to the consumer.[97] Moreover, a financial institution may provide a joint notice with one or more of its affiliates or other financial institutions as identified in the notice, as long as the notice is accurate with respect to all institutions to which it applies.[98]

The notice requirements of the GLBA and its implementing regulations have special rules for joint relationships, such as joint owners of an account. First, each joint consumer may exercise the right to opt out of the sharing of NPI.[99] The financial institution can treat the exercise of this right by one joint consumer as applying to all of the associated joint consumers, or it can permit each joint consumer to opt out separately as long as it permits one of the joint consumers to opt out on behalf of all associated joint consumers.[100] The financial institution may only provide one opt-out notice unless an associated consumer requests a separate opt-out notice.[101]

All notices provided under the GLBA must be in writing or, if the consumer agrees, in electronic format, so that each consumer can reasonably be expected to receive actual notice.[102] All notices are subject to a "clear and conspicuous" standard—they must be reasonably understandable and designed to call attention to the nature and significance of the information in the notice.[103]

Opt-Out Procedures

After delivery of the opt-out notice, the financial institution must give the consumer a reasonable opportunity to opt out of the disclosure of NPI before the financial institution discloses it to a nonaffiliated third party.[104] Likewise, the financial institution must comply with a consumer's opt-out direction as soon as reasonably practicable after receipt of such direction.[105] The consumer may exercise his or her opt-

---

[96] 16 C.F.R. Section 313.7(a)(1)(iii), (a)(2)(ii)(A)-(D).
[97] 16 C.F.R. Section 313.7(d).
[98] 16 C.F.R. Section 313.9(f).
[99] 16 C.F.R. Section 313.7(d)(2).
[100] 16 C.F.R. Section 313.7(d)(2)(i)-(ii), (3).
[101] 16 C.F.R. Section 313.9(g).
[102] 16 C.F.R. Section 313.9(a).
[103] 16 C.F.R. Section 313.3(b)(1), .4(a), .5(a)(1), .7(a)(1), .8(a)(1).
[104] 16 C.F.R. Section 313.10(a)(1)(iii).
[105] 16 C.F.R. Section 313.7(e).

28   CHAPTER 1

out right at any time, and the opt-out is effective until the consumer revokes the direction in writing (or electronically if the consumer agrees).[106]

Marketing Activities

No discussion about the GLBA would be complete without a discussion of the status of marketing activities under the Act and its implementing regulations. As mentioned earlier in this chapter, in 1999, a few instances of the disclosure of sensitive consumer information by financial institutions, primarily for marketing purposes, were highly publicized. In many of these instances, financial institutions were sharing consumer information, including credit or debit account numbers, with telemarketing firms that were engaged by the financial institution to sell other, nonproprietary products and services to consumers that the financial institution believed would be of interest to their consumer customer. State Attorneys General investigated these practices and lawsuits were initiated. Although these lawsuits were ultimately settled, the publicity garnered made the privacy of consumers' financial information the political topic of the day.

Although financial institution marketing practices came under intense scrutiny, Congress soon realized that consumers should not have the ability to opt out of the sharing of NPI for all marketing purposes. As such, Congress provided for two marketing instances in which the opt-out requirements of the Act would not apply. The first instance arises when a financial institution provides NPI to a nonaffiliated third party who performs marketing services or functions on a financial institution's behalf, including the marketing of the financial institution's own products or services.[107] The second instance arises when a financial institution enters into a written agreement with another financial institution whereby the financial institutions jointly offer, endorse, or sponsor a financial product or service (known as a "joint marketing agreement").[108]

Both of these exceptions to the opt-out requirements only apply if the initial privacy notice is provided, and if the financial institution and nonaffiliated third party enter into a contractual arrangement whereby the nonaffiliated third party is prohibited from disclosing or using the NPI in a manner other than to carry out the purposes for which the financial institution disclosed the NPI or a general exception to the notice and opt-out provisions.[109] It is also important to remember that,

---

[106] 16 C.F.R. Section 313.7(f), (g)(1).
[107] 16 C.F.R. Section 313.12(a)(1).
[108] 16 C.F.R. Section 313.12(b), (c).
[109] 16 C.F.R. Section 313.12(a)(1)(i)-(ii).

although the opt-out rights of the consumer do not apply in these instances, the financial institution must disclose these types of arrangements in its privacy notices.

Although Congress recognized that many financial institutions, especially those small in size, have a legitimate need to share NPI with nonaffiliated third parties that market financial institutions' own products or services and with other financial institutions that jointly offer financial products or services, so, too, did Congress recognize the importance and sensitivity of customers' account numbers. The general rule in the GLBA with respect to the sharing of account numbers with nonaffiliated third parties is that a financial institution must not disclose any account number or other form of access code for a consumer's credit card, deposit, or transaction account for use in telemarketing, direct mail marketing, or electronic mail marketing.[110]

Three exceptions apply to this general rule. First, disclosure of account numbers or access codes to consumer reporting agencies is permitted.[111] Second, disclosure to marketing services providers that market financial institutions' own products or services is permissible as long as the marketing services provider is not authorized to directly initiate charges to the account.[112] Third, the financial institution may share account numbers or access codes with participants in a private label credit card, affinity, or similar program in which the participants in the program are disclosed to the customer when the customer enters the program.[113]

The Act and its implementing regulations do, however, make it clear that nothing prohibits a financial institution from disclosing encrypted account numbers or access codes to nonaffiliated third parties as long as the financial institution does not provide to the nonaffiliated third party the means to decrypt the account number or access code.[114]

Safeguarding Information

Up to this point, the discussion of the GLBA and its implementing regulations has focused on the disclosure of NPI. However, the GLBA also delineates security, or safeguard requirements for the protection of customer records and information. Specifically, the GLBA requires the enforcement agencies delineated in the Act to establish standards

---

[110]GLBA, 15 U.S.C. Section 6802(d), http://www4.law.cornell.edu/uscode/15/6802.html.

[111]Id.

[112]16 C.F.R. Section 313.12(b)(1).

[113]16 C.F.R. Section 313.12(b)(2).

[114]16 C.F.R. Section 313.12(c)(1).

30   CHAPTER 1

relating to administrative, technical, and physical safeguards to (a) ensure the security and confidentiality of customer records or information, (b) protect against anticipated threats or hazards to the security or integrity of this information, and (c) protect against unauthorized access to or use of customer records or information.[115]

The enforcement agencies' standards center around the financial institution's creation, implementation, and maintenance of a comprehensive, written information security program that is appropriate for the financial institution's size and complexity, type of business, and sensitivity of the customer information.[116] In creating, implementing, and maintaining the information security program,[117] the financial institution is required to

- Designate an employee or employees to coordinate the program;[118]
- Identify internal and external risks to the security confidentiality and integrity of customer information;[119]
- Assess the sufficiency of any safeguards in place to control the identified risks;[120]
- Design and implement safeguards to control identified risks;[121]
- Regularly test or otherwise monitor the effectiveness of the safeguards;[122]
- Select and retain service providers that are capable of maintaining appropriate safeguards;[123]
- Require service providers to implement and maintain appropriate safeguards by contract;[124] and
- Evaluate and adjust the information security program in light of testing or monitoring results, material changes in business operations, or other circumstances that may have a material impact.[125]

---

[115]GLBA, 15 U.S.C. Section 6801(b)(1)-(3), http://www4.law.cornell.edu/uscode/15/6801.html.

[116]16 C.F.R. Section 314.3(a).

[117]For a detailed discussion of the development of security programs and a more in-depth discussion on the Safeguard Rule, see Jody R. Westby, ed., *International Guide to Cyber Security*, American Bar Association, Section of Science & Technology Law, Privacy & Computer Crime Committee, ABA Publishing, http://www.abanet.org/abapubs/books/security/.

[118]16 C.F.R. Section 314.4(a).

[119]16 C.F.R. Section 314.4(b).

[120]*Id.*

[121]16 C.F.R. Section 314.4(c).

[122]*Id.*

[123]16 C.F.R. Section 314.4(d)(1).

[124]16 C.F.R. Section 314.4(d)(2).

[125]16 C.F.R. Section 314.4(c).

The standards set minimum considerations for the required risk assessment. In each relevant area of a financial institution's operations, the financial institution must consider employee training and management, information systems (including network and software design, and processing, storage, transmission, and disposal of information), and the detection, prevention, and response to attacks, intrusions, or other systems failures.[126]

Enforcement

GLBA enforcement can be divided into three issue areas: Privacy Rule, Safeguards Rule, and Pretexting. Pretexting traditionally is defined as a practice in which a so-called information broker, under the pretext of being a customer, tricks a financial institution into revealing the financial information of its customers. The definition is expanded in some instances to include any instance in which companies or individuals who use false pretenses to obtain consumers' personal financial information, and/or knowingly solicit others to do so.

The Federal Trade Commission (FTC) has not yet brought any actions under the Safeguards Rule. It did, however, successfully bring enforcement action under the Privacy Rule. The FTC filed a complaint against 30 Minute Mortgage, Inc., a mortgage spamming operation, and an officer and director of the company for engaging in unfair and deceptive trade practices under the FTC Act, and for violating the GLBA, the Truth in Lending Act, and the GLBA Privacy Rule.[127] The FTC froze the company's assets and the defendants agreed to a Stipulated Order of Preliminary Injunction halting the deceptive practices. The complaint alleged that the mortgage company was sending spam messages advertising very low mortgage rates and claiming it was a "national mortgage lender." The company urged potential customers to fill out detailed applications containing sensitive information, including asset/account numbers, salary, social security numbers, and addresses, assuring them the sensitive information would be protected because it was transmitted through Secure Sockets Layer (SSL) technology. The FTC claimed the company was, in fact, not a mortgage company, but instead sent spam, collected sensitive information under false pretenses, and then offered it for sale. The FTC charged that these actions violated both the GLBA Pretexting and Privacy Rules.[128]

---

[126]16 C.F.R. Section 314.4(b)(1)-(3).

[127]*See FTC v. 30 Minute Mortgage, Inc., Gregory P. Roth, Peter W. Stolz*, Civil Action No. 03-60021, (SD FL 2003), http://www.ftc.gov/os/2003/03/30mincmp.pdf; *see also* "Deceptive Mortgage Scam Halted," Federal Trade Commission, Mar. 20, 2003, http://www.ftc.gov/opa/2003/03/thirty6.htm.

[128]*Id.*

32   CHAPTER 1

The defendants agreed to settle the FTC charges. The settlement requires them to post US $1 million bonds before sending unsolicited commercial emails, and it bars misrepresentations in the advertising or sales of any goods or services on the Internet and misrepresentations that relate to residential mortgages. It also bars the defendants from using or benefiting personally from the personal information that was deceptively collected.[129]

The FTC also filed three actions in 2001 concerning pretexting under the traditional definition involving trickery of a financial institution: *FTC v. Paula L. Garrett, d/b/a Discreet Data Systems;*[130] *FTC v. Victor L. Guzzetta, d/b/a Smart Data Systems;*[131] and *FTC v. Information Search, Inc., and David Kacala.*[132] In addition, *FTC v. Rapp individually and dba Touch Tone Information, Inc.,*[133] contained anti-pretexting allegations under Section 5 of the FTC Act[134] before the GLB Act was enacted.

The first three actions, filed concurrently in different federal district courts, involved the same basic facts. The defendants operated websites in which they advertised that they could obtain nonpublic, confidential, financial information. In FTC sting operations set up in cooperation with local banks, an FTC investigator posed as a consumer seeking account balance information on her "fiancé's" checking account. The investigator provided limited information about the account to the defendants. The defendants or persons they hired called the bank, identified themselves by the name of the supposed fiancé, and asked to check his balance. The defendants later provided the account balance information to the FTC investigator. All of the defendants ultimately settled with the FTC, agreeing to injunctive provisions concerning the practices that were the subject of the complaints and to monetary relief.

The *Touch Tone* case also involved the sale of private financial data obtained through false pretenses. The FTC alleged that the pretexting

---

[129]*See FTC v. 30 Minute Mortgage, Inc., Gregory P. Roth, Peter W. Stolz,* Civil Action No. 03-60021-CIV-LENARD-SIMONTON, Nov. 26, 2003 (Stipulated Final Judgment and Order for Permanent Injunction and Other Equitable Relief as to Defendant Peter W. Stolz), http://www.ftc.gov/os/2003/12/031126stipstolz.pdf; for links to similar final judgments for other defendants, *see* "Internet Mortgage Scam Halted," Federal Trade Commission, Dec. 9, 2003, http://www.ftc.gov/opa/2003/12/30mm2.htm.

[130]*FTC v. Paula L. Garrett, d/b/a Discreet Data Systems,* Civil Action No. H-01-1255 (SD TX 2002), http://www.ftc.gov/os/2002/03/index.htm#8.

[131]*FTC v. Victor L. Guzzetta, d/b/a Smart Data Systems,* Civil Action No. 01-2335 (DGT) (ED NY 2002), http://www.ftc.gov/os/2002/03/index.htm#8.

[132] *FTC v. Information Search, Inc., and David Kacala,* Civil Action No. AMD01-1121 (D MD 2002), http://www.ftc.gov/os/2002/03/index.htm#8.

[133]*FTC v. Rapp individually and dba Touch Tone Information, Inc.,* Civil Action No. 99-WM-783 (D CO 2000), http://www.ftc.gov/os/2000/06/index.htm#27.

[134]GLBA, 15 U.S.C. Section 45(a), http://www4.law.cornell.edu/uscode/15/45.html

was deceptive and that Touch Tone's disclosure and sale of consumers' private financial information obtained by pretexting without consumers' knowledge or consent was an unfair act in violation of the FTC Act. The matter also resulted in a settlement that included injunctive provisions and a suspended financial provision.

Relation to State Law

One of the more contentious provisions of the GLBA is the provision that deals with the operation of state law vis-à-vis the Act. One might expect that with the modernization of the financial services industry and the advent of new technologies enabling financial institutions to maintain a nationwide presence, as well as enabling consumers to choose financial institutions from across the nation, the provisions of the GLBA should be applied consistently throughout the country. However, the GLBA specifically allows states to pass legislation that provides greater consumer protections than the GLBA.[135]

The provision of the Act that preserves state laws that afford consumers greater protection was, in essence, a political compromise between proponents of consumer "opt-out" rights and proponents of a system that required financial institutions to obtain consumers' consent before sharing NPI (that is, "opt-in"). As discussed earlier, the general rule of the GLBA is that a financial institution can share NPI with nonaffiliated third parties after notice to the consumer and providing the consumer with a reasonable opportunity to opt out of such a disclosure. Perhaps because of the sheer coverage of the provisions of the GLBA and the vast privacy protections within, the "opt-in" proponents were satisfied with the opt-out standard as long as the states could choose to implement the opt-in framework, thus allowing for greater consumer protection.

Since passage of the GLBA and finalization of its implementing regulations, the privacy of consumer financial information in the United States has continued to be a hotly debated topic in governmental arenas throughout the country. To be sure, the pervasiveness of information-based crimes such as identity theft and computer hacking, along with the ever-present and growing use of new technologies, will keep the privacy debate at the forefront for the foreseeable future. Nevertheless, the GLBA paved the way for a new era in privacy protection in the United States, with its efficacy to be measured only by the passage of time.

Extraterritorial Application

There are extraterritorial application considerations with GLBA. These are discussed in more detail in Chapter 2, Section D.

---

[135]GLBA, 15 U.S.C. Section 6807, http://www4.law.cornell.edu/uscode/15/6807.html.

34   CHAPTER 1

d. Fair Credit Reporting Act

The Fair Credit Reporting Act[136] (Act) was intended, in large part, to (a) provide a framework for the credit reporting industry and (b) to protect consumers' privacy and provide them certain rights with respect to their credit information that is maintained by consumer reporting agencies, such as credit bureaus. According to the FTC, "[T]he confidentiality of consumer report information is a fundamental principle underlying the statute."[137] Consumer protections are primarily concerned with privacy and accuracy of consumer credit information. Since Congress passed FCRA in 1970, amendments to the Act have strengthened consumer protections.[138]

Under FCRA, the protected information is broadly defined, with exclusions:

(1) In general. The term "consumer report" generally means any written, oral, or other communication of any information by a consumer reporting agency bearing on a consumer's credit worthiness, credit standing, credit capacity, character, general reputation, personal characteristics, or mode of living which is used or expected to be used or collected in whole or in part for the purpose of serving as a factor in establishing the consumer's eligibility for

(A) credit or insurance to be used primarily for personal, family, or household purposes;

(B) employment purposes; or

(C) any other purpose authorized under section 604 [15 U.S.C. Section 1681b].

(2) Exclusions. The term "consumer report" does not include

(A) any

(i)   report containing information solely as to transactions or experiences between the consumer and the person making the report;

(ii)   communication of that information among persons related by common ownership or affiliated by corporate control; or

---

[136]Fair Credit Reporting Act, 15 U.S.C. Section 1681 *et seq.*, http://www4.law.cornell.edu/uscode/15/1681.html (hereinafter "FCRA").

[137]"Prepared Statement of the Federal Trade Commission on The Fair Credit Reporting Act," U.S. Senate Committee on Banking, Housing, and Urban Affairs, May 15, 2003 at 10, http://www.ftc.gov/os/2003/05/030515finalfcratestimony.pdf (hereinafter "FTC FCRA Statement").

[138]*Id.* at 7-9, 11-12.

(iii) communication of other information among persons related by common ownership or affiliated by corporate control, if it is clearly and conspicuously disclosed to the consumer that the information may be communicated among such persons and the consumer is given the opportunity, before the time that the information is initially communicated, to direct that such information not be communicated among such persons;

(B) any authorization or approval of a specific extension of credit directly or indirectly by the issuer of a credit card or similar device;

(C) any report in which a person who has been requested by a third party to make a specific extension of credit directly or indirectly to a consumer conveys his or her decision with respect to such request, if the third party advises the consumer of the name and address of the person to whom the request was made, and such person makes the disclosures to the consumer required under section 615 [15 U.S.C. Section 1681m].[139]

FCRA applies to how information is collected and used. It has always applied to insurance, employment, and other noncredit consumer transactions. Credit reports can generally be provided for purposes of making decisions about credit, insurance, employment, and certain ongoing account-monitoring and collection purposes. Consumer reporting agencies are also permitted to provide reports to persons who have a "legitimate business need" for the information.[140] "Target marketing" (making unsolicited calls or mailings to consumers based on information in their credit report) is not a permissible purpose, although certain prescreening calls and mailings are permissible.[141] In a matter in which a credit reporting agency sold marketing lists that were constructed using consumer report information, U.S. Court of Appeals for the D.C. Circuit upheld the FTC action by declaring:

[If consumer information is] so sensitive as to rise to the level of a consumer report ... [then it must] be kept private except under circumstances in which the consumer could be expected to wish otherwise, or by entering into some relationship with a

---

[139]FCRA, 15 U.S.C. Section 1681a(d), http://www.ftc.gov/os/statutes/fcra.htm.
[140]FTC FCRA Statement at 10; FCRA, 15 U.S.C. Section 1681b(a)(3), http://www4.law.cornell.edu/uscode/15/1681b.html.
[141]FTC FCRA Statement at 10, fnote 30. For additional information on allowable prescreening, *see id*. at 12-13.

business, could be said to implicitly waive the Act's privacy to help further that relationship.[142]

Indeed, recent amendments to FCRA provide an exception to affiliate-sharing restrictions for purposes of marketing solicitations in cases where a consumer has a "pre-existing business relationship" with the company.[143]

Other important consumer protection provisions in FCRA (a) provide consumers rights to ensure the accuracy of their credit information[144]; (b) include "right to know" provisions to enable consumers to know all the information in their files and receive "adverse action" notices when credit is denied based on, or in part on, their consumer credit report[145]; and (c) grant consumer dispute rights to resolve disputed information in the consumer's report.[146] 1996 amendments to FCRA essentially preempt state laws with respect to prescreening, the time for investigation of a dispute, adverse action notices, consumer summary of rights, and information sharing by affiliates.[147] Additional amendments in 2003 extend pre-existing FCRA preemptions of state laws restricting the sharing of consumer information among affiliated companies. These amendments also establish limits on affiliate sharing and the use of consumer report information for marketing purposes.[148]

In passing the GLBA, Congress was careful not to upset the operation of the immensely successful and long-standing FCRA. Congress recognized that the framework established in the FCRA for protecting information in a consumer's credit report by placing obligations on consumer reporting agencies, furnishers of information, and users of consumer reports had served the United States very well since the original enactment of FCRA in 1970. Although the GLBA slightly amended the FCRA by altering its regulatory enforcement landscape, the GLBA provides that, other than those slight amendments, nothing in the GLBA "shall be construed to modify, limit, or supersede the operation of" the FCRA.[149]

---

[142]FTC FCRA Statement at 11 (quoting *Trans Union Corp. v FTC*, 81 F.3d 228, 234 (D.C. Cir. 1996).

[143]Fair and Accurate Credit Transaction Act of 2003, Section 624, Pub. Law 108-159, Dec. 4, 2003 (hereinafter "FACTA") (amended FCRA, 15 U.S.C. Section 1681s-3).

[144]FCRA, 15 U.S.C. Section 1681(a)(1), http://www4.law.cornell.edu/uscode/15/1681.html.

[145]FCRA, 15 U.S.C. Section 1681g, http://www4.law.cornell.edu/uscode/15/1681g.html.

[146]FTC FCRA Statement at 16-17.

[147]*Id.* at 18.

[148]FCRA, Sections 624(c) and 625(b)(1)(H) (as amended by FACTA Section 214).

[149]FCRA, 15 U.S.C. Section 6806, http://www4.law.cornell.edu/uscode/15/6806.html.

Furthermore, the GLBA provides that no notice and opt-out is required when NPI is disclosed to a consumer reporting agency in accordance with the FCRA, or from a consumer report issued by a consumer reporting agency.[150] At this point, it is important to distinguish the information disclosure restrictions of the GLBA and FCRA. The GLBA governs disclosures of NPI to nonaffiliated third parties. The FCRA contains provisions restricting the sharing of information among affiliated companies.[151]

The FCRA's preemption provisions contrast with GLBA, which does not prohibit states from enacting more restrictive laws relating to sharing by financial institutions of nonpublic personal information with affiliated and non-affiliated third parties. Recent amendments to FCRA have failed to resolve the apparent conflict between preemption under FCRA and authorization for further state law regarding affiliate sharing under GLBA.[152]

Enforcement of FCRA is vested in the FTC, and the agency has undertaken significant efforts to educate the business and consumer communities on FCRA provisions. The Commission has published over 350 staff opinions, a staff guidance handbook, and six formal Commission interpretations.[153] The FTC has also conducted training for state officials.

Enforcement actions have focused on

- Compliance with the adverse action notice requirements on the part of creditors, employers, an Internet mortgage lender, and landlords
- Compliance with privacy and accuracy requirements by the national credit bureaus
- Compliance by resellers of consumer reports
- Compliance with the requirement that credit bureaus have personnel available at toll-free numbers printed on consumer credit reports

---

[150]FCRA, 15 U.S.C. Section 6802(e)(6)(A)-(B), http://www4.law.cornell.edu/uscode/15/6802.html.

[151]See FCRA, 15 U.S.C. Section 1681a(d)(2)(A)(i)-(iii), http://www4.law.cornell.edu/uscode/15/1681a.html.

[152]See, e.g., 16 C.F.R. Section 313.17; see also Gail Hillebrand, "After the FACT Act: What States Can Still Do to Prevent Identity Theft," Consumers Union, Jan. 2004, http://www.consumersunion.org/pub/core_financial_services/000756.html for an excellent discussion of FACTA amendments to FCRA, state preemption, and GLBA considerations.

[153]See http://www.ftc.gov/privacy/privacyinitiatives/credit.html for further details, including the full text of staff opinion letters and other materials.

■ Actions against reporters of information for reporting inaccurate delinquency information.[154]

FCRA was amended through passage of the Fair and Accurate Credit Transactions Act of 2003 (FACTA), enacted on December 4, 2003. The FACTA was intended to improve accuracy of and access to financial and credit information and help fight identity theft. As amended, FCRA now:

■ Requires that consumers receive notice and be offered an opportunity to opt out before most information relating to that consumer can be shared with an affiliate for marketing purposes
■ Restricts the transfer or sale of debt caused by identity theft
■ Imposes new responsibilities on those who supply information to consumer reporting agencies
■ Imposes new requirements on lenders, including the requirement to disclose credit scores to mortgage loan applicants and provide "Risk-Based Pricing Notices" to consumers who receive below-average credit terms due to information in a credit report
■ Eliminates the need to notify employees pursuant to FCRA's notice and disclosure requirements of investigations into wrongdoing
■ Gives every consumer the right to their credit report free of charge every year
■ Establishes a nationwide system of fraud alerts for consumers to place on their credit files
■ Creates a national system of fraud detection.[155]

As always, companies are advised to consult with experts confronted with detailed FCRA issues. That caveat, with an additional suggestion to follow regulatory developments, is especially important.

e. Health Insurance Portability and Accountability Act

The Health Insurance Portability and Accountability Act of 1996 (HIPAA)[156] directs the Secretary of Health and Human Services (HHS) to adopt three sets of regulations to protect private health information (PHI):

---

[154]FTC FCRA Statement at 19-22.

[155]*See* FACTA, Pub. Law 108-159, http://frwebgate.access.gpo.gov/cgi-bin/getdoc. cgi?dbname=108_cong_public_laws&docid=f:publ159.108.pdf.

[156]Health Insurance Portability and Accountability Act of 1996, Pub. Law 104-191, http://aspe.hhs.gov/admnsimp/pl104191.htm (hereinafter "HIPAA").

1. Standards for Electronic Transactions;[157]
2. Standards for Privacy of Individually Identifiable Health Information;[158] and
3. Security Standards.[159]

Generally speaking, the HIPAA regulations cover three kinds of "covered entities": providers that bill at least one HIPAA "standard transaction" electronically, all health plans, and health care clearinghouses.[160] By extension, HIPAA also applies to "business associates" of covered entities.[161] The relationship between a covered entity and a business associate is required to be covered by a contract, the minimum requirements for which are prescribed by regulation.[162]

The Standard Transactions rule establishes a nationwide system of electronic data interchange for health care "standard transactions."[163] The aim is to reduce costs by handling health care billing and insurance transactions electronically rather than by antiquated paper-based business processes. Because medical records in electronic form are so vulnerable to abuse, Congress in HIPAA also requires the Secretary to issue regulations to protect the privacy and security of medical records.[164]

---

[157]Health Insurance Reform: Standards for Electronic Transactions, Final Rule and Notice, 65 *Federal Register* 50,311-72, Aug. 17, 2000, (codified at 45 C.F.R. Part 160, Subpart A and Part 162, Subpart I), http://a257.g.akamaitech.net/7/257/2422/14mar20010800/edocket.access.gpo.gov/2003/C3-3876.htm, *amended by* Health Insurance Reform: Modifications to Electronic Data Transactions Standards and Code Sets, 68 *Federal Register* 8,381-99, Feb. 20, 2003, (codified at 45 C.F.R. pt. 162), http://a257.g.akamaitech.net/7/257/2422/14mar20010800/edocket.access.gpo.gov/2003/03-3876.htm, *amended by* Health Insurance Reform: Modifications to Electronic Data Transaction Standards and Code Sets, 68 *Federal Register* 11,445, Mar. 10, 2003, (codified at 45 C.F.R. Part 162), http://a257.g.akamaitech.net/7/257/2422/14mar20010800/ edocket.access.gpo.gov/2003/C3-3876.htm (hereinafter "HIPAA Standard Transactions Rule").

[158]Standards for Privacy of Individually Identifiable Health Information, 45 C.F.R. Parts 160, 164, http://www.hhs.gov/ocr/hipaa/finalreg.html (hereinafter "HIPAA Privacy Rule").

[159]Security Standards, 68 Federal Register 8,333-81, Feb. 20, 2003, (codified at 45 C.F.R. Parts 160, 162, 164), http://www.wedi.org/snip/public/articles/HIPAA_Security_Final_Rule_official_version.pdf (hereinafter "HIPAA Security Rule").

[160]HIPAA, 42 U.S.C. Section 1320d-1(a).

[161]45 C.F.R. Section 160.103 (definition).

[162]45 C.F.R. Section 164.504(e).

[163]The HIPAA Standard Transactions Rule was promulgated pursuant to HIPAA statutory provision, 42 U.S.C. Section 1320d-2(a)(2).

[164]*See* HIPAA Privacy Rule; HIPAA Security Rule; *see generally* Richard D. Marks, *Implementing HIPAA: Guidelines for Initiating HIPAA Systems Implementation Projects, Electronic Commerce & Law Report*, Bureau of National Affairs, Vol. 5, No. 18, May 3, 2000 at 468-74 (hereinafter "Marks: Implementing HIPAA"); Richard D. Marks, "Surviving Standard Transactions: A HIPAA Roadmap," *Privacy & Security Law Report*, Bureau of National Affairs, Vol. 2, No. 24 , June 16, 2003 at 661-71 (hereinafter "Marks: HIPAA Roadmap").

40   CHAPTER 1

Standard Transactions Rule

The Standard Transactions Rule—which went into effect October 16, 2003—standardizes the electronic process of enrolling patients for health insurance, verifying their eligibility for coverage, making and paying claims for health care, and performing related information exchanges efficiently, electronically, and without using paper.[165] To enforce this vision, the statute and implementing regulations require the health insurance industry to abandon the hodgepodge of proprietary transaction formats and codes and to move instead to new, government-prescribed "standard transactions."[166] The standard transactions listed in the statute are

- Health claims or equivalent counter information
- Health claims or attachments
- Enrollment and disenrollment in a health plan
- Eligibility for a health plan
- Health care payment and remittance advice
- Health plan premium payments
- First report of injury
- Health claim status
- Referral certification and authorization.[167]

The Standard Transactions Rule will require all affected companies to reprogram their business processes and computer systems to fit the rule. In turn, this will upset the privacy and security plans and systems these companies have in place. The implementation of this rule alone serves as an excellent example of why a cross-organizational team is a necessary part of developing a privacy plan and why a change management process is a critical implementation component.

Privacy Rule

The Standards for Privacy of Individually Identifiable Information (Privacy Rule) was originally published on December 20, 2000. The Privacy Rule was then amended on May 31, 2002, and again on August 14, 2002. It was issued in final form in October 2002, and it became effective April 14, 2003. The privacy regulations create a complex regulatory structure to protect private health information (PHI), also referred to as "individually identifiable information." They provide for notice of privacy practices[168] and afford individuals more control over

---

[165]Marks: HIPAA Roadmap at 661 (citing *South Carolina Medical Assn. v. Thompson*, 327 F.3d 346, 348 (4th Cir., Apr. 25, 2003)).
[166]HIPPA, 42 U.S.C. Section 1320d-2.
[167]HIPPA, 42 U.S.C. Section 1320d-1(c)(3)(B)(iii).
[168]45 C.F.R. Section 164.520.

the use and disclosure of their information. The privacy rule also requires covered entities to establish a privacy compliance program, including staff training.[169]

Although separate Privacy and Security Rules were issued, the Privacy Rule contains a "mini-security rule"[170] that states:

Standard. Safeguards. A covered entity must have in place *appropriate administrative, technical, and physical safeguards* to protect the privacy of protected health information.

Implementation Specification: Safeguards.

(i) A covered entity must *reasonably safeguard* protected health information from any intentional or unintentional use or disclosure that is in violation of the standards, implementation specifications, or other requirements of this subpart.

(ii) A covered entity must *reasonably safeguard* protected health information to limit incidental uses or disclosures made pursuant to an otherwise permitted or recorded use or disclosure.[171]

This mini-security rule applies to protected health information that is both in electronic and paper form. In determining the meaning of "appropriate safeguards" and "reasonably safeguard," courts may well look to the principles and safeguard requirements in the Security Rule. The Security Rule, however, applies only to information in electronic form, whereas the Privacy Rule's mini-security rule applies to information in electronic and paper form.[172]

Security Rule

The Security Regulations are intended to secure PHI (1) when it is in the custody of entities covered by the Act (health insurance providers as well as their "business associates," for example, data processors, lawyers, etc.), and (2) when PHI is in transit between covered entities or from covered entities to others. The objective of the security rule is to ensure the integrity, confidentiality, and availability of electronic PHI

---

[169]45 C.F.R. Section 164.530.

[170]Randy Gainer, Michael van Eckhardt, Rebecca Williams, and Richard D. Marks, "WiFi Devices in Hospitals Pose Major HIPAA Challenges," *Privacy & Security Law Report*, Bureau of National Affairs, Vol. 2, No. 21, May 26, 2003 at 575 (hereinafter "Gainer, Eckhardt, Williams, and Marks").

[171]45 C.F.R. Section 154.530(c) (emphasis added); *see also* Gainer, Eckhardt, Williams, and Marks at 576.

[172]*See* 45 C.F.R. Section 164.530(c); *see also* Gainer, Eckhardt, Williams, and Marks at 576.

that covered entities collect, maintain, use, or transmit. The rule covers data while both in storage and in transit and has 28 "standards" and 41 "implementation specifications." There are administrative, physical, and technical aspects to the rule. The rule requires an enterprise approach be taken with policies, procedures, change control mechanisms, risk analysis, review, and training.[173] The Security Regulation takes into account technical capabilities of record systems, costs of security measures, the need for personnel training, and the value of audit trails in computerized record systems. The Rule requires the maintenance of reasonable and appropriate administrative, physical, and technical safeguards to protect the integrity and confidentiality of PHI and to protect against reasonably anticipated threats or hazards to the security or integrity of PHI or its unauthorized use or disclosure.[174]

The core principles of the Security Rule require covered entities to:

- Ensure the confidentiality, integrity, and availability of all electronic protected health information the covered entity creates, receives, maintains, or transmits.
- Protect against any reasonably anticipated threats or hazards to the security or integrity of such information.
- Protect against any reasonably anticipated uses or disclosures of such information that are not required under the Security Rule.
- Ensure compliance with the Security Rule by its workforce.[175]

References to "ensure" and "any" in the Security Rule make the security standards of care a challenge to meet. The Rule, however, does offer some flexibility:

- Covered entities may use any security measures that allow the covered entity to reasonably and appropriately implement the standards and implementation specifications as specified in the Security Rule.
- In deciding which security measures to use, a covered entity must take into account the following factors:
  (i) The size, complexity, and capabilities of the covered entity.
  (ii) The covered entity's technical infrastructure, hardware, and software security capabilities.
  (iii) The costs of security measures.

---

[173]Linda A. Malek and Brian R. Krex, "HIPAA's security rule becomes effective 2005," *The National Law Journal*, Mar. 31, 2003 at B14; *see also* Chapter Three of this publication, Security Programs: Plans, Policies & Procedures.
[174]*See* HIPPA, 42 U.S.C. Section 1320d-2(d)(2).
[175]45 C.F.R. Section 164.306(a); *see also* Gainer, Eckhardt, Williams, and Marks at 576.

(iv) The probability and criticality of potential risks to electronic protected health information.[176]

While these general rules allow covered entities to take a flexible approach, flexibility does not mean laxity. For example, although a covered entity should consider the costs of security measures,[177] the size, complexity, and capabilities of the entity must also be considered,[178] which means that large entities may be given no leeway for failing to deploy expensive security technology.

The more detailed standards of the Security Rule are grouped under three headings: Administrative Safeguards, Physical Safeguards, and Technical Safeguards. Additionally, the security rules identify safeguards that are "required" and those that are "addressable." If HHS views the safeguard as essential, it is labeled "required." "Addressable" does not mean, however, that an entity need not consider the safeguard. Rather, it means that HHS believes that there may be many ways to implement the safeguard. An entity will have to justify any decision to do nothing regarding a safeguard described as "addressable" in the Security Rule.

The Privacy and Security Rules clearly have implementation considerations. Physical safeguards, for example, require covered entities to implement policies and procedures to safeguard equipment from unauthorized physical access, tampering, and theft.[179] This could mean special provisions to prevent the theft of wireless devices or access to PCs. Also, wireless local area networks (WLANs) should have security features to make it difficult for a thief to access PHI on a laptop, cell phone, or personal digital assistant (PDA). At a minimum, users should authenticate themselves by using passwords before accessing wireless devices, the portable device should be authenticated to a server before access is granted to the WLAN, and the cryptographic keys used by portable devices to access the WLAN must be changed frequently.[180] Data interceptions can occur by intercepting

---

[176]45 C.F.R. Section 164.306(b), see also Gainer, Eckhardt, Williams, and Marks at 576.

[177]45 C.F.R. Section 164.306(b)(2)(iii); see also Gainer, Eckhardt, Williams, and Marks at 576.

[178]45 C.F.R. Section 164.306(b)(2)(i); see also Gainer, Eckhardt, Williams, and Marks at 576.

[179]Id.

[180]Gainer, Eckhardt, Williams, and Marks at 576; see also Marianne Swanson, Security Self-Assessment Guide for Information Technology Systems, National Institute of Standards and Technology, Special Publication 800-26, Nov. 2001 at A-43, http://csrc.nist.gov/publications/nistpubs/; Gary Stoneburner, Alice Goguen, and Alexis Feringa, Risk Management Guide for Information Technology Systems, NIST Draft Special Publication 800-30, Rev A, Jan. 21, 2001 at 11, 19, 20, 34, http://csrc.nist.gov/publications/drafts.html; Tom Karygiannis and Les Owens, Wireless Network Security: 802.11, Bluetooth and Handheld Devices, NIST Special Publication 800-48, Nov. 2002, http://csrc.nist.gov/publications/nistpubs/. HHS's comments regarding the Security Rule cites various NIST publications four times. See Federal Register No. 34, Feb. 20, 2003 at 8334, 8346, 8350, 8352, 8355. HHS's repeated references to these publications suggest that they provide useful information to assist in understanding and complying with the Rules.

44   CHAPTER 1

the radio waves used to transmit WLAN data. There are additional security concerns regarding the use of 802.11b "Wi-Fi" wireless technology.[181] Skilled employees frequently install their own modems, and now some are even installing their own wireless access points, creating another security challenge and potential hole for breaches of PHI. Remote wireless access points also create compliance risks.[182]

Interrelation Between Security and Privacy Rules

Security and privacy are interrelated in the HIPAA statute and rules, as they should be in any adequate system of cyber security. Still, a legitimate criticism of HIPAA's implementation by HHS includes the delay in issuing the implementing regulations and failing to issue the security regulations—the framework for HIPAA privacy and transactions—before promulgating the privacy and transactions rules. The "final" privacy rule was issued on December 28, 2000 and became effective on April 14, 2001, and covered entities had to be in compliance by April 14, 2003 (except "small health plans," which have until April 14, 2004 to comply). The security rule was not finalized and issued until February 20, 2003 and becomes effective on April 21, 2005. Yet the "mini-security rule" in the privacy rule became effective on April 14, 2003, along with the rest of the privacy rule.

This piecemeal approach understandably leaves covered entities affected by the regulations—and, indeed, the entire health care industry—confused. Privacy depends upon security, yet covered entities had to meet the privacy requirements prior even to knowing what the final security rule would require. Moreover, the breadth and reach of the provisions and the criminal penalties for violations of the regulations have caused much confusion and angst throughout the health care industry and are indicative of the need for government regulators to better understand cyber security before promulgating such types of regulation.

The security and privacy rules, taken together, have great reach. For example, they require a high level of security for hospitals that are interconnected with each other, physicians' offices, academic medical centers, other research organizations or research networks, and with vendors (such as computer system vendors that maintain connections for troubleshooting, routine maintenance, or to supply upgrades).

---

[181]Gainer, Eckhardt, Williams, and Marks at 577. This article contains a detailed and excellent description of the technical security and compliance issues surrounding 802.11b and other wireless technologies. It argues the main reason that technical safeguards cannot be met using 802.11b technologies is that the encryption protocol used by these devices, "Wired Equivalent Privacy," is suspect.
[182]*Id.*

They require consideration of security in virtually all areas of the health care industry's use of technology.

HIPAA's new standard of care for privacy and security will, by virtue of its statutory preemption rules,[183] displace existing *state* law tort standards of care. This is true whether a state law cause of action is based on simple negligence, breach of confidentiality in the patient-physician relationship, invasion of privacy, or a related state law tort or consumer protection theory. In addition, the HIPAA statute includes administrative fines imposed by HHS and criminal penalties.[184]

Criminal and Civil Penalties

HIPAA compliance concerns take on an urgency because of HIPAA's criminal penalties. Wrongful disclosure of individually identifiable health information carries up to a year in prison and a penalty of up to US$50,000. If the wrongful disclosure is under false pretenses, the maximum term rises to five years, and the monetary penalty to US$100,000; add an intent to sell, transfer, or use for commercial advantage, personal gain, or to inflict malicious harm, and the prison term increases to a maximum of ten years, with a monetary penalty of up to US$250,000.[185]

It is unlikely that most doctors, nurses, hospital administrators, or information system staff members (to name a few) ever expected to be exposed to these levels of jeopardy. HIPAA also has civil penalties of US$100 for violation of a single provision, with an annual cap per entity of US$25,000 for violations of an identical requirement or prohibition.[186] Failure to implement the transaction sets is US$25,000 annually per set, for an annual maximum penalty for all nine sets of US$225,000.[187]

Covered entities that fail to comply with HIPAA's privacy and security standards also must consider potential liability in tort, including invasion of privacy (publication of private facts, false light, and unauthorized commercial use, as the case may be), defamation, and fraud. There is also potential exposure under consumer fraud statutes. And, of course, there are various potential causes of action for breach of contract, depending on the circumstances. Public companies in the health care industry may face additional exposure from shareholder suits if they fail to implement adequate information security programs.

---

[183] *See* HIPAA, 42 U.S.C. Section 1320d-7.

[184] *See* HIPAA, 42 U.S.C. Section 1320d-5, d-6.

[185] *See* HIPAA, 2 U.S.C. Section 1177(b).

[186] *See* HIPAA, 42 U.S.C. Section 1177(b).

[187] *Id.*

46   CHAPTER 1

The real breadth and reach of HIPAA may end up being determined through litigation.[188] Enforcement actions will also be a determining factor. Enforcement of the HIPAA privacy requirements has been delegated to HHS's Office of Civil Rights (OCR). Nearly 4,000 complaints have been filed with the OCR since the Privacy Rule's April 14, 2003 compliance date.[189]

There is little experience yet with the impact of HIPAA, and particularly its formidable security requirements, on health care in the United States. HIPAA's security requirements will have a significant ongoing financial and cultural impact on health care entities of all types and sizes. This change must be made, yet it will to some degree influence health care entities' ability to offer patients convenient, friendly facilities and services. We can expect that a few years' experience with HIPAA's new regime may convince Congress of the need to make changes to reduce HIPAA's compliance costs and covered entities' exposure to state court tort litigation resulting from the elevated standard of care that HIPAA creates under *state* law. Only time will tell.

f. Children's Online Privacy Protection Act

In October 1998, Congress passed the Children's Online Privacy Protection Act (COPPA).[190] The primary purpose of the Act was to protect the personal information of children under the age of thirteen by requiring the consent of their parents to collect and/or use any personal information collected from those children.[191] More specifically, "Congress enacted COPPA to prohibit unfair and deceptive acts or practices in connection with the collection, use or disclosure of personally identifiable information from and about children on the Internet."[192] The FTC was vested with regulatory and enforcement authority.[193] The FTC issued the Children's Online

---

[188]"True Scope of the HIPAA's Privacy Protection To Be Defined Through Lawsuits, Lawyers Say," *Privacy & Security Law Report*, Bureau of National Affairs, Vol. 3, No. 11, Mar. 15, 2004 at 305-06.
[189]"HIPAA Privacy Rule Compliance to Enter Enforcement Phase in 2004," *Privacy & Security Law Report*, Bureau of National Affairs, Vol. 3, No. 4, Jan. 26, 2004 at 106-07.
[190]Children's Online Privacy Protection Act, 15 U.S.C. Sections 6501-6506, 1998, http://www4.law.cornell.edu/uscode/15/6501.html (hereinafter "COPPA").
[191]*See* "The Children's Online Privacy Protection Act," Electronic Privacy Information Center, http://www.epic.org/privacy/kids/.
[192]"Children's Online Privacy Protection Rule," Final Rule, Federal Trade Commission, *Federal Register*, Vol. 64, No. 212, Nov. 3, 1999 at 59,888 (codified at 16 C.F.R. Part 312), http://www.ftc.gov/os/1999/10/64fr59888.pdf (hereinafter "COPPA Rule").
[193]COPPA, 15 U.S.C. Sections 6502, 6506, http://www4.law.cornell.edu/uscode/15/6502.html and http://www4.law.cornell.edu/uscode/15/6506.html. States Attorneys General can also enforce COPPA through civil action in certain cases. COPPA, 15 U.S.C. Section 6504, http://www4.law.cornell.edu/uscode/15/6504.html.

Privacy Protection Rule (COPPA Rule) to implement the Act.[194] It became effective on April 21, 2000 and gave specific guidance on how to comply with COPPA's requirements.[195]

Under the Act, it is "unlawful for an operator of a website or online service directed to children, or any operator that has actual knowledge that it is collecting personal information from a child, to collect personal information from a child in a manner that violates" the regulations promulgated by the FTC.[196] COPPA specifically applies to "operators of commercial websites and online services directed to children under 13 that collect personal information from children, and operators of general audience sites with actual knowledge that they are collecting information from children under 13."[197] Generally, those operators are required to:

(1) post clear and comprehensive Privacy Policies on the website describing their information practices for children's personal information;

(2) provide notice to parents, and, with limited exceptions, obtain verifiable parental consent *before* collecting personal information from children;

(3) give parents the choice to consent to the operator's collection and use of a child's information while prohibiting the operator from disclosing that information to third parties;

(4) provide parents access to their child's personal information to review and/or have deleted;

(5) give parents the opportunity to prevent further collection or use of the information; and

(6) maintain the confidentiality, security, and integrity of information they collect from children.[198]

Moreover, the Rule also "prohibits operators from conditioning a child's participation in an online activity on the child's providing more information than is reasonably necessary to participate in that activity."[199]

---

[194]COPPA Rule; "Children's Online Privacy Protection Rule, Final rule amendment, Federal Trade Commission, *Federal Register*, Vol. 67, No. 74, Apr. 17, 2002 at 18,818 (codified at 16 C.F.R. Part 312) (hereinafter "COPPA Sliding Scale Mechanism Rule").

[195]"Frequently Asked Questions about the Children's Online Privacy Protection Rule, Volume 1," Federal Trade Commission, http://www.ftc.gov/privacy/coppafaqs.htm (hereinafter "COPAA FAQ").

[196]COPPA, 15 U.S.C. Section 6502(a)(1), http://www4.law.cornell.edu/uscode/15/6502.html.

[197]COPPA FAQ, http://www.ftc.gov/privacy/coppafaqs.htm .

[198]*Id.* (emphasis in original).

[199]*Id.*

48   CHAPTER 1

The Rule also includes several exceptions that permit the collection of a youngster's e-mail address without getting prior consent of a parent. Specifically, prior consent of a parent generally is not a prerequisite when:

- an operator collects a child's or parent's e-mail address to provide notice and seek consent;
- an operator collects an e-mail address to respond to a one-time request from a child and then deletes it;
- an operator collects an e-mail address to respond more than once to a specific request—say, for a subscription to a newsletter;
- an operator collects a child's name or online contact information to protect the safety of a child who is participating on the site;
- an operator collects a child's name or online contact information to protect the security or liability of the site or to respond to law enforcement, if necessary, and does not use it for any other purpose.[200]

Because there are requirements and exceptions, companies concerned with this rule should seek expert advice. Another reason to seek advice is that COPPA requirements may change; the Rule is due for overall review in 2005.

Studies by the FTC, the University of Pennsylvania/Annenberg Center, and the Center for Media Education have shown that since the Rule took effect, many children's sites have reduced the amount of personal information that they collect from children. However, COPPA has not cured all problems. In April 2002, the FTC announced the results of its April 2001 COPPA compliance survey reviewing information collection practices on 144 children's websites.[201] The 2001 survey followed up on an earlier 1998 FTC survey and indicated that much progress has been made since the Rule went into effect in April 2000.[202] For example, survey data showed that the vast majority—nearly 90 percent—of the sites that collected personal information from children posted privacy policies on their sites, as opposed to only 24

---

[200]*How to Comply With The Children's Online Privacy Protection Rule: A Guide from the Federal Trade Commission, the Direct Marketing Association and the Internet Alliance* at 7, http://www.ftc.gov/bcp/conline/pubs/buspubs/coppa.pdf; *see also* "Children's Privacy: Education and Guidance," http://www.ftc.gov/privacy/privacyinitiatives/childrens_educ.html for additional guidance materials.

[201]*See Protecting Children's Privacy Under COPPA: A Survey on Compliance*, Staff Report, Apr. 2002, Federal Trade Commission, http://www.ftc.gov/os/2002/04/coppasurvey.pdf.

[202]*See Privacy Online: A Report to Congress*, June 1998, Federal Trade Commission.

percent in 1998. The survey also indicated that the types and amounts of information collected by websites are more limited than they used to be, suggesting a heightened sense of awareness of the safety and privacy concerns of collecting information from children.[203] At the same time, however, the survey showed that full compliance with the Rule has yet to be attained. For example, just over half the websites complied with a provision that requires the disclosure that websites are prohibited from conditioning a child's participation in an activity on the disclosure of more personal information than is reasonably necessary for the activity. Furthermore, just about half of the sites complied with the provision that requires them to inform parents of their right to review, request the deletion of, and refuse the further collection and use of their children's personal information.

The FTC is responsible for COPPA enforcement. Violations of the Act are to be treated as an unfair or deceptive act or practice proscribed under 15 U.S.C. Section 57a(a)(1)(B).[204] Each violation could result in civil penalties of up to US\$11,000.[205] As of April 2004, the FTC has brought ten enforcement cases, reinforcing the message that children's privacy must be respected. The issues have included allegations that the consent mechanism employed by the operator was not reasonably calculated to ensure that the person providing consent was the child's parent;[206] that children's data was collected without prior consent;[207] that the operator collected more information than was reasonably necessary for children to participate in a site's "Birthday Club" activity, and that the site's privacy policy statement did not clearly or completely disclose all of its information collection practices or make certain disclosures required by the Rule;[208] that the operator collected personal information from children under thirteen years of age without prior parental consent and shared that information with third parties without parental consent;[209] and that children's data was

---

[203]See *Protecting Children's Privacy Under COPPA: A Survey on Compliance*, Staff Report, Apr. 2002, Federal Trade Commission, http://www.ftc.gov/os/2002/04/coppa survey.pdf.

[204]COPPA, 15 U.S.C. Section 6505(c), http://www4.law.cornell.edu/uscode/15/6505.html; *see also* FTC Act, 15 U.S.C. Section 57a(a)(1)(b), http://www4.law.cornell.edu/uscode/15/57a.html.

[205]See COPPA FAQs, Question 14, http://www.ftc.gov/privacy/coppafaqs.htm.

[206]*U.S. v. Hershey Foods Corp.*, Civ. Action No. 4CV:03-350 (M.D. Penn., 2003), http://www.ftc.gov/os/2003/02/index.htm#27.

[207]*U.S. v. Mrs. Fields Famous Brands, Inc., et al.*, Civ. Action No. 2:03 CV205 JTG (Dist. of Utah, 2003), http://www.ftc.gov/os/2003/02/index.htm#27.

[208]*U.S. v. the Ohio Art Co.*, Civ. Action No. 3:02 CV 7203 (N.D. Ohio, 2002), http://www.ftc.gov/os/2002/04/index.htm#22.

[209]*U.S. v. Looksmart*, Ltd., Civ. Action No. 01-606-A (E.D. Va., 2001), http://www.ftc.gov/os/2001/04/index.htm#19.

collected without first sending the parents a notice, obtaining consent, and providing a mechanism to review or delete the information.[210]

The FTC also has brought actions which included FTC Act Section 5[211] counts concerning privacy policies as well as COPPA allegations.[212] In addition to civil penalties, the settlement agreements in these cases have included remedies such as creating a link from the offending website to www.ftc.gov/kidzprivacy, which provides educational information for children and their parents; requiring employee education about COPPA; submitting written compliance reports to the FTC; and deleting personal information about children that was collected without parental consent. The FTC has also surfed the Internet and sent warnings to websites that may be in violation.

There are extraterritorial application considerations with COPPA. These are discussed in more detail in Chapter Two, Section D.

As a possible alternative to FTC scrutiny, COPPA provides the opportunity for industry groups to get involved in self-regulation through the Rule's "safe harbor" provision. The COPPA safe harbor provision enables industry groups or others to apply for FTC approval of their self-regulatory programs to govern participants' compliance.[213] FTC-approved safe harbors provide website operators with the opportunity to tailor compliance obligations to their business models with the assurance that if they follow the safe harbor guidelines, they will be in compliance with the Rule. Websites participating in FTC-approved safe harbor programs will be subject to the review and disciplinary procedures provided in those guidelines in lieu of formal FTC action. To date, the FTC has approved safe harbor programs operated by the Children's Review Unit of the Council of Better Business Bureaus, Inc., the Entertainment Software Rating Board, and TRUSTe.

g. Electronic Communications Privacy Act

The Electronic Communications Privacy Act (ECPA) governs the circumstances under which individuals and the government may

---

[210]*U.S. v. UMG Recordings, Inc.*, Civ. Action No. CV-04-1050 JFW (Ex) (C.D. Cal., 2004), http://www.ftc.gov/os/caselist/umgrecordings/040217compumgrecording.pdf (hereinafter "UMG"); *U.S. v. Bonzi Software, Inc.*, Civ. Action No. CV-04-1048 RJK (Ex) (C.D. Cal., 2004), http://www.ftc.gov/os/caselist/bonzi/040217compbonzi.pdf (hereinafter "Bonzi").

[211]Under Section 5 of the FTC Act, the FTC has authority to take enforcement actions against unfair and deceptive trade practices; *see* 15 U.S.C. Section 45, http://www4.law.cornell.edu/uscode/15/45.html.

[212]*U.S. v. Frank, Inc.*, Civ. Action No. 01-1516-A (E.D. Va., 2001), http://www. ftc.gov/os/2001/10/index.htm#2; UMG; Bonzi.

[213]16 C.F.R. Section 312.10.

obtain access to "wire or electronic communications" that are kept and maintained by "electronic communications service" or by "remote computing services."[214] To analyze the statute, it is therefore necessary to understand these terms.

An electronic communications service means any service that provides to users the ability to send and receive wire or electronic communications.[215] Thus, Internet service providers (ISPs) and telephone companies are considered providers of such services. Banks can also be considered providers of electronic communications services.[216]

A remote computing service is defined as the "provision to the public of computer storage or processing services by means of an electronic communications system."[217] In other words, it is the computer service that stores, but is not responsible for sending, files. Of significance here is that the service has to be available to the public. Thus, assume that an organization accepts e-mails from the Internet sent to its employees and allows those employees to retain copies of those e-mails on the office's server. That organization is not a remote computing service, because it offers its storage space only to its own employees.

The purpose of the ECPA is to protect communications services from intrusions and to protect the information stored in those services. Thus, the ECPA makes it unlawful for unauthorized persons to access the communications service (to hack into it), and it also makes it unlawful for all persons, even those who are authorized to maintain the service, to read or alter the information in the service while that information is in "electronic storage."[218] Electronic storage is defined as "any temporary, intermediate storage of a wire or electronic communication incidental to the electronic transmission thereof" and "any storage of such communication by an electronic communication service for purposes of back-up protection."[219] As an example, suppose Sender A sends an e-mail to Sender B, who has an account with AOL. The communication will go to AOL's service, where it will be stored until Sender B retrieves it. While it is sitting on the server awaiting

---

[214]Electronic Communications Privacy Act, 18 U.S.C. Sections 2701-2712, http://www4.law.cornell.edu/uscode/18/2701.html (hereinafter "ECPA").

[215]18 U.S.C. §2510(15), http://www4.law.cornell.edu/uscode/18/2510.html.

[216]*See Organizacion JD Ltd. v. Dept of Justice*, 124 F.3d 354 (2d Cir. 1997).

[217]ECPA, 18 U.S.C. 2711(2), http://www4.law.cornell.edu/uscode/18/2711.html. The term "electronic communications system" is defined in 18 U.S.C. Section 2510 as "any wire, radio, electromagnetic, photo optical or photo electronics facilities for the transmission of wire or electronic communications, and any computer facilities or related electronic equipment for the electronic storage of such communications," http://www4.law.cornell.edu/uscode/18/2510.html.

[218]ECPA, 18 U.S.C. Section 2701, http://www4.law.cornell.edu/uscode/18/2701.html.

[219]18 U.S.C. Section 2510(17), http://www4.law.cornell.edu/uscode/18/2510.html.

52   CHAPTER 1

retrieval, it is considered in electronic storage. While it is traveling either from the sender to the server or from the server to the sender, it is in transit.[220]

The statute divides information kept by electronic communications services into three types and gives each type a different degree of protection. There is subscriber information, which includes the name and address of the account subscriber, as well as the type of service, the method of payment for the service, and the records of how the subscriber connected to the service (including the Internet protocol (IP) address assigned at the time of the connection).[221] The government may obtain this information by serving a subpoena on the service and does not need to notify the account holder that it is getting this information.[222]

The statute also deals with what is often referred to as transaction records, that is, information that does not include the content of the e-mail but is not defined as subscriber information. Information concerning the cell-sites that process cell phone calls is considered transactional information. Information about websites that have been visited may also fit in this category.[223] To obtain this information, the government must, at the very least, obtain a court order, which the court can only issue upon being shown that there are "reasonable grounds" to believe that the information sought is "relevant and material to an ongoing criminal investigation."[224]

Finally, the statute addresses when the government can obtain the actual content of the communication. Here, the statute divides the communications into two: those that are unopened and have been in electronic storage less than 180 days and those that are unopened and have been in storage more than 180 days. In the case of the former, the government can only obtain those communications pursuant to a search warrant, which requires that the government demonstrate probable cause to believe that a crime has been committed and that the contents of the e-mails contain evidence of that crime.[225]

If the unopened e-mails are more than 180 days old, then they receive somewhat less protection. In this instance, while the

---

[220]The access of electronic communications that are in transit is governed by the federal wiretap statute. 18 U.S.C. Section 2510 *et seq.*

[221]ECPA, 18 U.S.C. Section 2703(c)(2), http://www4.law.cornell.edu/uscode/2703.html.

[222]ECPA, 18 U.S.C. Section 2703(c)(3), http://www4.law.cornell.edu/uscode/18/2703.html.

[223]ECPA, 18 U.S.C. Section 2703(c)(1), http://www4.law.cornell.edu/uscode/18/2703.html.

[224]ECPA, 18 U.S.C. Sections 2703(c)(1)(B), 2703(d), http://www4.law.cornell.edu/uscode/18/2703.html.

[225]ECPA, 18 U.S.C. Section 2703(a), http://www4.law.cornell.edu/uscode/18/2703.html.

government can still obtain them by way of search warrant, it also can compel disclosure of the contents of the communications by way of a subpoena or a court order. The statute then requires that the subscriber be notified unless the prosecutor obtains permission from the court to delay notification.[226] In order to delay notification, however, the government must demonstrate that notification would endanger someone's life, seriously jeopardize the investigation, or result in flight from prosecution, destruction or tampering with evidence, or intimidation of witnesses.[227]

Finally, the statute provides reduced protection when the e-mails have been opened but the subscriber has not deleted them from the server. Then, the communications are considered stored in a remote computing service and are treated as if they were over 180 days old.[228] In other words, the government can obtain them through a subpoena or court order.

The statute provides the subscriber with a means to combat or protest government acquisition of his records. First, in those instances in which the subscriber receives notification of the government's request from the communications service for records, the subscriber may make a motion to quash the subpoena or vacate the court order. He will be successful in preventing the government from acquiring the records if he can demonstrate that the records are not relevant to a legitimate law enforcement inquiry or that the government has failed to comply with the ECPA.[229]

The statute also allows the ISP, the subscriber, or any other "aggrieved person" to sue for violations of the ECPA and guarantees that, if they win, they receive at least US$1000.[230] The statute does permit the person being sued to raise the defense that he or she relied in good faith on a court order or subpoena, or believed that he or she had either legislative or statutory authorization to act.[231]

There are several useful websites that discuss the ECPA and contain useful resources:

---

[226]ECPA, 18 U.S.C. Sections 2703(b)(2), 2705(a), http://www4.law.cornell.edu/uscode/18/2703.html and http://www4.law.cornell.edu/uscode/18/2705.html.

[227]ECPA, 18 U.S.C. Section 2705(a), http://www4.law.cornell.edu/uscode/18/2705.html.

[228]ECPA, 18 U.S.C. Section 2703(b), http://www4.law.cornell.edu/uscode/18/2703.html.

[229]ECPA, 18 U.S.C. Section 2704(b), http://www4.law.cornell.edu/uscode/18/2704.html.

[230]ECPA, 18 U.S.C. Section 2707, http://www4.law.cornell.edu/uscode/18/2707.html. The statute exempts the federal government from any such lawsuit. 18 U.S.C. Section 2707(a). However, it does require federal agencies to initiate disciplinary proceedings if a court determines that the relevant agent acted willfully in violating the provisions of the ECPA. 18 U.S.C. Section 2707(d).

[231]ECPA, 18 U.S.C. Section 2707(e), http://www4.law.cornell.edu/uscode/18/2707.html.

http://www.cybercrime.gov/s&smanual2002.htm
http://www/epic/org
http://www.cdt.org
http://www.consumerprivacyguide.com/law/ecpa.shtml.

h. Economic Espionage Act of 1996

The Economic Espionage Act of 1996 (EEA) protects the privacy of trade secrets and facilitates the criminal prosecution of trade secret theft.[232] Before the EEA became law, there was no federal law that specifically criminalized the theft of commercial trade secrets. Federal prosecutors had to rely on laws such as the Interstate Transportation of Stolen Property Act, the Computer Fraud and Abuse Act, and Mail and Wire Fraud statutes.[233]

Even though most states do recognize a civil cause of action through either tort misappropriation or contract claims, many companies choose not to pursue these remedies. The reasons are fourfold: (1) the civil remedies are often simply not enough to compensate a company for the loss of the market edge the trade secrets provided; (2) the defendants are frequently judgment-proof; (3) civil litigation is exceedingly costly and risky; and (4) companies and individuals seldom have the resources or investigative capacity crucial to obtaining a successful judgment.[234]

In 1996, Congress recognized the swelling importance of trade secrets to the U.S. economy and the inadequate means of protecting them. It saw the need for a statute explicitly criminalizing trade secret theft and enacted the EEA, which became effective on October 11, 1996.[235] Congress intentionally defined "trade secret" broadly:

---

[232]Economic Espionage Act of 1996, 18 U.S.C. Sections 1831-1839, http://www4.law.cornell.edu/uscode/18/1831.html (hereinafter "EEA").

[233]James H. A. Pooley, Mark A. Lemley and Peter J. Toren, "Understanding the Economic Espionage Act of 1996," 1997 at 1, http://www.utexas. edu/law/journals/tiplj/volumes/vol5iss2/lemley2.htm (hereinafter "Pooley, Lemley, and Toren"); see also "Economic Espionage Act of 1996," http://rf-web.tamu.edu/security/SECGUIDE/T1threat/Legal.htm (citing Annual Report to Congress on Foreign Economic Collection and Industrial Espionage, June 1997, National Counterintelligence Center, and The Economic Espionage Act of 1996: A Brief Guide, National Counter Intelligence Center); President William J. Clinton, Presidential Statement on the Signing of the Economic Espionage Act of 1996, Oct. 11, 1996, http://www.opsec.org/opsnews/Dec96/protected/EEA96.html.

[234]Pooley, Lemley, and Toren at 4, http://www.utexas.edu/law/journals/tiplj/volumes/vol5iss2/lemley2.htm.

[235]George "Toby" Dilworth, "The Economic Espionage Act of 1996: An Overview," U.S. Attorneys' Bulletin, U.S. Dept. of Justice, May 2001 at 2, http://www.cybercrime.gov/usamay2001_6.htm (hereinafter "Dilworth"); see also Computer Crime and Intellectual Property Section (CCIPS), "VIII. Theft of Commercial Trade Secrets," Apr. 23, 2001, http://www.cybercrime.gov/ipmanual/08ipma.htm (hereinafter "CCIPS EEA").

[T]he term "trade secret" means all forms and types of financial, business, scientific, technical, economic, or engineering information, including patterns, plans, compilations, program devices, formulas, designs, prototypes, methods, techniques, processes, procedures, programs or codes, whether tangible or intangible, and whether how stored, compiled, or memorialized physically, electronically, graphically, photographically, or in writing if—

(A) the owner thereof has taken reasonable measures to keep such information secret; and

(B) the information derives independent economic value, actual or potential, from not being generally known to, and not being readily ascertainable through proper means by, the public.[236]

The second part of the definition places a burden on the owner to take reasonable efforts to maintain the secrecy of the information. This second part also requires that the information obtain independent economic value from not being "generally known" or "readily ascertainable" by the public. The value of the information may be actual or potential to qualify under this definition.[237] Some factors a court may consider when determining whether an owner has made reasonable efforts to keep the information secret are whether the owner:

- Implemented and enforced policies concerning the secret information;
- Trained employees, consultants, and licensees to keep the information confidential;
- Mandated nondisclosure and confidentiality agreements for all employees, consultants, and licensees with access to the information;
- Restricted access to areas with secret information;
- Controlled the number of copies of sensitive documents;
- Made sensitive documents difficult to photocopy;
- Encrypted electronic information;
- Allowed access to confidential information on a "need-to-know" basis only.[238]

---

[236]EEA, 18 U.S.C. Section 1839, http://www4.law.cornell.edu/uscode/18/1839.html.
[237]CCIPS EEA, VIII.8.B.2.c at 7-10.
[238]Dilworth at 4-5.

56   CHAPTER 1

The level of security measures must be reasonable under the circumstances, and there is no definite level of security that will make information a trade secret. Rather, this is a fact-specific inquiry, where more valuable information and information that is at a higher risk of being stolen requires more stringent security measures.[239]

Similarly, the question as to whether information is "generally known" or "reasonably ascertainable" by the public is a slippery concept. For example, the court in *United States v. Hsu* stated that "what is 'generally known' and 'reasonably ascertainable' about ideas, concepts, and technology is constantly evolving in the modern age. With the proliferation of the media of communication on technological subjects, and (still) in so many languages, what is 'generally known or reasonably ascertainable' to the public at any given time is necessarily never sure."[240]

A Two-Part Prohibition

The EEA contains two separate provisions criminalizing the theft of trade secrets. The first is Section 1831, which deals with economic espionage carried out to benefit a foreign government, foreign instrumentality, or foreign agent. The other provision, Section 1832, prohibits the commercial theft of trade secrets that either a foreign or domestic perpetrator performs for some economic or commercial advantage.[241]

To prove a violation of Section 1832, the burden is on the government to prove beyond a reasonable doubt that

- The defendant stole or, without authorization of the owner, obtained, duplicated, destroyed, or conveyed information;
- The defendant knew the information was proprietary;
- The information was a trade secret;
- The defendant acted with the intent to economically benefit someone other than the owner;
- The defendant knew or intended that the owner of the trade secret would be injured; and
- The trade secret was related to or included in, a product that was produced for or placed in interstate or foreign commerce.[242]

---

[239]CCIPS EEA at VII.8.B.2.c at 7.

[240]*United States v. Hsu*, 40 F.Supp.2d 623, 630 (E.D.Pa. 1999).

[241]Dilworth at 3; *see also* CCIPS EAA at 2-5.

[242]Dilworth at 3; *see also* CCIPS EEA at 4-5; Jody R. Westby, "Protection of Trade Secrets and Confidential Information: How to Guard Against Security Breaches and Economic Espionage," *Intellectual Property Counselor*, Jan. 2000 at 6.

To prove a violation of Section 1831, the government must prove that

- The defendant stole, or without authorization obtained, destroyed, or conveyed information;
- The defendant knew or believed the information was a trade secret;
- The defendant knew or intended that the offense would benefit any foreign government, instrumentality, or agent.[243]

The EEA defines the term "foreign instrumentality" to mean "any agency, bureau, ministry, component, institution, association, or any legal, commercial, or business organization, corporation, firm, or entity that is substantially owned, controlled, sponsored, commanded, managed, or dominated by a foreign government."[244] "Substantial" control, sponsorship, etc. in this context means "material or significant, not technical or tenuous."[245]

Misappropriation and Knowledge

Because a defendant may steal a trade secret without the owner ever losing custody or control over that trade secret, Congress also prohibited the copying, duplication, sketching, drawing, photographing, downloading, uploading, altering, destruction, photocopying, replicating, transmitting, delivering, sending, mailing, communication, or conveying of trade secrets.[246] Under this element, the government must prove that the defendant did not have "authorization" to act as the defendant did.[247] The legislative history defines "authorization" as "the permission, approval, consent or sanction of the owner."[248] For example, an employee who has the authorization to possess a trade secret during the regular course of employment may nevertheless violate the EEA by "conveying" that trade secret to a competitor without the employer's authorization.[249]

For the government to prove knowledge on the part of the defendant, the defendant must have a firm belief that he or she is taking a trade secret. Someone taking a trade secret because of ignorance, mistake, accident, or a reasonable belief that the information is not proprietary is not liable under the EEA.[250]

---

[243]Dilworth at 6.

[244]EEA, 18 U.S.C. Section 1839(1), http://www4.law.cornell.edu/uscode/18/1839.html.

[245]Dilworth at 6 (citing 142 Cong. Rec. S12201, 12202 (daily ed. Oct. 2, 1996)).

[246]EEA, 18 U.S.C Section 1832(a)(2), http://www4.law.cornell.edu/uscode/18/1832.html.

[247]CCIPS EEA, VIII.B.2.a at5.

[248]Id. (citing 142 Cong. Rec. S12202, 12212 (daily ed. Oct. 2, 1996)).

[249]CCIPS EEA, VIII.B.2.a at 5.

[250]CCIPS EEA, VIII.B.2.a at 5-6.

58   CHAPTER 1

Penalties

Penalties for violation of Section 1831 (benefiting a foreign government) by an individual are a fine not more than US$500,000 or imprisonment for not more than fifteen years, or both. An organization that violates Section 1831 may be fined not more than US$10 million.[251] The penalty for violation of Section 1832 by an individual is imprisonment of not more than ten years and an unspecified fine. An organization that violates Section 1832 may be fined not more than US$5,000,000.[252] The EEA also provides that courts shall order the forfeiture of any proceeds or property derived from the theft as well as the property used to carry out the offense.[253]

Sections 1831 and 1832 may apply to trade secret theft occurring outside the United States in two situations. First, the EEA applies if the offender is a citizen or resident alien of the United States or an organization organized under U.S. law. The EEA also controls offenses committed outside the United States if an act in furtherance of the offense was committed in the United States.[254]

Conspiracies

The EEA also provides criminal punishment for conspiracies to misappropriate trade secrets.[255] Under this provision, it does not matter whether or not the defendant actually received a trade secret.[256] The elements of the crime are (a) an agreement, (b) an unlawful purpose, (c) voluntary participation of the defendant, (d) intention of the defendant to enter into the agreement and intention to steal the trade secrets, and (e) that at least one co-conspirator made some affirmative step toward carrying out the conspiracy.[257]

Protective Orders and Confidentiality

There is a major problem with trying trade secret cases because there is a possibility that the trade secrets themselves may be disclosed during the trial.[258] Therefore, Congress directed courts to take all necessary actions, including issuing protective orders, to maintain the confidentiality of trade secrets during proceedings under the EEA.[259]

---

[251]EEA, 18 U.S.C. Section 1831, http://www4.law.cornell.edu/uscode/18/1831.html.

[252]EEA, 18 U.S.C. Section 1832, http://www4.law.cornell.edu/uscode/18/1832.html.

[253]EEA, 18 U.S.C. Section 1834, http://www4.law.cornell.edu/uscode/18/1834.html.

[254]EEA, 18 U.S.C. Section 1837, http://www4.law.cornell.edu/uscode/18/1837.html.

[255]See EEA, 18 U.S.C. Sections 1831-1832.

[256]United States v. Martin, 228 F.3d 1, 13 (1st Cir. 2000).

[257]Id.

[258]Dilworth at 7-8.

[259]EEA, 18 U.S.C. Section 1835, http://www4.law.cornell.edu/uscode/18/1835.html.

i. Trade Secrets

Generally, trade secrets are protected by state statutes, state common law, misappropriation claims, or state contractual claims. Federal law, through the Economic Espionage Act, also protects trade secrets. Thirty-eight states have enacted some form of the Uniform Trade Secrets Act (UTSA),[260] which was drafted by the National Conference of Commissioners on Uniform State Laws (NCCUSL).

The UTSA has a two-part definition of "trade secret." The first part requires that the information obtain "independent economic value" from not being known or discoverable by others.[261] The second part requires the owner of the information to employ reasonable efforts to keep the information secret.[262] The UTSA states that "'trade secret' means information, including a formula, pattern compilation, program device, method, technique, or process, that: (i) derives independent economic value, actual or potential, from not being generally known to, and not being readily ascertainable by proper means by, other persons who can obtain economic value from its disclosure or use, and (ii) is the subject of efforts that are reasonable under the circumstances to maintain its secrecy."[263]

The Restatement of Torts states the definition of "trade secret" as

> [A]ny formula, pattern, device or compilation of information which is used in one's business, and which gives him an opportunity to obtain an advantage over competitors who do not know or use it. It may be a formula for a chemical compound, a process of manufacturing, treating or preserving material, a pattern for a machine or other device, or a list of customers.[264]

The Third Restatement of Unfair Competition states that "a trade secret is any information that can be used in the operation of a business or other enterprise and that is sufficiently valuable and secret to afford an actual or potential economic advantage over others."[265]

---

[260]Richard M. Peterson, "Protecting Your Secret Recipe: Trade Secrets, Espionage and Preserving Your Product in Associations," "Definitions and Elements," *Forum Magazine*, May 2002, http://www.centerline.org/knowledge/article.cfm?ID=2236&.

[261]Uniform Trade Secrets Act, Drafted by the National Conference of Commissioners on Uniform State Laws, as amended 1985, Section 1(4)(i), http://nsi.org/Library/ Espionage/usta.htm (hereinafter "USTA").

[262]USTA Section 1(4)(ii), http://nsi.org/Library/Espionage/usta.htm.

[263]USTA Section 1(4), http://nsi.org/Library/Espionage/usta.htm.

[264]Andrew Beckerman-Rodau, "Protection of Ideas, Trade Secret Law, Patent Law & Trademark Law," Section II.A.2, 1996, http://www.law.suffolk.edu/arodau/articles/ kiev-cle.html (hereinafter "Beckerman-Rodau").

[265]Restatement of the Law Third, Unfair Competition, Chapter 2, "Trade Secret Law," American Law Institute, Jan. 1995, http://my.execpc.com/~mhallign/unfair.html.

Factors a Court Will Apply to Determine Whether Information is a Trade Secret

Courts generally consider six factors in deciding whether certain material is a trade secret.[266] These are:

- The extent to which the information is known outside the owner's business. The greater the knowledge outside the business, the less likely it is that courts will consider the information to be a trade secret.
- The extent to which the information is known by the owner's employees or others involved in the owner's business. The more employees who know the information, the less likely it is that courts will consider the information to be a trade secret.
- The extent of measures taken to keep the information secret. The greater the security measures taken, the more likely it is that courts will consider the information to be a trade secret.
- The value of the information to the owner and the owner's competitors. The more valuable the information, the more likely it is that courts will consider the Information to be a trade secret.
- The amount of money and effort expended by the owner in developing the information. The more money and effort expended, the more likely it is that courts will consider the information to be a trade secret.
- The relative ease or difficulty for another to acquire the information. The easier it is to acquire the information, the less likely it is that courts will consider the information to be a trade secret.

Reasonable Efforts and Misappropriation

Information qualifies as a trade secret for only as long as the owner takes reasonable steps to keep the information secret.[267] This secrecy requirement is not absolute. Rather, "reasonable" in this context mandates that a court weigh the commercial value of the information against the time, expense, and effort expended to safeguard the information.[268] Therefore, the more valuable the information, the greater the measures the owner must take to protect the information

---

[266]Beckerman-Rodau at Section II.B; *Internet Law and Business Handbook*, Chapter II, "Standards," Ladera Press, 2001 (hereinafter "Internet Law and Business Handbook"); Legal Ideas, "Trade Secret Protection," *Legal Ideas*, 1998, http://members. aol.com/cynthiabs/ secret.html.

[267]Internet Law and Business Handbook at Chapter II, "Exclusive Rights."

[268]Beckerman-Rodau at Section II.B.3.

for those efforts to be considered "reasonable." A partial list of factors a court considers when evaluating whether reasonable efforts have been made is listed above.

An action for trade secret misappropriation is usually predicated upon one of two different theories. The first is that the defendant acquired the trade secret by "improper means."[269] The second is that the defendant acquired the trade secret in violation of a valid nondisclosure or confidentiality agreement.[270]

The UTSA defines "misappropriation" to mean either

- Acquisition of a trade secret belonging to another, by a person who knows or has reason to know that the trade secret was acquired by improper means, OR
- Disclosure or use of a trade secret of another without express or implied consent by a person who
  1. used improper means to acquire knowledge of the trade secret, OR
  2. at the time of the use or disclosure knew or had reason to know that his knowledge of the trade secret was
     (i)   derived from or through a person who utilized improper means to acquire it,
     (ii) acquired under circumstances giving rise to a duty to maintain its secrecy or limit its use (such as under a nondisclosure agreement), or
     (iii) derived from or through a person who owed a duty to the person seeking relief to maintain its secrecy or limit its use, OR
  3. before a material change of his position, knew or had reason to know that it was a trade secret and that knowledge of it had been acquired by accident or mistake.[271]

The UTSA defines "improper means" as "theft, bribery, misrepresentation, breach or inducement of a breach of duty to maintain secrecy, or espionage through electronic or other means."[272]

Remedies

The UTSA provides for three civil remedies for trade secret theft: injunctive relief, damages, and attorney's fees.[273] The UTSA provides that damages may include both the trade secret owner's actual loss from the misappropriation and the unjust enrichment of the defendant.

---

[269]Beckerman-Rodau at Section II.F.1.

[270]*Id.*

[271]USTA, Section 1(2), http://nsi.org/Library/Espionage/usta.htm.

[272]USTA, Section 1(1), http://nsi.org/Library/Espionage/usta.htm.

[273]USTA, Sections 2-4, http://nsi.org/Library/Espionage/usta.htm.

62   CHAPTER 1

Alternatively, a court may award damages in the amount of a reasonable royalty for the use or disclosure of the trade secret.[274] In addition, if a court determines that the misappropriation is willful and malicious, the court may award exemplary damages up to twice the amount of actual damages, unjust enrichment damages, or reasonable royalty damages.[275]

The prevailing party in such litigation may be entitled to attorney's fees if

- a claim of misappropriation is made in bad faith,
- a motion to terminate an injunction is made or resisted in bad faith, or willful and malicious misappropriation exists.[276]

j. CAN-SPAM Act of 2003

Spam is unsolicited email that is sent in bulk through "open relays." In response to increasing complaints about spam messages and growing costs and risks associated with it, the U.S. Congress passed the Controlling the Assault of Non-Solicited Pornography and Marketing Act of 2003, commonly known as the CAN-SPAM Act. The Act went into effect on January 1, 2004.[277] The CAN-SPAM Act establishes civil and criminal penalties for various types of email activity. It preempts U.S. state spam laws except those that prohibit "falsity or deception in any portion of a commercial electronic mail message."[278]

Although the CAN-SPAM Act does not prohibit all forms of unsolicited commercial email, it does require uniform notice and opt-out features. The opt-out information must include a physical mailing address and an indication that the message is a solicitation.[279] For now, the form of the solicitation indicator is at the discretion of the sender. The Act specifically precludes the FTC from requiring specific labeling on commercial messages except for those pertaining to "sexually oriented" material.[280] Opt-out requests must be honored within ten

---

[274]USTA, Section 3(a), http://nsi.org/Library/Espionage/usta.htm.

[275]USTA, Section 3(b), http://nsi.org/Library/Espionage/usta.htm.

[276]USTA, Section 4, http://nsi.org/Library/Espionage/usta.htm.

[277]Controlling the Assault of Non-Solicited Pornography and Marketing Act of 2003, Pub. Law 108-187, http://thomas.loc.gov/cgi-bin/bdquery/z?d108:s.00877: (hereinafter "CAN-SPAM Act"); for good overviews of the CAN-SPAM Act, see "SPAM — Unsolicited Commercial E-Mail," Electronic Privacy Information Center, http://www.epic.org/privacy/junk_mail/spam/; Ron Plesser, Jim Halpert, Stu Ingis, and Alisa Bergman, "The New Federal Spam Law and Compliance Challenges it Poses," Security & Law Report, Bureau of National Affairs, Vol. 2, No. 50, Dec. 22, 2003.

[278]CAN-SPAM Act, Section 8(b), http://thomas.loc.gov/cgi-bin/bdquery/z?d108:s.00877:.

[279]CAN-SPAM Act, Section 5(a), http://thomas.loc.gov/cgi-bin/bdquery/z?d108:s.00877:.

[280]CAN-SPAM Act, Section 13(b), http://thomas.loc.gov/cgi-bin/bdquery/z?d108:s.00877:.

days.[281] Certain deceptive spam tactics are prohibited, such as (a) using false and misleading header or message information, (b) disguising the origin of spam messages by routing them through other computers or retransmitting them, and (c) using domain names, originating e-mail addresses, or Internet protocol addresses obtained through false pretenses or misrepresentation.[282]

The Act directs the FCC to establish regulations to protect consumers from unwanted mobile service commercial messages.[283] Violations of the CAN-SPAM Act are deemed to be unfair or deceptive acts or practices to be enforced by the Federal Trade Commission.[284] The CAN-SPAM Act also gives other agencies with specific jurisdiction over specific industries, such as the FCC and SEC, authority to enforce the law.[285] The civil penalties (irrespective of which agency enforces the CAN-SPAM Act) are those allowable under the FTC Act for unfair or deceptive acts, which are $10,000 for each violation.[286] State Attorneys General, state agencies, and Internet Service Providers can also file civil actions to enforce the CAN-SPAM Act and seek injunctive relief as well as civil damages, up to a capped amount.[287]

3. U.S. REGULATORY ACTION

a. Federal Trade Commission

The FTC has shown a significant interest in the protection of consumer privacy online since it held an early public workshop on Consumer Protection and the Global Information Infrastructure in April 1995. This workshop has been followed by surveys, studies of privacy policies, reports, and additional workshops, the most recent of which, in May and June of 2003, focused on technologies for protecting personal information on the Internet.[288]

---

[281]CAN-SPAM Act, Section 5(a)(4), http://thomas.loc.gov/cgi-bin/bdquery/z?d108:s.00877:.

[282]CAN-SPAM Act, Section 5, http://thomas.loc.gov/cgi-bin/bdquery/z?d108:s.00877:.

[283]CAN-SPAM Act, Section 14, http://thomas.loc.gov/cgi-bin/bdquery/z?d108:s.00877:.

[284]CAN-SPAM Act, Section 7(a), http://thomas.loc.gov/cgi-bin/bdquery/z?d108:s.00877:. The FTC has authority to enforce unfair and deceptive practices pursuant to the FTC Act, 15 U.S.C. 57a(a)(1)(b).

[285]CAN-SPAM Act, Section 7(b), http://thomas.loc.gov/cgi-bin/bdquery/z?d108:s.00877:.

[286]CAN-SPAM Act, Section 7(d), http://thomas.loc.gov/cgi-bin/bdquery/z?d108:s.00877:; FTC Act, 15 U.S.C. Section 45, http://www4.law.cornell.edu/uscode/15/45.html.

[287]CAN-SPAM Act, Section 7(f), (g), http://thomas.loc.gov/cgi-bin/bdquery/z?d108:s.00877:.

[288]See, for example, *Privacy Online: A Report to Congress*, Federal Trade Commission, June, 1998, http://www.ftc.gov/reports/privacy3/priv-23a.pdf; *Privacy Online: Fair Information Practices in the Online Marketplace*, Federal Trade Commission, May 2000, http://www.ftc.gov/reports/privacy2000/privacy2000.pdf.

64   CHAPTER 1

This interest is motivated in part by statutes that the FTC enforces, such as the Gramm-Leach-Bliley Act (GLBA) and the Children's Online Privacy Protection Act (COPPA). However, the FTC's core statutory mandate has provided a broader, and potentially more significant, role for the agency in the still developing area of online privacy protection. The Commission enforces Section 45(a) of the Federal Trade Commission Act (FTC Act), which contains a broad mandate prohibiting "unfair or deceptive acts or practices in or affecting commerce."[289] Generally, the Commission will find deception if there is a representation, omission, or practice that is likely to mislead the consumer acting reasonably in the circumstances, to the consumer's detriment.[290] An unfair or unlawful act or practice, as codified in Section 45(n) of the FTC Act, is one that "causes or is likely to cause *substantial injury* to consumers which is *not reasonably avoidable* by consumers themselves and *not outweighed by countervailing benefits* to consumers or to competition."[291]

The first Internet privacy action brought under the Unfair Methods of Competition section of the FTC Act, Section 45, was *In the Matter of GeoCities*,[292] finalized in February 1999. This matter, which resulted in a consent order, involved a situation in which GeoCities disclosed personally identifiable information (PII)[293] gathered on its website to

---

[289]Federal Trade Commission Act, 15 U.S.C. Section 45(a), http://www4.law.cornell.edu/uscode/15/45.html (hereinafter "FTC Act").

[290]FTC Policy Statement on Deception, appended to Cliffdale Associates, Inc., 103 FTC 110, 174 (1984). The FTC Policy Statement on Deception can be located at http://www.ftc.gov/bcp/policystmt/ad-decept.htm.

[291]FTC Act, 15 U.S.C. Section 45(n), http://www4.law.cornell.edu/uscode/15/45.html (emphasis added to stress the three elements of the legal test).

[292]*In the Matter of GeoCities*, File No. 9823015, Docket No. C-3850, http://www.ftc.gov/os/1999/02/9823015cmp.htm; *In the Matter of GeoCities*, File No. 9823015, Agreement Containing Consent Order, http://www.ftc.gov/os/1998/08/geo-ord.htm (consent order accorded final approval on Feb. 12, 1999). Details of all FTC privacy actions can be found in the Privacy Initiatives area of the agency's website at http://www.ftc.gov/privacy.

[293]Specific definitions of PII vary. As one example, from the definitions section of the Consent and Order from *In the Matter of Microsoft Corporation*:

"Personally identifiable information" or "personal information" shall mean individually identifiable information from or about an individual including, but not limited to: (a) a first and last name; (b) a home or other physical address, including street name and name of city or town; (c) an email address or other online contact information, such as an instant messaging user identifier or a screen name that reveals an individual's email address; (d) a telephone number; (e) a Social Security Number; (f) a persistent identifier, such as a customer number held in a "cookie" or processor serial number, that is combined with other available data that identifies an individual; or (g) any information that is combined with any of (a) through (f) above.

In the Matter of Microsoft Corporation, File No. 012 3240, Docket No. C-4069, http://www.ftc.gov/os/2002/12/microsoftcomplaint.pdf; *In the Matter of Microsoft Corporation*, File No. 012 3240, Agreement Containing Consent Order, http://www.ftc.gov/os/2002/08/microsoftagree.pdf (consent order accorded final approval on December 20, 2002).

third parties, in violation of the explicit terms of its stated privacy policies. This information was shared with third parties in the normal course of Geocities's business. *FTC v. Toysmart* involved another type of violation of privacy policy statements concerning PII. Toysmart's privacy policy stated that PII gathered through the website would never be shared with third parties.[294] That was true in normal operations, but the company attempted to sell its customer database to a third party when it ran into financial difficulties. In addition, the FTC has brought cases in which companies stated that they would share data, but did so with organizations outside the scope of the sharing statement. For example, *In the Matter of The National Research Center For College and University Admissions, Inc., et al.*,[295] involved a situation in which the respondents were said to have provided PII to commercial marketers in violation of privacy policy promises that the data would be shared only with education-related organizations.

The FTC has not limited its efforts to examining deliberate sharing of information in violation of privacy policies and then ordering remedial action concerning the policies. The FTC has gone beyond examining and enforcing promises made in a website's privacy policy. In three recent and important cases, the FTC has taken additional, significant steps. The FTC has made it clear that it will review corporate privacy and security procedures where personal data have been, or may be, disclosed inadvertently because of a lack of commonly accepted privacy and security practices, and mandate remedial action with ongoing FTC review in those instances. Eli Lilly & Co. maintained websites that collected personal information from visitors, with promises of confidentiality. Two of those websites offered an e-mail service to remind consumers to refill prescriptions. Shortly after introducing a new computer program that would access subscribers' e-mail addresses, the company sent an e-mail informing users of the reminder service that it would be terminated. The notification message included the e-mail addresses of all 669 subscribers in the To: line of the e-mail message.

In the complaint, the FTC alleged that Lilly's claim of privacy and confidentiality was deceptive because the company failed to maintain

---

[294]*U.S. v. Toysmart*, Civil Action No. 00-11341-RGS, D.Mass. (2000), http://www.ftc.gov/os/2000/07/toysmartcomplaint.htm.
[295]*In the Matter of The National Research Center For College and University Admissions, Inc., et al.*, File No. 022 3005, Docket No. C-4071 and C-4072, NRCCUA Complaint, http://www.ftc.gov/os/2003/01/nrccuacmp1.htm, American Student List Complaint, http://www.ftc.gov/os/2003/01/aslcmp.htm; *In the Matter of The National Research Center For College and University Admissions, Inc., et. al*, File No. 022 3005, Agreement Containing Consent Order as to NRCCUA and Munce, http://www.ftc.gov/os /2002/10/nrccuamunceagree.pdf, Agreement Containing Consent Order as to American Student List, http://www.ftc.gov/os/2002/10/nrccuaagree.pdf (consent order accorded final approval on January 29, 2003).

66   CHAPTER 1

or implement internal measures appropriate under the circumstances to protect sensitive consumer information.[296] It is also important to note that Eli Lilly had a policy on the privacy of this information; the employee made a mistake. According to the FTC, that was no excuse. The FTC's complaint alleged the company's claim of privacy and confidentiality of this information was deceptive *because of "failure to maintain or implement internal measures appropriate under the circumstances" to support the policy.*[297] According to the FTC, Eli Lilly failed to (1) provide appropriate training for employees regarding consumer privacy and information security; (2) provide appropriate oversight and assistance for the employee who sent out the e-mail, who had had no prior experience in creating, testing, or implementing the type of computer program used; and (3) implement appropriate checks and controls on the process, such as reviewing the computer program with experienced personnel and pre-testing the program internally before sending out the e-mail.

The consent order[298] in the matter barred misrepresentations about the extent to which Lilly maintains and protects the privacy or confidentiality of any personal information collected from or about consumers. However, more importantly, in understanding the scope of FTC actions in the area of privacy protection, it also directly addressed security practices at the company. It required Lilly to establish and maintain a four-stage information security program. This program was to be designed to establish and maintain reasonable and appropriate administrative, technical, and physical safeguards to protect consumers' personal information against any reasonably anticipated threats or hazards to its security, confidentiality, or integrity, and to protect such information against unauthorized access, use, or disclosure.

Lilly involved inadvertent disclosure of sensitive information by a company. The FTC addressed a situation involving hacking in *In the Matter of Guess?, Inc. and Guess.com.*[299] According to the complaint, a visitor to the website was able to manipulate SQL strings in a URL and thereby view information, including credit card numbers, in the Guess.com customer database. The Commission, in issuing its complaint, determined that SQL injection attacks, as this technique is

---

[296]*In re Eli Lilly and Co.*, File No. 012 3214, Docket No. C-4047, http://www.ftc.gov/os/2002/01/lillycmp.pdf.
[297]*Id.* at para. 7.
[298]*In re Eli Lilly and Co.* , Agreement Containing Consent Order, FTC No. 0123214, Jan 18, 2002, http://www.ftc.gov/os/2002/01/lillyagree.pdf (consent order accorded final approval on May 10, 2002).
[299]*In the Matter of Guess?, Inc. and Guess.com*, File No. 022 3260, Docket No. 0223260, http://www.ftc.gov/os/2003/06/guesscmp.pdf.

known, were well documented in security literature. Therefore, the failure to safeguard against this type of intrusion attacks was a violation of statements on the website that the company had implemented reasonable and appropriate measures to protect the personal information that they obtained from consumers through their website.[300]

As in *Lilly*, the ensuing consent order mandated specific security remedies and follow-up FTC oversight. Guess? was to create a comprehensive information security program involving administrative, technical, and physical safeguards to protect customer information that it gathered. The company also had to commission biannual security assessments by an outside expert and make the assessments and other security-related documents available to FTC staff upon request.[301]

The FTC also scrutinized internal security issues involving privacy protections in the Microsoft Passport program, which includes Passport, Passport Wallet, and Kids Passport. Passport is a service that collects information from consumers and then allows them to sign in at any participating site with the use of a single name and password. Passport Wallet collects and stores consumers' credit card numbers and billing and shipping addresses, so that consumers do not have to input this information every time they make a purchase from a site. Kids Passport was promoted as a way for parents to create accounts for their children that limited the information that could be collected from them.

In August 2002, the Commission announced a settlement regarding claims made by the company about the information collected from consumers through its Passport services.[302] The Commission's complaint alleged that Microsoft misrepresented the privacy afforded by these services, including the extent to which Microsoft kept the information secure. For example, in various online statements, Microsoft said that the Passport service "achieves a high level of Web Security by using technologies and systems designed to prevent unauthorized access to your personal information."[303] In fact, the Commission alleged that Microsoft failed to employ reasonable and appropriate measures to protect the personal information collected in connection with these services because it failed to (1) implement procedures needed to prevent or detect unauthorized access, (2)

---

[300]*Id.*

[301]*In the Matter of Guess?, Inc. and Guess.com*, File No. 022 3260, Agreement Containing Consent Order, http://www.ftc.gov/os/2003/06/guessagree.pdf (Consent agreement placed on public record on June 18, 2003).

[302]*In the Matter of Microsoft Corporation*, File No. 012 3240, Docket No. C-4069, http://www.ftc.gov/os/2002/12/microsoftcomplaint.pdf (hereinafter "Microsoft Complaint"); *In the Matter of Microsoft Corporation*, File No. 012 3240, Agreement Containing Consent Order, http://www.ftc.gov/os/2002/08/microsoftagree.pdf (consent order accorded final approval on December 20, 2002).

[303]Microsoft Complaint at para. 3.

monitor the system for potential vulnerabilities, and (3) perform appropriate security audits or investigations.

The Commission's order against Microsoft contained strong relief designed to provide significant protections for consumer information. First, it prohibited any misrepresentations about the use of and protection for personal information. Second, it required Microsoft to implement a comprehensive information security program similar to the program required under the FTC's Gramm-Leach-Bliley Safeguards Rule. Finally, to provide additional assurances that the information security program complies with the consent order, Microsoft must have its program certified as meeting or exceeding the standards in the order by an independent professional every two years. The provisions of the order will expire after twenty years.

Microsoft is an important case because the action was brought, and settlement reached, even though no known breach of the system existed. The Commission found the mere potential for injury actionable when sensitive information and security promises are involved, and when the potential for injury is significant. This determination is an extremely important principle. It is not enough to make promises about protecting personal information, and then just hope that nothing bad happens or, if it does, that no one finds out. Fulfilling privacy and security promises requires affirmative steps to ensure that personal information is appropriately protected from security risks.

Certain lessons can be drawn from examining FTC Section 5 privacy cases. At the most basic level, privacy policies must be clear and accurate; say what you do and do what you say. Companies must make sure they know what information is collected, how it is stored, and how it is used, and write privacy policies accordingly. They must keep data secure where privacy policies promise confidentiality.

Data for which protection is promised must be secure from both deliberate and inadvertent disclosure. The latter admittedly is difficult to guarantee, as arguably no computer system is 100 percent secure. However, companies must take demonstrably reasonable measures viewed in light of overall systems and privacy requirements to safeguard confidential data. The best way to ensure that privacy policies reflect reality, and that systems designs take privacy issues into account, is to develop a cross-organizational policy when it comes to safeguarding sensitive consumer data. Representatives from management, legal, marketing, IT, security, and Web design must be included to (i) determine current information practices, (ii) assess what laws may apply, (iii) develop and draft clear data security policies and practices, and (iv) develop and draft a clear privacy policy. These representatives must support the policies and practices with formal employee education on data security issues and make sure that outside contractors are aware of the relevant issues if they handle system development or management where privacy is an issue. These topics are covered in more depth in the Plans, Policies, and Procedures and Implementation chapters of this book.

b. Federal Communications Commission

The Federal Communications Commission (FCC) has used its broad authority over telecommunications carriers and providers of cable television to regulate these companies' privacy practices. This includes customer personal information, cable subscriber information, and telemarketing and junk fax activities. In addition, nearly every company that telemarkets is subject to the FCC's telemarketing rules, which were expanded in July 2003 to include a national "Do Not Call" program.

CPNI Regulations of Telecommunications Carriers

The federal Communications Act limits how telecommunications common carriers may use and disclose Customer Proprietary Network Information (CPNI).[304] CPNI includes most billing information and other information available to a carrier due to the customer-carrier relationship, such as the type of telecommunications service used by a customer and the kinds of calls the customer tends to make. Common carriers have paid substantial fines for violations of the CPNI rules.

Detailed CPNI rules are currently in effect.[305] In July 2002, the FCC further clarified how carriers and other businesses may use CPNI.[306] Carriers must provide customers notice and an opportunity to opt out of marketing if they or their affiliates wish to use CPNI to market communications-related services (for example, phone services, Internet services, caller ID boxes, etc.). Notice and opt-in approval are required, however, if a carrier intends to disclose CPNI to an affiliate that is not providing communications-related services or to an unrelated third party. The FCC provides a "total service approach" exception to these rules that allows carriers to use CPNI to market to existing customers— even if carriers have not provided customers specific notice or received their approval—if the marketed product falls into a category of

---

[304]*See* Communications Act, 47 U.S.C. Section 222, http://www4.law.cornell.edu/uscode/47/222.html.
[305]*See Customer Proprietary Network Information*, 47 C.F.R. Section 64.2001 *et seq.*
[306]*See Third Report and Order and Third Further Notice of Proposed Rulemaking*, CC Docket Nos. 96-115, 96-149, 00-257, FCC 02-214 (July 25, 2002), http://hraunfoss.fcc.gov/edocs_public/attachmatch/FCC-02-214A1.pdf.

telecommunications service that the customer already purchases from that carrier.[307]

Subscriber Privacy Rules for Cable Network Operators

The Communications Act requires cable network operators to provide their subscribers conspicuous, detailed notice about their collection, use, and disclosure of information identifying subscribers—both at the time of subscription and on an annual basis thereafter.[308] Without consent, an operator may not collect or disclose subscriber information except as necessary to provide cable service or pursuant to other statutory exceptions. In addition, a cable operator must grant subscribers reasonable access to their personal information and destroy information once it is no longer necessary for the purpose for which it was collected. Subscribers may bring civil suits for damages.[309] The FCC does not have enforcement authority over this provision of the Act.

The subscriber privacy rules have implications for cable operators providing Internet services. A recent FCC ruling has helped clarify whether current federal law regulating the cable industry, and the subscriber privacy rules in particular, apply when a cable operator offers Internet services over its cable network. In March 2002, the agency issued a ruling that cable modem service is an "interstate information service," not a "cable service."[310] Nonetheless, the agency concluded that cable modem service falls into the statutory category of "other service[s]" provided over cable systems to which the subscriber privacy rules apply.[311] Thus, cable operators must comply with the subscriber privacy rules when offering Internet access via cable modem.

FCC Telemarketing and Junk Fax Rulemaking

The FCC's telemarketing rules generally apply to U.S. companies that telemarket to consumers for commercial purposes.[312] These rules implemented the Telephone Consumer Protection Act (TCPA),[313] which gave the FCC power to regulate interstate and most intrastate telemarketing. The rules require companies, among other things, not to

---

[307]47 C.F.R. Section 64.2005.

[308]Communications Act, 47 U.S.C. Section 631.

[309]*See* Communications Act, 47 U.S.C. Section 631(f).

[310]*See Declaratory Ruling and Notice of Proposed Rulemaking,* GN Docket No. 00-185, CS Docket No. 02-52, FCC 02-77 (March 15, 2002), http://hraunfoss.fcc.gov/edocs_public/attachmatch/FCC-02-77A1.pdf.

[311]*Id.*

[312]*See Restrictions on Telephone Solicitation,* 47 C.F.R. Section 64.1200.

[313]Telephone Consumer Protection Act, 47 U.S.C. Section 227, http://www4.law.cornell.edu/uscode/47/227.html.

call before 8:00 a.m. in the morning or after 9:00 p.m. in the evening, to keep an internal record of consumers who ask not to be called again, and to refrain from sending commercial faxes without the recipient's prior express consent. A general exception exists for telemarketing calls to a business's established customers. The FCC, the states, and private parties have authority to enforce the TCPA.

The FCC has recently implemented updates to its telemarketing rules, establishing a national "Do Not Call" program. Congress required the FCC to harmonize its telemarketing rules with the sweeping new regulations adopted in January 2003 by the Federal Trade Commission (FTC).[314] Most notably, the FTC's revised Telemarketing Sales Rule (TSR) established a national "Do Not Call" list, which went into effect in October 2003.[315] Under the national "Do Not Call" program, covered businesses must check the national "Do Not Call" registry on a quarterly basis, determine whether a target consumer has registered not to receive telemarketing calls, and, if so, refrain from calling that consumer. FCC rules impose "Do Not Call" obligations on those entities exempt from FTC jurisdiction (for example, common carriers, banks, some financial service companies, and insurance companies). Consequently, nearly all U.S. businesses will be required to check the federally maintained "Do Not Call" list, as well as any state lists that might apply, before initiating a telemarketing campaign. The FTC, FCC, and the states will jointly enforce "Do Not Call" rules.

C. Seal Programs

Many companies participate in privacy seal programs as a means of building consumer trust. Seal programs are believed to provide a level of assurance that companies posting the seal "say what they do and do what they say" regarding privacy in their data collection policies and practices. Privacy seal programs often assist companies in conducting internal assessments of their information practices and counsel companies as they draft their privacy policies. They can also verify that posted policies are implemented through seeding and auditing procedures.

Seal programs such as TRUSTe (www.truste.org) and Better Business Bureau Online, known as BBBOnline (www.bbbonline.org), also provide consumers with a forum for dispute resolution—a place to bring concerns

---

[314]*Do Not Call Implementation Act*, P.L. 108-10 (2003); http://www.mbaa.org/industry/docs/03/hr395_0213.pdf.

[315]*Telemarketing Sales Rule*, 16 C.F.R. Part 310. Consumers may register for the "Do Not Call" program beginning July 2003, but telemarketers do not have to consult the national DNC list until October 2003.

72   CHAPTER 1

about the company's implementation of their privacy policy and complaints when a policy is not followed, or information has been shared or handled inappropriately. Although the actions of seal programs related to consumer complaints do not have the force of law, they can have implications for a company's public and consumer relations.

The majority of complaints fielded by TRUSTe have been related to consumers who had received unsolicited commercial e-mail, allegedly as a result of their interactions with a website. Other complaints have stemmed from users who wish to "unsubscribe" from a site and were unable to do so. Still others came from those who wished to have their personally identifiable information deleted from a company's database.

BBBOnline most often fields inquiries related to how a consumer would remove an e-mail address from a marketing list, fraud and scam questions, opt-out maintenance questions, and inquiries about credit information and protection.

The main components of each program are

1. BBBONLINE PRIVACY PROGRAM

- Awards a compliance seal to businesses that meet the core privacy principles, such as notice, choice, access, and security
- Provides dispute resolution
- Monitors compliance through required annual company assessments of online privacy practices.
- Imposes consequences for noncompliance, such as seal withdrawal, negative publicity, and referral to government enforcement agencies.

2. TRUSTe PRIVACY PROGRAM

- Awards privacy seal or "trustmark" to companies that adhere to their principles of disclosure, choice, access, and security
- Monitors compliance through periodic reviews
- "Seeds" websites to ensure their practices are in compliance with stated policies
- Requires compliance reviews by a CPA firm
- Provides alternative dispute resolution.[316]

D. State Legal Landscape

Privacy issues are an increasingly hot topic in U.S. state legislatures. Two different and, quite often, conflicting themes are shaping the development of the law at the state level. The first is the ever-increasing impact of the electronic age on personal privacy. The

---

[316]Barbara S. Wellbery and Miriam H. Wugmeister, "Privacy: The U.S., E.U., Latin America, and Asia," at 7.

U.S. Legal Framework   73

second is the struggle to enhance security, especially following the terrorist attacks on September 11. Clearly, a patchwork of federal and state laws is not the most effective means to address the privacy issues involved, especially from the vantage point of businesses with multistate or multinational operations.

It is beyond the scope of this guide to list and detail each state law and regulation dealing with privacy issues. Such compilations do exist and would serve as an excellent reference tool for those charged with complying with the laws of multiple states.[317] State laws cover a wide range of privacy issues. Some laws are of general applicability to business activities, but many are targeted at specific industries. The following is intended to provide a summary of the areas of state privacy law of most interest to the corporate world. Omitted from this summary are laws relating to privacy matters that would not ordinarily be of concern to businesses and their counsel, such as laws relating to identity theft, limitations on government action, use of personal information by government, and access to arrest and conviction records. Finally, other sections of this book give special consideration to customer and employee records, as well as credit information. Accordingly, state laws relating to those subject areas are not covered in this section.

1. ELECTRONIC SURVEILLANCE

Telephone monitoring and recording are regulated in each state. A substantial majority of the fifty U.S. states (thirty-eight plus the District of Columbia) have so-called one-party consent statutes, which permit a party to a conversation to record a telephone conversation without the other party's consent. Eleven states require the consent of all parties before a telephone conversation is recorded.[318] Video surveillance is addressed by only a handful of states. In the states in which a statute exists, most prohibit the use of a camera to photograph or videotape people in some state of undress. For example, Connecticut prohibits video surveillance in employee locker rooms and rest rooms.[319]

---

[317]*See, e.g.,* "Compilation of State and Federal Privacy Laws," *Privacy Journal,* 2002, http://www.privacyjournal.net/work1.htm (hereinafter "Privacy Journal"); *see also* Electronic Privacy Information Center, "Privacy Laws by State," http://www. epic.org/privacy/consumer/states.html (providing an electronic posting of categories of protected information; taken from foregoing "Compilation of State and Federal Privacy Laws").

[318]Privacy Journal at 67-69 (California, Connecticut, Delaware, Florida, Illinois (however, monitoring of an employee's calls with customers is permissible for quality control and training purposes, provided that the employee has notice), Massachusetts, Maryland, Montana, New Hampshire, Pennsylvania, and Washington).

[319]Connecticut General Statutes Section 31-48b(b).

74   CHAPTER 1

Delaware prohibits the installation of a device for photographing in any private place without consent.[320] Several states make it illegal to install a video device in a fitting or dressing room, bathroom, or other place where a person may be undressed and expects privacy.[321]

Monitoring of an employee's e-mail is an evolving area of state law. To date, only Connecticut and Delaware have adopted laws to limit or prevent an employer from e-mail monitoring. Connecticut requires employers to give employees prior written notice if e-mail (or other electronic) monitoring may occur.[322] Delaware also requires a one-time written notice, which must be signed by the employee, describing the monitoring that may occur.[323] Legislation has been introduced on this topic in several other states. Case law in state courts (discussed further below) has sided with employers, generally holding that employees do not have a reasonable expectation of privacy in their e-mail communications at work.

2. SOCIAL SECURITY NUMBERS

A few states have made it illegal for businesses to require a customer's social security number when transacting business. In Ohio, a business may not record, with limited exceptions, the SSN of a customer in a credit card transaction.[324] In Rhode Island, a business may not require a SSN when a purchase is made.[325] In Virginia, it is unlawful to refuse service if a SSN is not furnished, unless such disclosure is specifically required by federal or state law.[326]

3. TESTING IN EMPLOYMENT (INCLUDING POLYGRAPHS)

Laws in this area fall into two general categories—those pertaining to tests used in pre-employment screening and those dealing with testing of employees in connection with their employment activities. In the first category, several states have made it unlawful to use genetic test results in making employment decisions or prohibit discrimination in employment based on genetic characteristics.[327] In Florida, a person

---

[320]Delaware Code Annotated Title 11, Section 1335(a)(2).

[321]Privacy Journal at 21-24 (California, Florida, Georgia, Louisiana, Massachusetts, Michigan, Mississippi, Missouri, New York, Ohio, Oregon, Virginia, and Wisconsin).

[322]Connecticut General Statutes Section 31-48d(3)(b)(1).

[323]See Delaware Code Annotated Title 19, Section 705, 2003.

[324]Ohio Revised Code Annotated 1349.17.

[325]Rhode Island General Laws 6-13-17.

[326]Virginia Code Section 2.1-385.

[327]Privacy Journal at 45-49 (Arizona, California, Connecticut, Delaware, Illinois, Iowa, Kansas, Maine, Massachusetts, Michigan, Missouri, Nevada, New Hampshire, New Jersey, New York, North Carolina, Oklahoma, Oregon, Rhode Island, Texas, Vermont, and Wisconsin).

must be informed if genetic information was used to deny employment.[328] A number of states regulate other types of pre-employment testing. Connecticut and Vermont, for example, require employers to inform applicants in writing that a urinalysis test will be used in the employment decision, and regulate the administration of the test.[329] Montana, New Mexico, Vermont, and Washington prohibit HIV testing as a condition of employment.[330] Finally, many states specifically prohibit or limit the use of polygraph examinations in connection with employment applications.[331]

Testing of employees, and the use of the test results in making employment-related decisions, is regulated to varying degrees in several states. Although there is not a uniform approach in the states, testing for drug and alcohol use is generally permissible. Several states require an employer to notify the employee in advance that testing can occur and how the results will be used.[332] With limited exceptions, random testing is prohibited in Connecticut (employers must have reasonable suspicion of use that adversely affects or could adversely affect job performance), Minnesota (numerous procedural safeguards), Montana (reasonable suspicion required), Oregon (use of breathalyzers in the workplace is limited), Rhode Island (reasonable grounds required), and Vermont (reasonable suspicion and adverse affect required).[333]

---

[328]Florida Statutes Section 760.40.

[329]Connecticut General Statutes Section 31-51t; Vermont Statutes Title 21, Section 511.

[330]Montana Code Section 50-16-1009; New Mexico Statutes Annotated Section 28-10A-1; Vermont Statutes Title 21, Section 495(6); Washington Revised Code Section 49.60.172.

[331]Alaska Statutes Section 23.10.037; Arizona Revised Statutes Section 32.2701 (only inquiries regarding political, sexual, religious or organized labor activities prohibited); California Labor Code Section 432.2; Connecticut General Statutes Section 31-51g; Delaware Code Title 19, Section 704; D.C. Code Section 36-801; Georgia Code Section 43-36-1 (limitations similar to Arizona); Hawaii Revised Statutes Section 378.1; Idaho Code Section 44-903; Iowa Code Section 730.4; Maine Revised Statutes Title 32, Section 7166; Maryland Code of Labor and Employment, Section 3-702; Massachusetts General Laws Chapter 149, Section 19B; Minnesota Statutes Section 181.75; Nebraska Revised Statutes Section 81-1932; New York Labor Law Section 733; Oregon Revised Statutes Section 659.225; Pennsylvania Statutes Title 18, Section 7321; Rhode Island General Laws Section 28-6.1-1; Tennessee Code Section 62-27-123 (limitations upon use of test); Utah Code Section 34-37-16; Vermont Statutes Title 21, Section 5a; Washington Revised Code Section 49.44.120; West Virginia Code Section 21-5-5a.

[332]Privacy Journal at 70-71; *see also* "Post 9/11 Anxiety Increases Substance Abuse—Legal Issues Surround Drug and Alcohol Testing," *HR Managers' Legal Reporter*, Issue 396 at 5, http://www.eapage.com/post911anxiety.doc (*e.g.*, Connecticut, Hawaii, Iowa and Vermont).

[333]Privacy Journal at 70 (with limited exceptions, random testing is prohibited in Connecticut (must have reasonable suspicion of use that adversely affects or could adversely affect job performance), Minnesota (numerous procedural safeguards), Oregon (use of breathalyzers in the workplace is limited), and Rhode Island (reasonable suspicion required)).

76   CHAPTER 1

As in the pre-employment context, many states regulate the use of polygraphs by employers. States that distinguish between pre-employment polygraph examinations and using polygraph tests for employees (or using the results of such a test in the employment context) are few in number. Louisiana permits the use of polygraph examinations in the pre-employment context, but refusal to take a test after being hired cannot be used as grounds for termination of employment.[334] Other states that restrict the use of polygraph tests only with respect to employees, as opposed to applicants, include Michigan,[335] Montana,[336] and Nevada.[337] A majority of states either do not have statutes regulating the use of polygraphs of employees by employers or permit such use with some conditions or limitations.[338] The most common conditions are requiring the consent of the employee to be obtained prior to the test, providing limitations on the scope of inquiry in conducting the test, and providing that the employee receive the results of the test.

4. LAWS TARGETED AT SPECIFIC INDUSTRIES

Cable and Satellite Television
In addition to federal law, five states (California, Connecticut, Illinois, New Jersey, and Wisconsin) and the District of Columbia have statutes targeted at cable television or satellite operators that seek to limit the companies from collecting or using information regarding the viewing habits of subscribers or disclosing other personally identifiable information relating to their customers.[339]

Video Rentals and Sales
California, Connecticut, Delaware, Iowa, Louisiana, Maryland, Michigan, New York, Oklahoma, and Rhode Island have enacted statutes that preclude or limit the disclosure of personally identifiable information in the context of sales or rentals of videos.[340]

---

[334]Louisiana Statutes Section 36-A:2848.

[335]Michigan Compiled Laws Section 37.201.

[336]Montana Code Section 39.2-304.

[337]Nevada Revised Statutes Section 613.480 (polygraph tests are limited to investigations of embezzlement).

[338]Privacy Journal at 45-49 (Alabama, Arkansas, California, Florida, Illinois, Iowa, Kentucky, Louisiana, Mississippi, Nebraska, Nevada, New Jersey, New Mexico, North Dakota, Oklahoma, South Carolina, Tennessee, Texas, Utah, Virginia, Wisconsin).

[339]Privacy Journal at 9.

[340]Privacy Journal at 42-43 (California, Connecticut, Delaware, Iowa, Louisiana, Maryland, Michigan, New York and Rhode Island have enacted statutes that preclude or limit the disclosure of personally identifiable information in the context of sales or rentals of videos).

Financial Institutions

Disclosure of customer financial information by financial institutions is restricted by only a handful of states, although there appears to be a trend toward further regulation at the state level. Alaska, Connecticut, Illinois, Maine, Maryland, and North Dakota are the most aggressive in limiting disclosure of financial information without the consent of the customer. Other states limit a financial institution from disclosing financial records to any state agency without following specified procedures.[341]

Insurance Companies

GLBA requires states to create privacy rules for insurers. By July 1, 2001, all states had either a privacy regulation or a statute in place. Many states adopted either the 1982 or 2000 National Association of Insurance Commissioners (NAIC) Model Rule. Section 17 of the 2000 Model Rule limits disclosure of "personal health information" unless the consumer authorizes such disclosure. Nonetheless, there remain many variances in the state regulations that have been adopted.[342]

Telemarketing

At least twenty-eight states have adopted some form of "do not call" law directed at the telemarketing industry. Many more states are expected to enact similar statutes in the near future. Many laws provide exceptions for certain types of telemarketing, such as fundraising by charitable organizations. Extending these laws to cover calls made to cell phones and unsolicited facsimile transmissions is also becoming more widespread.[343]

Internet Advertising

The scourge of "spam" has been addressed by at least 35 states. The federal CAN-SPAM Act of 2003 preempted state spam laws, except for those that prohibit "falsity or deception in any portion of a commercial electronic message."[344] The CAN-SPAM Act also provides a right of action for civil suits brought by state Attorneys General, or state

---

[341]See especially, Disclosure of Customer Information, North Dakota Century Code, Chapter 6-08.1-03 (2003), http://www.state.nd.us/lr/cencode/T06C081.pdf. For information regarding California privacy protections to consumer financial information, see http://www.privacyprotection.ca.gov/financial/financial.htm; see also, http://www.privacyrights.org for an excellent compitation of California privacy information.

[342]P.D. Squire, "Privacy of Health Information by way of the GLBA: The NIAC Model Act on Privacy of Consumer Financial Information," Jan. 1, 2001, http://www.ebglaw.com/article_389.htm.

[343]Privacy Journal at 67-69 (California, Connecticut, Florida, Illinois, Nevada, New York, Washington).

[344]CAN-SPAM Act, Section 8(b), http://thomas.loc.gov/cgi-bin/bdquery/z?d108:s.00877:

78   CHAPTER 1

agencies if they have reason to believe that an interest of the residents of that state has been or is threatened or adversely affected by false and deceptive emails.[345] Thus, many states are updating their spam laws to impose "super penalties" upon false and deceptive spam messages.[346]

5. REPORTING

In 2002, a hacker broke into a California state database and gained access to confidential personnel data on more than 250,000 state employees. The state was not even aware of the breach for more than a month and then waited another two weeks before notifying employees of the security breach. In response, the California legislature passed Senate Bill (SB) 1386, which requires notification to any California resident when it is known or reasonably believed that certain types of unencrypted personal information have been disclosed as a result of a security breach. Failure to provide such notification can result in civil actions for damages and injunctive relief against the business.[347]

6. STATE ATTORNEYS GENERAL ACTIONS AND CASE RULINGS

Privacy Policies

Investigations and enforcement actions at the state level in recent years have been focused predominately on the failure of businesses to adhere to their own privacy policies. Even the American Civil Liberties Union (ACLU) was a target of such an investigation in March 2003 for mistakenly making available the e-mail distribution list for its online "Safe and Free Newsletter" to each of the 860 recipients. The investigation came on the heels of a settlement with the New York Attorney General's office in January 2003 for a privacy violation involving personal information obtained from people who bought products through the ACLU's website.[348]

State and local prosecutors have also investigated or brought actions against businesses for using personally identifiable information

---

[345]CAN-SPAM Act, Section 7(f), http://thomas.loc.gov/cgi-bin/bdquery/z?d108:s.00877:
[346]For a comprehensive listing of spam laws globally, including U.S. state laws, *see* David E. Sorkin, "Spam Laws," http://www.spamlaws.com.
[347]Security Breach Information Act (SB 1386), Feb. 12, 2002, http://info.sen.ca.gov/pub/01-02/bill/sen/sb_1351-1400/sb_1386_bill_20020926_chaptered.html; Devon Hewitt, "New California privacy law has nationwide ripple," *Washington Technology*, July 7, 2003 at 12; Keith Poulsen, "California disclosure law has national reach," *SecurityFocus Online*, Jan. 6, 2003, http://online.securityfocus.com/news/1984. The law became effective July 1, 2003 for those conducting business in California.
[348]*See* "State Settles Online Privacy Act Case," Office of New York State Attorney General Eliot Spitzer, Jan. 14, 2003, http://www.oag.state.ny.us/press/2003/jan/jan14a_03.html.

obtained from their websites in violation of published privacy policies or misrepresenting the type of information collected and retained. Many of these proceedings are brought under laws prohibiting deceptive trade practices and are the state corollary to the many actions brought by the FTC at the federal level. The lesson for businesses is to ensure that any privacy policy adopted is clear and complete, and then is followed.

Moreover, a business should give adequate notice of any change in a previously published privacy policy to those affected. What constitutes adequate notice is not always clear. In June 2002, the New York Attorney General's office announced the settlement with Juno of an action brought against Juno for failing adequately to notify its customers of changes made in the terms of its service agreement.[349] Juno had sent members an e-mail with the new version of the policy and had posted the changes on its website, but this did not satisfy the State of New York. Under the settlement agreement, Juno agreed to provide subscribers with notice of material changes at least 30 days prior to the effective date by e-mail, U.S. mail, or a "pop-up" screen. In addition, Juno must post a notice on its website and clearly and conspicuously identify the nature of the change and provide a comparison to the prior version.[350]

Monitoring of Employee E-mail

The relatively few published state court decisions regarding the monitoring of employee e-mail have generally held that employees do not have a reasonable expectation of privacy in the use of e-mail at work.[351] As a consequence, employers may review employee e-mail to prevent inappropriate use of the employer's e-mail system. Nevertheless, employers are advised to put an e-mail policy into place to further reinforce the fact that employees have no expectation of privacy when using e-mail at work.[352]

---

[349]See "Settlement with Internet Service Provider Ensures that Consumers Receive Notice of Changes to Service Agreement," Office of New York State Attorney General Eliot Spitzer, May 7, 2002, http://www.oag.state.ny.us/press/2002/may/may07b_02.html.

[350]Collier Shannon Scott, PLLC, *Privacy Law in Q4 2002*, p. 37.

[351]*McLaren v. Microsoft Corp.*, 1999 Tex. App. LEXIS 4103 (Tex. Ct. App., May 28, 1999); *Thomasson v. Bank of America*, No. A061120 (Cal. Ct. App. 1994), app. den., 1995 Cal. LEXIS 1843 (1995).

[352]Kathleen M. Porter, David Wilson, and Jacqueline Scheib, "Work Station or purgatory? Steps Toward a Company Policy on E-Mail and Using the Net," *Business Law Today*, July/Aug. 2002 at 59-62.

E. Conclusion

The U.S. legal framework concerning privacy is complex. Although the United States does not have an omnibus privacy law like the EU and Canada, compliance with the patchwork of sectoral laws and regulations, state laws, and state and federal constitutional provisions is challenging. New sectoral laws, such as HIPAA and GLBA, and their corresponding regulations have a broad reach and significantly affect business operations and privacy plans, policies, and procedures. Workplace privacy considerations vary significantly between the United States and the EU, creating special problems for multinational corporations. Companies must also take care to ensure their privacy program meets the legal threshold of economic espionage and trade secret laws to enable them to seek civil damages or criminal penalties. Numerous legal provisions have been added since the September 11 attacks that pose increased burdens on companies and raise thorny and unsettled privacy issues.

The U.S. privacy legal framework is far from settled. Recent actions taken by the FTC indicate priority attention will continue to be given to privacy, and state action appears to be increasing. It is important that companies stay abreast of legal developments and ensure that their privacy plans, policies, and procedures meet corporate legal compliance and contractual requirements.

CHAPTER ❖ 2

International Legal Framework

A. Overview

The U.S. approach to privacy of self-regulation and sectoral legislation is not the universal method for managing privacy issues. Many countries have enacted general, universally applicable laws that govern the collection, use, and dissemination of personal information and have appointed a Privacy Commissioner or similar oversight mechanism to ensure compliance. In other jurisdictions rules may be developed in conjunction with industry and with Privacy Commissioner oversight. Of course, many countries have chosen not to address privacy legislation at all. While this chapter is necessarily a summary, an attempt has been made to address all jurisdictions with meaningful privacy legislation.

For the purposes of the following review, it should be noted that no effort has been made to review the criminal laws of various jurisdictions to provide a systematic overview of the right to privacy in a criminal context, as that is beyond the scope of this book. In addition, privacy issues in the context of litigation are not considered. Also, most jurisdictions with privacy legislation have particular elements upon which they focus, such as personal identification numbers (for example, Japan, the Philippines, Canada) or air passenger information databases (for example, the EU and Canada); we have not attempted to provide a systematic review of such local "hot-button" issues.

82   CHAPTER 2

B. Multinational Laws, Treaties, and Agreements

1. UNITED NATIONS

A right to privacy is declared in both the *Universal Declaration of Human Rights*[1] and the *International Covenant on Civil and Political Rights*,[2] among other UN texts, but it is not fleshed out in any meaningful way. On December 14, 1990, the United Nations adopted its *Guidelines concerning Computerized personal data files* (UN Computerized Guidelines).[3] Legislation enacted in harmony with the UN Computerized Guidelines would create an obligation that the data collected be secure, accurate, and limited, and would provide a right of access and rectification for the data subject. The UN Guidelines are nonbinding on the Member states.

2. ORGANISATION FOR ECONOMIC CO-OPERATION AND DEVELOPMENT

The Organisation for Economic Co-operation and Development (OECD)[4] has been a frontrunner in the privacy and security arenas and has contributed mightily to the development of the global legal framework in both areas. In 1980, the OECD developed its *Guidelines on the Protection of Privacy and Transborder Flows of Personal Data* (OECD Privacy Guidelines).[5] Recognizing that privacy is dependent upon the security of information, in 1992, the OECD adopted *Guidelines for the Security of Information Systems*.[6]

---

[1]*Universal Declaration of Human Rights*, United Nations, General Assembly, Resolution 217 A (III), Dec. 10, 1948, http://www.un.org/ Overview/rights.html.

[2]*International Covenant on Civil and Political Rights*, General Assembly Resolution 2200A (XXI), Dec. 16, 1966 (adopted), Mar. 23, 1976 (entry into force), http://193.194.138.190/html/menu3/b/a_ccpr.htm.

[3]*United Nations guidelines concerning Computerized personal data files*, United Nations, General Assembly, Dec. 14, 1990, http://www.europa.eu.int/comm/internal_market/privacy/instruments/un_en.htm.

[4]There are currently 30 OECD member countries, 20 of which signed the original OECD convention on 14 December 1960. Recent entrants include Mexico (1994), the Czech Republic (1995), Hungary (1996), Poland (1996), Korea (1996), and the Slovak Republic (2000). Seventy other countries have active relationships with the OECD. *See* Organisation for Economic Co-operation and Development, "Ratification of the Convention on the OECD," http://www.oecd.org/document/58/0,2340,en_2649_34483_1889402_1_1_1_1,00.html.

[5]*Guidelines on the Protection of Privacy and Transborder Flows of Personal Data*, Organisation for Economic Co-operation and Development, Sept. 23, 1980, http://uhoh.org/oecd-privacy-personal-data.pdf (hereinafter "OECD Privacy Guidelines").

[6]*See Guidelines for the Security of Information Systems*, Organisation for Economic Co-operation and Development, Nov. 1992, http://www.oecd.org/document/19/0,2340,en_2649_34255_1815059_1_1_1_37409,00.html (hereinafter "OECD 1992 Security Guidelines").

The OECD Security Guidelines suggested that its Member States develop procedures to facilitate mutual legal assistance in dealing with cybercrimes.[7] Pursuant to Recommendation of the OECD Council, in 1997, the OECD initiated a review of the progress Member states had made toward implementing the 1992 OECD Security Guidelines.[8] The review revealed that countries had experienced difficulties in developing laws and procedures relating to information security because of "differences in the various legal systems and how they deal with security matters ... such as ... computer crimes."[9] Thus, the OECD Council's Recommendation suggested that the OECD Security Guidelines be reviewed every five years "with a view to improving international co-operation on issues relating to the security of information systems."[10] However, the general consensus was that the 1992 OECD Security Guidelines were still adequate and did not need to be revised.[11]

The OECD Security Guidelines were reviewed again in 2001; this review resulted in the 2002 release of a new version, the *OECD Guidelines for the Security of Information Systems and Networks: Towards a Culture of Security*.[12] The OECD Council adopted these new 2002 OECD Security Guidelines as a Recommendation of the Council at its 1037th Session on July 25, 2002.[13] They are intended to "respond to an ever changing security environment by promoting the development of a culture of security."[14] The 2002 OECD Security Guidelines are covered in more depth in the sister publication to this handbook, the *International Guide to Cyber Security*.[15]

The 2002 OECD Security Guidelines present excellent model security principles for all countries to follow when they consider and adopt privacy and security policies, laws, and regulations. They offer particularly valuable guidance to developing countries that desire to

---

[7] *See Id.*

[8] *See* Organisation for Economic Co-operation and Development, *Directorate for Science, Technology and Industry—Committee for Information, Computer and Communications Policy, Review of the 1992 Guidelines for the Security of Information Systems*, 1997, (hereinafter "OECD 1997 Security Guidelines Review"); *see also* OECD 1992 Security Guidelines.

[9] OECD 1997 Security Guidelines Review at 10.

[10] *Id.* at 5.

[11] *Id.* at 18.

[12] *See* Organisation for Economic Co-operation and Development, *OECD Guidelines for the Security of Information Systems and Networks: Towards a Culture of Security*, July 25, 2002, http://www.oecd.org/document/42/0,2340,en_2649_34255_15582250_1_1_1_1,00.html (hereinafter "OECD 2002 Security Guidelines").

[13] *Id.*, Preface at 3.

[14] *Id.*, Section I at 8.

[15] *See* Jody R. Westby, ed., *International Guide to Cyber Security*, American Bar Association, Section of Science & Technology Law, Privacy & Computer Crime Committee, ABA Publishing, 2004, http://www.abanet.org/abapubs/books/security/.

enact laws and regulations in these areas that are consistent with the global legal framework.

With respect to privacy, the preface of the OECD Privacy Guidelines states:

> [T]here is a danger that disparities in national legislations could hamper the free flow of personal data across frontiers; these flows have greatly increased in recent years and are bound to grow further with the widespread introduction of new computer and communications technology. Restrictions on these flows could cause serious disruption in important sectors of the economy, such as banking and insurance.
>
> For this reason OECD Member countries considered it necessary to develop Guidelines which would help to harmonise national privacy legislation and, while upholding such human rights, would at the same time prevent interruptions in international flows of data. They represent a consensus on the basic principles which can be built into existing national legislation, or serve as a basis for legislation in those countries which do not yet have it.[16]

The basic principles of the Privacy Guidelines are broken into four parts: (1) Basic Principles of National Application, (2) Basic Principles of International Application: Free Flow and Legitimate Restrictions, (3) National Implementation, and (4) International Cooperation:

Basic Principles of National Application

- *Collection Limitation Principle.* There should be limits to the collection of personal data, and any such data should be obtained by lawful and fair means and, where appropriate, with the knowledge or consent of the data subject.
- *Data Quality Principle.* Personal data should be relevant to the purpose for which they are to be used, and, to the extent necessary for those purposes, should be accurate, complete, and kept up-to-date.
- *Purpose Specification Principle.* The purposes for which personal data are collected should be specified not later than at the time of data collection, and the subsequent use limited to those purposes or compatible purposes, with changes of purpose specified on each occasion.
- *Use Limitation Principle.* Personal data should not be disclosed, made available, or otherwise used for purposes other than those specified.

---

[16]OECD Privacy Guidelines at Preface.

- *Security Safeguards Principle.* Personal data should be protected by reasonable security safeguards against such risks as loss or unauthorized access, destruction, use, modification, or disclosure of data.
- *Openness Principle.* There should be a general policy of openness about developments, practices, and policies with respect to personal data. Means should be readily available to establish the existence and nature of personal data, and the main purposes of their use, as well as the identity and usual residence of the data controller.
- *Individual Participation Principle.* An individual should have the right to (1) obtain from a data controller confirmation of whether or not the data controller has data relating to him, and (2) have communicated to him data relating to him in an intelligible form within a reasonable time and manner and at a charge that is not excessive. If such a request is denied, he should be able to challenge both the denial and the data relating to him. If the challenge is successful, the data should be erased, rectified, completed, or amended.
- *Accountability Principle.* A data controller should be accountable for complying with measures that give effect to these principles.

Basic Principles of International Application: Free Flow and Legitimate Restrictions

- Member countries should take into consideration the implications for other Member countries of domestic processing and re-export of personal data.
- Member countries should take all reasonable and appropriate steps to ensure that transborder flows of personal data, including transit through a Member country, are uninterrupted and secure.
- A Member country should refrain from restricting transborder flows of personal data between itself and another Member country, except where the latter does not yet substantially observe these Guidelines or where the re-export of such data would circumvent its domestic privacy legislation. A Member country may also impose restrictions with respect to certain categories of personal data for which its domestic policy legislation includes specific regulations in view of the nature of those data and for which the other Member country provides no equivalent protection.
- Member countries should avoid developing laws, policies, and practices in the name of protection of privacy and individual liberties, which would create obstacles to transborder flows of

personal data that would exceed requirements for such protection.

National Implementation

- In implementing the foregoing principles, Member countries should establish legal, administrative, or other procedures or institutions for the protection of privacy and individual liberties with respect to personal data. Member countries should in particular endeavor to (a) adopt appropriate domestic legislation; (b) encourage and support self-regulation, whether in the form of codes of conduct or otherwise; (c) provide for reasonable means for individuals to exercise their rights, (d) provide for adequate sanctions and remedies in case of failures to comply with measures that implement the national and international principles; and (e) ensure that there is no unfair discrimination against data subjects.

International Cooperation

- Member countries should, where requested, make known to other Member countries details of the observance of the principles in these Guidelines. Member countries should also ensure that procedures for transborder flows of personal data and for the protection of privacy and individual liberties are simple and compatible with those of other Member counties that comply with these Guidelines.
- Member countries should establish procedures to facilitate information exchange related to these Guidelines and mutual assistance in the procedural and investigative matters involved.
- Member countries should work toward the development of principles—domestic and international—to govern the applicable law in the case of transborder flows of personal data.[17]

Thus, the OECD Privacy Guidelines recognize that, although there is a general interest in protecting privacy among the OECD Member States, the Guidelines are intended to be flexible enough to adapt to the solution chosen by each Member State. The OECD Privacy Guidelines apply to personal data (in both the public and private sectors) that, because of how it is processed or used, may pose a danger to privacy and individual liberties. The Guidelines are technology-neutral and non-binding, and are intended to serve as a framework for individual nation states and self-regulating entities or corporations in

---

[17]OECD Privacy Guidelines, Parts Two to Four at 3-4.

developing their own privacy policies. In fact, the Electronic Privacy Information Center has recommended that the OECD Privacy Guidelines be the framework for proposed WHOIS guidelines on privacy and data protection for domain name registrants.[18]

The OECD has made available a Privacy Policy Statement Generator (in both paper and electronic forms), which contains a questionnaire allowing organizations to develop a standard Privacy Policy that conforms to the OECD Guidelines.[19]

3. COUNCIL OF EUROPE

The Council of Europe (CoE) is an intergovernmental organization formed in 1949 whose aims are to protect human rights, democracy, the rule of law, and to promote awareness and encourage the development of Europe's cultural identity and diversity.[20] In 1950, the CoE's *Convention for the Protection of Human Rights and Fundamental Freedoms* stipulated in Article 8 a right to privacy and the right to be free from interference of this right by public authority except where necessary, among other things, for national or economic security or to prevent crime.[21] Article 10 provides for a freedom of expression. The European Commission of Human Rights and the European Court of

---

[18]"WHOIS," Electronic Privacy Information Center, http://www.epic.org/privacy/whois/ ("The OECD [Privacy Guidelines] offer a sound framework for sensible WHOIS policies on privacy and data protection. The OECD Privacy Guidelines offer important international consensus on and guidelines for privacy protection and establish eight principles for data protection that are widely used as the benchmark for assessing privacy policies and legislation. These principles are Collection Limitation; Data Quality; Purpose Specification; Use Limitation; Security Safeguards; Openness; Individual Participation; and Accountability."). WHOIS is a database of domain names registered by Network Solutions (now owned by Verisign) that includes the majority of U.S. registered domain names. The database contains information about the domain name, such as its expiration date and assigned owner's contact information. *See* http://www.networksolutions.com/en_US/whois/index.jhtml for the WHOIS search site and http://searchnetworking.techtarget.com/gDefinition/0,294236,sid7_gci213362,00.html for a more detailed overview of the database.

[19]"What is the OECD Privacy Statement Generator?" Organisation for Economic Co-operation and Development, http://www.oecd.org/document/39/0,2340,en_2649_34255_28863271_119669_1_1_1,00.html.

[20]The founding members of the Council of Europe were Belgium, Denmark, France, Ireland, Italy, Luxembourg, the Netherlands, Norway, Sweden, and the United Kingdom. *See* Council of Europe, "Communications and Research," http://www.coe.int/T/E/Communication_and_Research/Contacts_with_the_public/About_Council_of_Europe/An_overview/.

[21]*Convention for the Protection of Human Rights and Fundamental Freedoms as Amended by Protocol No. 11, with Protocol Nos. 1, 4, 6, 7, 12, and 13*, Article 8, Feb. 2003, http://www.echr.coe.int/Convention/webConvenENG.pdf ("Everyone has the right to respect for his private and family life, his home and his correspondence.").

88   CHAPTER 2

Human Rights have interpreted these rights expansively and the restrictions upon them narrowly. The Convention is not limited to state action, but also covers situations where the state should reasonably have prohibited certain private actions.[22]

In 1981, the CoE enacted the *Convention for the Protection of Individuals with regard to Automatic Processing of Personal Data* (CoE Personal Data Convention).[23] In 1999, the CoE amended the Convention, allowing the European Communities to accede[24] and issued *Guidelines for the Protection of Individuals with Regard to the Collection and Processing of Personal Data on Information Highways.*[25] In 2001, the CoE adopted the *Additional Protocol to the Convention for the Protection of Individuals with regard to Automatic Processing of Personal Data regarding supervisory authorities and transborder data flows.*[26]

The CoE Personal Data Convention, as amended, applies to all personal data files regardless of form.[27] The term "automatic processing" is defined in the Convention to include storage, processing, altering, erasing, retrieval, or dissemination of data.[28] The 1999 Amendments to the CoE Personal Data Convention specifically state that:

> [Signatories] will also apply this Convention to information relating to groups of persons, associations, foundations, companies, corporations, and any other bodies consisting

---

[22]*See, e.g.,* Theodor Meron, "The Implications of the Convention on the Development of Public International Law," Ad Hoc Committee of Legal Advisers on Public International Law, Contribution of the CAHDI to the Celebration of the 50th Anniversary of the European Convention on Human Rights, CAHDI (2000), 4 rev, Apr. 4, 2000, at 13, http://www.legal.coe.int/international/docs/2000/CAHDI(2000)4reve.pdf.

[23]*Convention for the Protection of Individuals with regard to Automatic Processing of Personal Data,* Council of Europe, ETS No. 108, 28.I.1981, 1981, http://conventions. coe.int/ Treaty/EN/Treaties/Html/108.htm (hereinafter "CoE Personal Data Convention").

[24]*Amendments to the Convention for the protection of individuals with regard to automatic processing of personal data* (ETS No. 108) *allowing the European communities to accede,* Council of Europe, 28.I.1981, June 15, 1981, http://www.coe.int/ T/E/Legal_affairs/Legal_co-operation/Data_protection/Documents/International_legal_ instruments/Amendements%20to%20the%20Convention%20108.asp (hereinafter "CoE 1999 Amendments to CoE Personal Data Convention").

[25]*Guidelines for the Protection of Individuals with Regard to the Collection and Processing of Personal Data on Information Highways,* Council of Europe, R(99)5, Feb. 23, 1999, http://www.coe.fr/cm/ta/rec/1999/99r5.htm.

[26]*Additional Protocol to the Convention for the Protection of Individuals with regard to Automatic Processing of Personal Data regarding supervisory authorities and transborder data flows,* Council of Europe, ETS No. 181, 8.XI.2001, Jan. 28, 1991, http:// conventions.coe.int/Treaty/EN/Treaties/Html/181.htm (hereinafter "CoE Additional Protocol to Personal Data Convention").

[27]CoE 1999 Amendments to Personal Data Convention at Article 1 (amending Article 3 of original CoE Personal Data Convention).

[28]CoE Personal Data Convention, Article 2 c, "Definitions."

directly or indirectly of individuals, whether or not such bodies possess legal personality.[29]

The Convention sets forth several criteria for automatic processing of personal data. Data must be obtained and processed fairly and lawfully, consistent with the purpose for which the data is stored. The data holder must keep the data up-to-date and accurate and, when the purpose for which the data was collected has expired, delete the identity of the data subject.[30] Proper security measures must be taken to protect the data against accidental or unauthorized destruction or loss, unauthorized access, modification, or disclosure.[31] Data subjects are entitled to discover whether a file concerning them is being kept and, if so, to obtain rectification and removal of data under the appropriate circumstances.[32] Governments are not permitted to create exceptions to these requirements, except for public safety, national or economic security, to protect the data subject or the rights and freedoms of others, or to repress criminal activities.[33]

Except under specific circumstances, states that are parties to the Convention shall not prohibit or require special authorization from each other when transferring data across each others' borders.[34] The state parties must provide each other with mutual assistance in data transfer and data protection activities.[35] The 2001 Additional Protocol to the Convention restricts transborder flows of data to non-signatory countries only if that country "ensures an adequate level of protection for the intended data transfer."[36]

4. EUROPEAN UNION

a. Data Protection Directive

In 1995, the European Union (EU)[37] raised global awareness of privacy issues with the adoption of the EU Data Protection

---

[29]CoE 1999 Amendments to Personal Data Convention at Article 1 b.

[30]CoE Personal Data Convention, Article 5, "Quality of data."

[31]CoE Personal Data Convention, Article 7, "Data security."

[32]CoE Personal Data Convention, Article 8, "Additional safeguards for the data subject."

[33]CoE Personal Data Convention, Article 9, "Exceptions and restrictions."

[34]CoE Personal Data Convention, Article 12, "Transborder flows of personal data and domestic law."

[35]CoE Personal Data Convention, Article 13, "Co-operation between Parties."

[36]CoE Additional Protocol to Personal Data Convention, Article 2.

[37]The European Union is an international organization of European countries committed to reducing economic barriers among themselves. Formerly the European Economic Community, the EU was formally created through the Treaty of Maastricht in 1992. By 2004, it will have over 25 members, with most new additions coming from Eastern Europe. See "The European Union at a glance," http://europa.eu.int/abc/index_en.htm.

Directive.[38] In adopting the Directive, the EU wanted to ensure that "fundamental" privacy rights were protected when personal information was processed, regardless of the national citizenship of the individual data subjects, without restricting the free flow of personal information within the EU. The Directive became effective on October 25, 1998. Similar to the CoE Additional Protocol to the Personal Data Convention, the Data Protection Directive prohibits the transfer of protected personal information outside the EU unless the receiving country affords similar legal protections.

The Data Protection Directive, like all EU Directives, is not self-executing. Instead, it requires EU Member States to pass harmonized national legislation enacting its terms. It is important to realize that the national laws that have been enacted in each of the EU Member States are not identical. There are, for instance, local variations in administrative requirements and penalties for noncompliance. Thus, understanding the terms of the Directive by no means guarantees that a business understands all of the steps it must take to comply with each national law. To complicate matters more, not all of the Member States have implemented the Directive. The Commission of the European Communities' *First Report on the Implementation of the Data Protection Directive (95/46/EC)* notes:

> Experience with the implementation of the Directive is so far very limited. Only [a] few Member States implemented the Directive on time. Most Member States only notified implementing measures to the Commission in the years 2000 and 2001, and Ireland has still not notified its recent implementation.[39]

---

[38]*Directive 95/46/EC of the European Parliament and of the Council of 24 October 1995 on the protection of individuals with regard to the processing of personal data and on the free movement of such data,* Official Journal L 281/31, Nov. 23, 1995, http://europa.eu.int/smartapi/cgi/sga_doc?smartapi!celexapi!prod!CELEXnumdoc& lg=EN&numdoc=31995L0046&model=guichett (hereinafter "EU Data Protection Directive").

[39]Commission of the European Communities, *Report from the Commission: First report on the implementation of the Data Protection Directive (95/46/EC),* COM (2003) 265 final, May 15, 2003, para. 3.1 at 7, http://europa.eu.int/eur-lex/en/com/rpt/2003/com2003_ 0265en01.pdf; *see also* Douwe Korff, *EC Study on Implementation of Data Protection Directive: comparative summary of national laws,* Human Rights Centre, Colchester, UK, Sept. 2002, http://europa.eu.int/comm/internal_market/privacy/docs/lawreport/ consultation/univessex-comparativestudy_en.pdf. For up-to-date information regarding the status of implementation of the Data Protection Directive in the Member States, *see* "Status of implementation of Directive 95/45 on the Protection of Individuals with regard to the Processing of Personal Data," http://europa.eu.int/comm/internal_ market/privacy/law/implementation_en.htm.

The EU Directive applies to most commercial uses of personal information.[40] The Directive establishes limitations and obligations on "controllers" (entities directing the collection, use, or transfer of personal information) and "processors" (entities utilizing personal information at another party's direction) with respect to the "processing" (virtually any collection, use, transfer, or destruction of personal information) of "personal data" (any information from which a particular individual may be identified). Non-compliance with the Directive is punishable by the imposition of civil fines, injunctions requiring changes in business practices, seizure of data processing hardware or data assets, prohibitions on data processing, and, in some instances, criminal penalties.[41]

Key Principles

The EU Data Protection Directive, like other privacy laws, is organized around certain key principles of information use. These can be summarized as follows:

Notice

Data subjects (individuals to whom personal information relates) must be informed of:

- The identity of the collector of their personal information;
- The uses or purposes for which the information is collected;
- How the data subject may exercise any available choices regarding the use or disclosure of personal information;
- Where and to whom information may be transferred; and
- How data subjects may access their personal information held by an organization.[42]

Consent

In general, the "unambiguous consent" of a data subject is required before any personal information concerning such an individual may be processed.[43] The precise meaning of "unambiguous consent" is somewhat vague, however; it is not precise, and it is not firmly established whether its standard can be met by inference or implication. "Special categories of information" relating to race, religion, political or philosophical beliefs, health, union membership, sex life, and criminal history have additional processing restrictions

---

[40] Article 3, Section 2 identifies applicability to personal data by automated means and filing systems while not applying to (1) public security and criminal investigations and (2) natural persons' personal use.
[41] EU Data Protection Directive, Articles 2 and 3.
[42] EU Data Protection Directive, Article 10.
[43] EU Data Protection Directive, Article 7.

that place additional responsibilities on businesses seeking to comply with the EU Data Protection Directive.[44] Data subjects also have the right to opt-out of having personal information used for direct marketing purposes.[45]

Consistency

Controllers and processors may use personal information only in strict accordance with the terms of the notice given to data subjects, and any choices such data subjects have exercised with respect to its use.[46]

Access

Controllers must give data subjects access to the personal information held about them and must allow data subjects to propose corrections to inaccurate information.[47]

Security

Organizations must provide adequate security, using both technical and other means, to protect the integrity and confidentiality of personal information. The sufficiency of such means is measured with respect to the state of the art. In practice, a "reasonable" level of information security is a constantly rising standard, subject to ever more rigorous controls and requirements.[48]

Onward Transfer

Personal information may not be transferred to a third party unless that third party has been contractually bound to use the data consistently with the notice given to data subjects, any choices the subjects have made with respect to their data's use or disclosure, and applicable law.[49]

Enforcement

The Directive grants a private right of action to data subjects when organizations do not follow the law.[50] In addition, each EU country has established a Data Protection Authority—a regulatory enforcement agency—that has the power to investigate complaints, levy fines, initiate criminal actions, and demand changes in businesses' information-handling practices.[51] These Authorities are described below.

---

[44]EU Data Protection Directive, Article 8.
[45]EU Data Protection Directive, Article 14.
[46]EU Data Protection Directive, Article 6.
[47]EU Data Protection Directive, Article 12.
[48]EU Data Protection Directive, Article 17.
[49]EU Data Protection Directive, Articles 6, 7, 17, and 26.
[50]EU Data Protection Directive, Articles 22 and 23.
[51]EU Data Protection Directive, Article 29.

The Role of Data Protection Authorities

Pursuant to Article 28 of the Data Protection Directive, each EU Member State has established a Data Protection Authority whose role is to oversee compliance with that country's data protection law. The authority has investigative powers of access to data, powers to collect all information necessary to perform its supervisory duties, powers of intervention, and powers to engage in legal proceedings where national provisions have been violated.[52] In addition, each Data Protection Authority is a member of the Working Party on the Protection of Individuals with regard to the Processing of Personal Data (Article 29 Working Party). This body was established by Article 29 of the Directive to examine questions regarding the application of national measures, determine the level of protection in the EU and third countries, advise the EU Commission on proposed amendments to the Directive, and render opinions on European Community codes of conduct.

International Data Transfer Restrictions

In addition to regulating much of the interaction between a business and its data subjects (any individuals from or about whom it collects and uses personal information, including its customers and employees), the EU Directive also regulates how companies operating in multiple jurisdictions worldwide may move personal information within their organizations and among their various affiliates, subsidiaries, and business partners.[53]

Transfers of personal information relating to EU-based data subjects to non-EU countries are generally prohibited (subject to some exceptions) unless the country of destination has "adequate" (that is, substantially similar) legal protections for privacy, as compared with the EU.[54] Only a few countries are considered by the EU to have legal protection equivalent to the Data Protection Directive.[55] Transfers to any other countries may only take place with the consent of the data subject, or where other "guarantees" exist that personal information will be treated according to the EU standard. EU regulators have the legal authority to prohibit transfers of personal information where such guarantees cannot be demonstrated.[56] This requirement is very problematic for many businesses and may require significant technological, organizational, and/or contractual changes.

---

[52]EU Data Protection Directive, Article 28.

[53]EU Data Protection Directive, Articles 25 and 26.

[54]EU Data Protection Directive, Article 25.

[55]*See, e.g.,* "Commission decisions on the adequacy of the protection of personal data in third countries," http://europa.eu.int/comm/internal_market/privacy/adequacy_en.htm.

[56]EU Data Protection Directive, Article 26.

94   CHAPTER 2

The two possible responses to the Directive's transfer restrictions are the EU Model Clauses and the U.S./EU Safe Harbor Agreement. These mechanisms are discussed in more detail below. Recent work on "binding rules" by the Article 29 Working Group can also be utilized.

U.S./EU Safe Harbor Agreement

The EU Data Protection Directive went into effect in October 1998 and prohibits the transfer of personal data to non-EU countries not meeting the European privacy standard for data protection. Although the United States and the European Union share the goal of enhancing privacy protection for their citizens, the United States takes an approach to privacy that is different from that taken by the European Union. The United States uses a sectoral approach that relies on a mix of legislation, regulation, and self-regulation. The European Union, however, relies on comprehensive legislation that, for example, requires creation of government data protection agencies, registration of databases with those agencies, and, in some instances, prior approval before personal data processing may begin. As a result of these different privacy approaches, the Directive could have significantly hampered the ability of U.S. companies to engage in many transatlantic transactions.

To bridge the different privacy approaches and provide a streamlined means for U.S. organizations to comply with the Directive, the U.S. Department of Commerce, in consultation with the European Commission, developed the so-called Safe Harbor Privacy Principles.[57] The Safe Harbor—approved by the EU in July 2000[58]—is an important way for U.S. companies to avoid experiencing interruptions in their business dealings with the EU or facing prosecution by European authorities under European privacy laws. The Safe Harbor is, however, a very unusual legal mechanism. Essentially, by a sub-treaty

---

[57]The full text of the Safe Harbor Privacy Principles (and associated materials) is available at http://www.export.gov/safeharbor/sh_documents.html (hereinafter "Safe Harbor Privacy Principles"). Further information about joining the Safe Harbor and how it works may be found at "Safe Harbor Workbook," U.S. Dept. of Commerce, Export Portal, http://www.export.gov/safeharbor/sh_workbook.html and "Safe Harbor Overview," U.S. Department of Commerce, Export Portal, http://www.export.gov/safeharbor/sh_overview.html.

[58]*Commission Decision of 26 July 2000 pursuant to Directive 95/46/EC of the European Parliament and of the Council on the adequacy of the protection provided by the safe harbour privacy principles and related frequently asked questions issued by the US Department of Commerce,* 2000/520/EC (notified under document number C(2000) 2441), Official Journal L 215, 25/08/2000 at 7-47, http://europa.eu.int/smartapi/cgi/sga_doc?smartapi!celexapi!prod!CELEXnumdoc&lg=en&numdoc=32000D0520&model =guichett (hereinafter "EU Safe Harbor Decision") (Safe Harbor Privacy Principles are at Annex I of this Decision).

agreement, the EU and the United States have created a means by which the U.S. government will enforce an EU law against a U.S. company that violates that law while acting in the United States, and only as a result of voluntary participation by the U.S. company.

By self-certifying that its operations are compliant with the terms of the Safe Harbor, a U.S. company will be deemed to provide adequate protection under the Directive. Under the Safe Harbor Privacy Principles, in the absence of being subject to the jurisdiction of European data protection authorities, an American company importing personal information on European citizens must

- Comply with the Safe Harbor Privacy Principles, according to the guidance offered in the Frequently Asked Questions (which are appended to the EU Decision);
- Self-certify, on a voluntary basis, with the United States Department of Commerce its adherence, in its U.S. operation, to the Principles; and
- Provide an independent third-party verification that the company adheres to the Principles. This step can be accomplished by joining a self-regulatory privacy program that adheres to the Safe Harbor. Joining such an organization can, by itself, also qualify the company for the Safe Harbor. BBBOnline and the U.S. Direct Marketing Association's Safe Harbor certification program have been cited as representative of the types of programs contemplated.

In effect, the U.S. and EU governments are encouraging self-regulation by deferring to nongovernment programs to enforce suitable standards on participating companies.[59]

At the time of publication, more than 476 companies participate in the Safe Harbor. Benefits to U.S. companies participating in the Safe Harbor include the following:

- The Safe Harbor Privacy Principles will bind all EU Member States;
- Assumption of adequate protection and data flows for those companies;
- Waiver or automatic approval of Member State requirements for data transfers; and
- U.S. jurisdiction in most legal actions brought by EU citizens against U.S. companies.[60]

---

[59]Additional information on BBBOnline and the DMA's program can be obtained at http://www.bbbonline.org and http://www.the-dma.org/safeharbor/.

[60]"Safe Harbor Overview," U.S. Department of Commerce, Export Portal, http://www.export.gov/safeharbor/sh_overview.html.

96   CHAPTER 2

Perceived shortcomings of the Safe Harbor include a limited scope and exposure to federal oversight:

- The Safe Harbor only covers transfers between the United States and the EU;
- Significant sectors of the economy (for example, financial services) are not eligible for the Safe Harbor; and
- Certification with the Safe Harbor exposes corporations to possible Federal Trade Commission (FTC) enforcement actions for any violation of the Safe Harbor principles.[61]

Companies subject to explicit U.S. federal regulations regarding the privacy of personal information (such as the Health Insurance Portability and Accountability Act (HIPAA) and the Gramm-Leach-Bliley Act (GLBA))[62] may in the future be eligible to self-certify their compliance with the applicable laws and gain the Safe Harbor recognition that would permit their transactions with European personal information to occur.[63] However, such a change would require a formal decision of the EU Commission, and no such decision is currently expected. In the meantime, companies participating in the Safe Harbor are subject to the jurisdiction of the FTC for unfair or deceptive trade practices, under the U.S. Federal Trade Commission Act (FTC Act), or, in some instances, subject to the jurisdiction of the U.S. Department of Transportation.[64] Failure of a company that has joined the Safe Harbor to abide by its stated privacy policy is actionable under the FTC Act as an unfair or deceptive trade practice.[65] In addition, companies would be subject to sanctions under other applicable laws.

---

[61] Aaron Lukas, "Safe Harbor or Stormy Waters? Living with the EU Data Protection Directive," Cato Institute, *Center for Trade Policy Studies,* No. 16, Oct. 30, 2001 at 25-26, http://www.freetrade.org/pubs/pas/tpa-016.pdf.

[62] The European Commission has deferred a review of whether the privacy provisions of GLBA are "adequate" pending implementation and possible further legislative action in the United States.

[63] Although the Safe Harbor Privacy Principles allow for "adequacy" determinations for U.S. business sectors that are subject to particular sectoral privacy laws, no determination has yet been made of the adequacy of any particular law.

[64] *See* EU Safe Harbor Decision at Annex III, "Safe Harbor Enforcement Overview," at 22, Annex VII, at 45; Federal Trade Commission Act, 15 U.S.C. Section 45. Note that banks, savings & loans, and entities such as stockyards and meat packers are excluded from the scope of the FTC Act and, therefore, are not eligible to participate in the Safe Harbor program. *See* EU Safe Harbor Decision, Annex VII at 45.

[65] *See* draft Safe Harbor FAQ No. 11: Dispute Resolution and Enforcement, available at http://www.ita.doc.gov/td/ecom/RedlinedFAQ11Enforc300.htm. Note that entities that are eligible for Safe Harbor membership because they are subject to the jurisdiction of the Department of Transportation may be subject to enforcement actions brought by that Department.

Currently, European officials in those Member States that have implemented the EU Data Protection Directive are authorized to enforce those laws against American companies (or their trading partners) involved in exporting personal information. To date, few conspicuous actions have been taken, but continued non-compliance with EU data protection laws is expected to be met with an increase in such actions. While data protection authorities have brought actions against U.S. companies for violations of the Data Protection Directive, no cases have yet been brought for violations of the Safe Harbor Privacy Principles.[66]

The European Commission conducted an initial assessment of the Safe Harbor program and its working implementation. The findings, released in early 2002, indicate that the elements of the Safe Harbor framework are in place and that the framework simplifies and reduces uncertainties for U.S. companies importing data from the EU. However, it states that a substantial number of organizations that have certified their compliance with the Safe Harbor are not providing the expected level of transparency with respect to their overall commitment or the content of their privacy policies. The assessment report suggests that the questions raised should be revisited.[67]

Model Clauses and other contractual Solutions for Exporting Personal Information

The EU Directive provides a number of exceptions to its general prohibition on the export of personal information to countries lacking "adequate" legal protections for privacy. One such exception is where a controller of personal information "adduces sufficient guarantees" with respect to privacy protection, which "may in particular result from appropriate contractual clauses."[68]

To provide a contractual mechanism for facilitating the export of personal information to third countries that do not ensure an adequate level of protection, the EU Commission rendered two Decisions, each

---

[66]Some well-publicized enforcement actions have been brought against U.S. companies; for instance, American Airlines was forced to change its practices with respect to passenger information by the Swedish privacy authority, and Microsoft was fined $60,000 in Spain for the illegal export of human resources data concerning its Spanish employees. *See, e.g.,* Declan McCullagh, "US Twitchy on EU Data Privacy," Oct. 16, 1998, *Wired,* http://www.wired.com/news/business/0,1367,15671,00.html; Gregory Dalton, "Privacy Law Worries U.S. Businesses," October 26, 1998, *InformationWeek,* http://www.informationweek.com/706/06iulaw.htm; Peter P. Swire, "The Great Wall of Europe," Feb. 15, 1998, *CIO,* http://www.cio.com/archive/enterprise/ 021598_intellectual.html.
[67]"Working Document on Functioning of the Safe Harbor Agreement," Article 29 Data Protection Working Party, 11194/02/EN, WP 62, July 2, 2002, http:// europa.eu.int/comm/internal_market/privacy/docs/wpdocs/2002/wp62_en.pdf.
[68]EU Data Protection Directive, Article 26 (2).

with approved "standard contractual clauses." The *Commission Decision of 15 June 2001 on standard contractual clauses for the transfer of personal data to third countries, under Directive 95/46/EC* has an attached Annex of Standard Contractual Clauses for the transfer of personal data from a controller in the EU to a controller in a third country.[69] The preamble of the Decision notes:

> This Decision does not cover the transfer of data by controllers established in the Community to recipients established outside the territory of the Community who act only as processors. Those transfers do not require the same safeguards because the processor acts exclusively on behalf of the controller. The Commission intends to address that type of transfer in a subsequent decision.[70]

Thus, the EU Commission rendered *Commission Decision of 27 December 2001 on standard contractual clauses for the transfer of personal data to processors established in third countries, under Directive 95/46/EC.* The Annex attached to the Decision contains standard contractual clauses for the transfer of personal data from an EU controller to a processor in a third country that does not provide adequate data protection.[71] If used, these standard contractual clauses meet all requirements under the Directive for "adducing sufficient guarantees" for privacy. The legal effect of the Commission's decision is that no data protection authority in an EU Member State may object to an export of personal information that is conducted pursuant to a contract incorporating the appropriate standard contractual clauses.

The standard clauses essentially ensure that any entity obtaining personal information from an EU-based company (including an affiliate of a U.S. company) would have to restrict its use and disclosure of that information to the same extent allowed under European law. However, the standard clauses arguably extend the obligations and restrictions on companies well beyond the requirements of the Directive and have

---

[69]*Commission Decision of 15 June 2001 on standard contractual clauses for the transfer of personal data to third countries, under Directive 95/46/EC,* Commission of the European Communities, (notified under document number C(2001) 1539), (2001/497/EC), http:// europa.eu.int/eur-lex/pri/en/oj/dat/2001/l_181/l_18120010704en00190031.pdf (hereinafter "EU Decision with Standard Clauses for Controller-to-Controller Data Transfers").

[70]*Id.* at para. 8.

[71]*Commission Decision of 27 December 2001 on standard contractual clauses for the transfer of personal data to processors established in third countries, under Directive 95/46/EC,* Commission of the European Communities (notified under document number C(2001) 4540) (2002/16/EC), http://europa.eu.int/eur-lex/pri/en/oj/dat/2002/l_006/l_00620020110en00520062.pdf (hereinafter "EU Decision with Standard Clauses for Controller-to-Processor Data Transfers").

therefore been much criticized by U.S. businesses and the U.S. government. The clauses require, for instance, that the exporter and importer of personal information agree to be subject to joint and several liability in the event of any misuse of such information.[72] This term could result in a U.S.-based importer of personal information being held liable for the misdeeds of a third-party exporter in Europe over which the U.S. company had no control. Other controversial requirements of the EU Model Clauses are that all European data subjects must be granted third-party beneficiary rights,[73] and that importers of personal information in non-EU jurisdictions must agree to make themselves and their non-EU operations subject to audits of the processing activities by EU data protection authorities.[74]

The standard contractual clauses are also controversial because of the seemingly de facto mandatory requirement of their use. The Directive, and each national law that implements it, contains provisions allowing for the export of personal information when the protection of such information is guaranteed by contract. These laws do not, however, require the use of *specific* contracts. Indeed, since the publication of the standard clauses, the EU Commission has endeavored to point out that under these provisions the use of the standard clauses is not mandatory. However, because of the limited resources available to most data protection authorities, they do not have the ability to review other privately developed contracts to determine their "adequacy" under the Directive. Accordingly, many such data protection authorities have indicated that while they will accept the use of the standard clauses, they will not necessarily accept the use of other contracts and will not, in any event, grant a prior review of such alternative contracts. The effect of such a position is to leave businesses with no confidence that alternative contracts will be accepted as legally adequate.

A group of seven business associations, led by the International Chamber of Commerce, has been negotiating with the European Commission regarding approval of a set of alternative standard contractual clauses for transfers of personal data from Europe to data controllers outside the EU. As of August 2003, it seemed that the clauses might obtain the support of the European Commission, but final

---

[72]*See* EU Decision with Standard Clauses for Controller-to-Controller Data Transfers, Annex, Clause 6; EU Decision with Standard Clauses for Controller-to-Processor Data Transfers, Annex, Clause 6.
[73]*See* EU Decision with Standard Clauses for Controller-to-Controller Data Transfers, Annex, Clause 3; EU Decision with Standard Clauses for Controller-to-Processor Data Transfers, Annex, Clause 3.
[74]*See* EU Decision with Standard Clauses for Controller-to-Controller Data Transfers, Annex, Clause 5; EU Decision With Standard Clauses for Controller-to-Processor Data Transfers, Annex, Clause 5.

100   CHAPTER 2

approval remains uncertain. The clauses have a number of significant improvements in various important areas (for example, liability and audit rights) as compared with the Commission's clauses.[75]

Actions by Non-EU European Countries and Associated Territories

Largely because of the EU Directive's prohibition on the transfer of personal information to countries with inadequate legal protection—and the fear in many countries of the potential adverse economic impact that could result from the interruption of data flows from EU countries—a number of other countries have passed essentially identical national data protection legislation so as to ensure uninterrupted data flows from the EU. These countries can be roughly divided into two categories: (1) EU trading partners that wish to ensure that data flows will not be interrupted, and (2) countries actively harmonizing their national legislation with the EU model in hopes of gaining membership in the EU.

The first non-EU countries that passed substantially similar legislation were the non-EU members of the European Economic Area (EEA),[76] Iceland,[77] and Norway.[78] These countries were considered most vulnerable to interruptions of trade with the EU. They were soon followed by European Free Trade Agreement countries Switzerland[79] and Liechtenstein.

The application for membership in the EU by a number of Eastern European countries has been preceded by those countries' adoption of data protection laws very similar in substance to the EU Directive. These countries include the Czech Republic,[80]

---

[75]*See* Christopher Kuner, *European Data Privacy Law and Online Business,* Oxford University Press, 2003 (contains commentary on the clauses). Mr. Kuner leads the negotiations on behalf of the ICC. The latest public version of the alternative clauses is available at http://www.iccwbo.org/home/e_business/word_documents/Final%20version%20July %202002%20Model%20contract%20clauses.pdf.

[76]European Economic Area, http://europa.eu.int/comm/external_relations/eea/.

[77]Act on Protection of Individuals with Regard to the Processing of Personal Data No. 77/2000, Republic of Ireland, http://www.mannvernd.is/english/laws/Act. DataProtection.html (English translation).

[78]The Norwegian data protection law is located at http://www.lovdata.no/all/ hl-20000414-031.html (in Norwegian).

[79]*Commission Decision of 26 July 2000 pursuant to Directive 95/46/EC of the European Parliament and of the Council on the adequate protection of personal data provided in Switzerland,* Commission of the European Communities (notified under document number C(2000) 2304) (2000/518/EC), http://www.edsb.ch/e/gesetz/eu/ adequacy.pdf.

[80]Act "On Personal Data Protection," 2000. The law is unavailable online in English. For a summary of Czech privacy legislation, see the EPIC and Privacy International summary available at *Privacy and Human Rights 2000: An International Survey of Privacy Laws and Developments,* "Country Reports," "Czech Republic," http://www. privacyinternational.org/survey/phr2000/countriesag.html#Heading11.

Cyprus, Estonia,[81] Hungary,[82] Latvia,[83] Lithuania,[84] Malta, and Poland.[85]

In addition, the Channel Islands of Guernsey and Jersey, plus the Isle of Man, adopted similar laws to protect their ability to conduct trade with Europe, because their semi-autonomous status excludes them from the automatic application of U.K. law.[86]

Most developing countries do not have privacy or data protection laws. Even more developed areas, such as Bermuda, do not have data protection laws. However, it is worth noting that in 1999, Bermuda passed a "private law" applying the substance of the EU Directive to a single company. This was an effort, on the part of the company, to ensure that its data transfers from the EU to Bermuda would be considered "adequate" under the Directive. Bermudian law allows for the passage of private laws where they will help to foster business growth. There is reference in paragraph 26 of the Bermudian Electronic Transactions Act 1999 empowering the Minister to promote privacy regulations. Apparently, no such regulations have yet been promulgated.[87]

---

[81]Personal Data Protection Act, 1996. The law is unavailable online in English. For a summary of Estonian privacy legislation, see the EPIC and Privacy International summary available at *Privacy and Human Rights 2000: An International Survey of Privacy Laws and Developments*, "Country Reports," "Republic of Estonia," http://www.privacyinternational.org/survey/phr2000/countriesag.html#Heading14.

[82]The law is unavailable online in English. *See Commission Decision of 26 July 2000 pursuant to Directive 95/46/EC of the European Parliament and of the Council on the adequate protection of personal data provided in Hungary,* Commission of the European Communities (notified under document number C(2000) 2305) (2000/519/EC), http://europa.eu.int/eur-lex/pri/en/oj/dat/2000/l_215/l_21520000825en00040006.pdf.

[83]*See* "Regulatory developments, Latvia Master Report," http://www.eu-esis.org/esls2reg/LVreg1.htm (for a general discussion of this law; law is unavailable online).

[84]Law on Legal Protection of Personal Data, 1996. The law is unavailable online in English. For a summary of Lithuanian privacy legislation, see the EPIC and Privacy International summary available at *Privacy and Human Rights 2000: An International Survey of Privacy Laws and Developments*, "Country Reports," "Republic of Lithuania," http://www.privacyinternational.org/survey/phr2000/countrieshp.html#Heading10.

[85]Law on the Protection of Personal Data Protection, 1997. The law is unavailable online in English. For a summary of Polish privacy legislation, see the EPIC and Privacy International summary available at *Privacy and Human Rights 2000: An International Survey of Privacy Laws and Developments*, "Country Reports," "Republic of Poland," http://www.privacyinternational.org/survey/phr2000/countrieshp.html#Heading20.

[86]Isle of Man Data Protection Act 2002, http://www.gov.im/odps/legislation/dpact2002.xml; Bailiwick of Guernsey Data Protection Law 2001, http://www.dpcommission.gov.gg/2001%20Law/2001%20Law.htm. Jersey Data Protection Law 1987 is available at http://www.dataprotection.gov.je/.

[87]Bermuda, Electronic Transactions Act of 1999, Part VI, Para. 26, Aug. 5, 1999, http://www.fortknox.bm/NXT/gateway.dll?f=templates&fn=default.htm.

102   CHAPTER 2

While the influence of the EU Directive can be seen spreading to more and more countries,[88] it should be stressed that privacy is regulated in each of these countries by national laws; differences and variations exist from one country to another. Across all of the EU Member States, non-EU European states, and other countries around the world that have passed laws reacting to the EU Directive, there is a growing recognition of the increased need for international legal harmonization to ensure data flows and preclude privacy concerns from creating barriers to free trade. The question that remains is whether the legal harmonization will gravitate toward the EU's emphasis on formal nationwide government regulation or the United States' reliance on a combination of self-regulation and targeted government enforcement of industry-specific privacy regulations.

b. Privacy in Electronic Communications

The EU took the data protection concept a step further with its *Directive 97/66/EC of the European Parliament and of the Council of 15 December 1997 concerning the processing of personal data and the protection of privacy in the telecommunications sector.* This Directive applied the principles of the EU Data Protection Directive and expanded them into specific rules for the telecommunications sector. Recognizing the developments in markets and advances in technologies for electronic communications services (beyond telephony), the EU replaced the 1997 Directive with *Directive 2002/58/EC of the European Parliament and of the Council of 12 July 2002 concerning the processing of personal data and the protection of privacy in the electronic communications sector (Directive on privacy and electronic communications)* (EU Electronic Communications Directive).[89]

Privacy Protections

This Directive establishes certain protections regarding electronic mail, telephone communications, traffic data, calling line identification, and unsolicited communications. The Directive was to be implemented in the Member States by October 31, 2003. As with the Data Protection

---

[88]"As Data Privacy Laws Evolve Globally Many Nations Consider European Model," *Privacy & Security Law Report,* Bureau of National Affairs, Vol. 2, No. 16, Apr. 21, 2003 at 425-28; "European Data Protection Law Seen as Spilling into Latin America," *Privacy & Security Law Report,* Bureau of National Affairs, Vol. 2, No. 16, Apr. 21, 2003 at 428-30.

[89]*Directive 2002/58/EC of the European Parliament and of the Council of 12 July 2002 concerning the processing of personal data and the protection of privacy in the electronic communications sector (Directive on privacy and electronic communications),* Official Journal L 201/37, July 31, 2002, at 37-47 (replacing EU Directive 97/66/EC), http:// europa.eu.int/smartapi/cgi/sga_doc?smartapi!celexapi!prod!CELEXnumdoc&lg=en& numdoc=32002L0058&model=guichett (hereinafter "EU Electronic Communications Directive").

Directive, the Electronic Communications Directive sets forth a strong presumption in favor of privacy. Article 5 states:

Article 5—Confidentiality of the communications

1. Member States shall ensure the confidentiality of communications and the related traffic data by means of a public communications network and publicly available electronic communications services, through national legislation. In particular, they shall prohibit listening, tapping, storage or other kinds of interception or surveillance of communications and the related traffic data by persons other than users, without the consent of the users concerned, except when legally authorised to do so in accordance with Article 15(1). This paragraph shall not prevent technical storage which is necessary for the conveyance of a communication without prejudice to the principle of confidentiality.[90]

There is tension, however, between the privacy afforded in Article 5 and the restrictions to these protections afforded in Article 15:

Article 15—Application of certain provisions of Directive 95/46/EC.

1. Member States may adopt legislative measures to restrict the scope of the rights and obligations provided for in Article 5, Article 6, Article 8(1), (3) and (4), and Article 9 of this Directive when such restriction constitutes a necessary, appropriate and proportionate measure within a democratic society to safeguard national security (that is, State security), defence, public security, and the prevention, investigation, detection, and prosecution of criminal offences or of unauthorised use of the electronic communications system, as referred to in Article 13(1) of Directive 95/46/EC. To this end, Member States may, among other things, adopt legislative measures providing for the retention of data for a limited period justified on the grounds laid down in this paragraph. All the measures referred to in this paragraph shall be in accordance with the

---

[90]EU Electronic Communications Directive, Article 5(1); *see* Daniel J. Solove and Marc Rotenberg, *Information Privacy Law*, Aspen Publishers, 2003, http://www.epic.org/bookstore/epic_books.html (hereinafter "Solove and Rotenberg").

104   CHAPTER 2

general principles of Community law, including those referred to in Article 6(1) and (2) of the Treaty on European Union.[91]

Other specific privacy protections included in the EU Electronic Communications Directive include Article 7, which allows a customer to receive nonitemized bills,[92] and Article 9 on "Location Data and Itemized Billing." This Article states that location data (other than traffic data) can only be processed when they are made anonymous, or with the consent of the subscriber to the extent and for the duration necessary for provision of a value-added service. Before obtaining consent, the provider must inform the subscriber of the type of location data that will be processed and whether they will be transmitted to a third party to provide the value-added service.[93] The Directive also regulates the collection of traffic data, including "cookies."[94]

Privacy Risks Through Data Retention

During the discussion of the EU Electronic Communications Directive, the Council of Ministers began advocating the inclusion of data retention provisions that would require ISPs and communications providers to store logs of all telephone calls, e-mails, faxes, and Internet activity for law enforcement purposes. These proposals were strongly resisted. Following the September 11 terrorist attacks, however, the Parliament came under extreme pressure from Member States (especially the United Kingdom and the Netherlands) to include data retention provisions in the Directive to strike "the right balance between privacy and the needs of law enforcement agencies in the light of the battle against terrorism." In the end, the Directive was adopted with the data retention provisions.[95]

The data retention provisions allow Member States to enact laws mandating the retention of the traffic and location data of all communications taking place over mobile phones, landline telephones, faxes, e-mails, chat rooms, the Internet, or any other electronic communications medium.[96] Countries may require providers to

---

[91] EU Electronic Communications Directive, Article 15(1); Solove and Rotenberg.

[92] EU Electronic Communications Directive, Article 7; Solove and Rotenberg.

[93] EU Electronic Communications Directive, Article 9; Solove and Rotenberg.

[94] EU Electronic Communications Directive, Article 6; Solove and Rotenberg.

[95] "Data Retention," "Origins of the EU Directive 2002/58/EC," Electronic Privacy Information Center, http://www.epic.org/privacy/intl/data_retention.html (hereinafter "Origins of the EU Directive 2002/59/EC"); *see* EU Electronic Communications Directive, Article 15(1).

[96] Origins of the EU Directive 2002/58/EC; EU Electronic Communications Directive, Article 15(1).

record, index, and store their subscribers' communication data. The data that can be retained include all traffic data as well as location data (geographic position).[97] The contents of communications are not covered by the Directive.

The data retention provisions have been strongly criticized by industry, consumers, privacy advocates, and civil libertarians. Industry complains that the retention requirements will impose costly compliance requirements and burden their operations. Others complain that the amount of data that can be retained—and the information derived from them—is a real threat to privacy and subject to potential abuses.[98]

Non-Compliance and Enforcement

On December 5, 2003, the European Commission (EC) launched infringement proceedings against nine EU Member States for failure to implement the EU Electronic Communications Directive, also known as the "e-Privacy Directive." The EC did not, however, give the Member States a new deadline for harmonization of national laws and implementation of the Directive.[99]

The European Court of Justice's (ECJ) decision on the EU Data Protection Directive created an important precedent in the scope of the Directive. The ECJ interpreted the Data Protection Directive expansively and ruled that posting personal information on websites constitutes automatic processing within the meaning of the Directive and thereby puts the data within the scope of the Directive's privacy obligations. In addition, the ECJ held that Member States may require privacy protections for personal data beyond those that the Directive requires. Even the EC argued that the Directive was intended to have a *harmonizing* impact, rather than serve as a floor from which Member States can impose additional restrictions.[100]

---

[97]Origins of the EU Directive 2002/58/EC; EU Electronic Communications Directive, Article 2(b) and (c).

[98]For a comprehensive listing of documents, news, and background on the EU Electronic Communications Directive, *see* "Data Retention," Electronic Privacy Information Center, http://www.epic.org/privacy/intl/data_retention.html.

[99]"Nine EU Nations Get EC Challenge Over Failure to Adopt Privacy Directive," *Privacy & Security Law Report,* Bureau of National Affairs, Vol. 2, No. 48, Dec. 8, 2003 at 1368-69. The nine states are Belgium, Germany, Greece, France, Luxembourg, the Netherlands, Portugal, Sweden, and Finland.

[100]Alan Charles Raul, Edward R. McNicholas, and Julie Dwyer, "European Court of Justice's Landmark Decision on EU Data Protection Directive Accords Broad Scope to EU Privacy Regime, Addresses Applicability to Internet," *Privacy & Security Law Report,* Bureau of National Affairs, Vol. 2, No. 48, Dec. 8, 2003 at 1387-89.

106   CHAPTER 2

C. Other Non-U.S. Countries

1. THE AMERICAS

a. Canada

The Canadian Charter of Rights and Freedoms[101] does not contain an express right to privacy, although it has been interpreted as containing certain protections against unreasonable intrusion into personal privacy. Canadian federal statutory law deals with privacy and personal information primarily in two statutes, one addressing governmental and public sector collection and the other dealing with private sector issues. Canada also has an Access to Information Act,[102] which permits third parties to access certain information in the hands of government under circumscribed conditions. Finally, Canada has federal legislation addressing privacy issues sectorally, principally in the area of health care information.

Canada's Privacy Act, which the Supreme Court of Canada has held is quasi-constitutional,[103] specifically states that no personal information shall be collected by a federal government institution unless it relates directly to an operating program or activity of that institution. Personal information should be collected from the data subject wherever possible. Once collected, personal information should only be used for the purpose for which it was collected or for uses consistent with that purpose, and should only be retained as long as necessary. The head of a government institution collecting personal information must create personal information banks and must publish an index of such personal information banks every year, indicating the data collected, the institution that has control of the bank, and other relevant information about the banks, so that data subjects may exercise their right of access to the information bank. Any complaint under the Privacy Act is to be addressed to Canada's Privacy

---

[101]Canadian Charter of Rights and Freedoms, http://lois.justice.gc.ca/fr/charte/const_en.html.

[102]Access to Information Act (R.S. 1985, c. A-1), http://laws.justice.gc.ca/en/A-1/text.html.

[103]A "quasi-constitutional" statute in Canadian law is a statute that contains fundamental principles of law that are meant as an interpretive guide to all other statutes, and where the text of a specific statute conflicts with a quasi-constitutional document, the latter prevails. *See Lavigne v. Canada (Office of the Commissioner of Official Languages)*, 2002, SCC 53 at para. 23-24, http://www.lexum.umontreal.ca/csc-scc/en/pub/2002/vol2/html/2002scr2_0773.html (where the Supreme Court describes the Privacy Act as "fundamental in the Canadian legal system" and ascribes it quasi-constitutional status).

Commissioner, and both the Privacy Commissioner and the data subject have limited rights to seek judicial review before the Federal Court of Canada of refusals to provide access.[104]

Although Canada has more closely followed the EU's direction in enacting privacy laws that have an omnibus approach with significant protections afforded to personally identifiable information, it differs in that it allows provincial privacy laws to trump the national law. Thus, while all personal information may be protected, it may not necessarily be protected under national law. The *Personal Information Protection and Electronic Documents Act* (PIPEDA) provides that personally identifiable information cannot be collected, used, or disclosed without the subject individual's knowledge and consent.[105] PIPEDA was adopted in April 2000 and came into force on January 1, 2001. At such time, the law only applied to "federal works, undertakings or businesses," including businesses in federally regulated industries (such as air and rail transportation, telecommunications, broadcasting, and banking and financial services) and to personal information (including health information) traded for consideration across provincial or national borders.[106]

As of January 1, 2004, PIPEDA also applies to all unregulated private sector organizations engaged in commercial activity in Canada, including all provincially regulated commercial enterprise,[107] unless a province enacts a law that is "substantially similar" to PIPEDA. The office of the Canadian Privacy Commissioner has determined "substantially similar" to mean "equal or superior to PIPEDA in the

---

[104]Privacy Act, 1980-81-82-83, c. 111, Sch. li "1," http://www.privcom.gc.ca/legislation/02_07_01_e.asp.

[105]Theodore C. Ling, Michael J. Miasek, and Arlan Gates, "Canadian Privacy Commissioner Sets High Standards for Handling of Customer Personal Information: The Air Canada Case," *Baker & McKenzie—Canada*, Apr. 2002 at 1, http://www.bakernet.com/ecommerce/cnda_publ_airc_020401.pdf (hereinafter "Ling, Miasek, and Gates"); *see also* Patricia Wilson, "Privacy Law in Canada," Jan. 15, 2003, http://www.osler.com/index.asp?navid=1086&layid=1124&csid1=1299 (hereinafter "Privacy Law in Canada").

[106]Theodore C. Ling, Michael J. Miasek, and Arlan Gates, "The European Commission Ruling on Canadian Private Sector Privacy Legislation and Its Impact on International Data Transfers," *Internet and E-Commerce Law in Canada*, Vol. 3, No. 8, Oct. 2002 at 1-2, http://www.bakernet.com/ecommerce/cnda_publ_eubt_021001.pdf.; Privacy Law in Canada.

[107]Ling, Miasek, and Gates at 1-2, http://www.bakernet.com/ecommerce/cnda_publ_airc_020401.pdf; Privacy in Canada. Note that Canadian law does not contain the same concepts of the primacy of federal legislation as American law, and that there may be a constitutional challenge with respect to the legality of the federal government's attempt to force provincial governments to enact "substantially similar" legislation.

108   CHAPTER 2

degree and quality of privacy protection provided."[108] Recently, British Columbia[109] and Alberta[110] enacted private sector privacy bills intended to meet this test. Quebec already has an *Act Respecting the Protection of Personal Information in the Private Sector*,[111] which has been in effect since 1994 and which is "substantially similar."[112] Alberta's privacy bill excludes protection of health information because it is already protected under Alberta's *Health Information Act*.[113]

Violations of PIPEDA are monitored by the Privacy Commissioner, to whom any initial complaint must be made. If an organization is found by the Privacy Commissioner to have violated PIPEDA and does not correct the situation within 45 days of the Commissioner's report, the Commissioner and the data subject may seek an order from the Federal Court of Canada enjoining the organization to comply and awarding damages. The Privacy Commissioner may also conduct privacy audits of any organization regulated by PIPEDA at his own instigation and make recommendations that can be made enforceable by Federal Court order.

PIPEDA has been recognized by the EU as providing adequate protection for personal information under the Canadian "Safe Harbor" rules of its Data Protection Initiative without the need for additional legislation or protections.[114] As such, with the advantage of the North

---

[108]*See, e.g., Report to Parliament Concerning Substantially Similar Provincial Legislation,* Privacy Commissioner of Canada, June 2003 at 2, http://www.privcom.gc.ca/legislation/leg-rp_030611_e.pdf (hereinafter "Privacy Commissioner Report to Parliament"); *see also* Michael J. Miasek and Arlan Gates, "British Columbia and Alberta Introduce Private Sector Privacy Bills," *Baker & McKenzie—Canada,* June 2003 at 2, http://www.bakernet.com/ecommerce/cnda_publ_bcab_030601.pdf (hereinafter "Miasek and Gates").

[109]Personal Information Protection Act, Province of British of Columbia, SBC 2003, http://www.qp.gov.bc.ca/statreg/stat/P/03063_01.htm.

[110]Personal Information Protection Act, C P-6.5, http://www.qp.gov.ab.ca/documents/Acts/P06P5.cfm?frm_isbn=0779726316.

[111]An Act Respecting the Protection of Personal Information in the Private Sector, 1994, Province of Quebec, R.S.Q., chapter P-39.1, http://publicationsduquebec.gouv.qc.ca/dynamicSearch/telecharge.php?type-2&file=/P_39_1/P39_1_A.html.

[112]Privacy Commissioner Report to Parliament at 4; Miasek and Gates at 3.

[113]*Id.* at 1; text of the Health Information Act available at http://www.qp.gov.ab.ca/documents/acts/H05.cfm.

[114]*Commission Decision of 20 December 2001 pursuant to Directive 95/46/EC of the European Parliament and of the Council on the adequate protection of personal data provided by the Canadian Personal Information Protection and Electronic Documents Act (notified under document number C(2001) 4539),* Official Journal L 002, Apr. 1, 2002 at 13-16, http://europa.eu.int/smartapi/cgi/sga_doc?smartapi!celexapi!prod!CELEXnumdoc&lg=EN&numdoc=32002D0002; *see also Opinion 2/2001 on the Adequacy of the Canadian Personal Information and Electronic Documents Act,* Article 29 Data Protection Working Party, 5109/00/EN, WP 39, Jan. 26, 2001, http://europa.eu.int/comm/internal_market/privacy/docs/wpdocs/2001/wp39en.pdf.

American Free Trade Agreement (NAFTA) and EU approval for data flows, Canada has become an attractive site for data warehousing and processing transactions.

Canadian Provincial Legislation

Many Canadian provinces have enacted privacy laws that are limited to information in the hands of government or health care information (health care in Canada is controlled by the provincial governments). Only British Columbia, Alberta, and Quebec have enacted legislation regulating information in the hands of private entities.

While British Columbia and Alberta's legislation are both similar in many respect to PIPEDA, it remains to be seen if either law will receive the "substantially similar" imprimatur and therefore trump application of PIPEDA to privacy issues in British Columbia or Alberta, which commenced as of January 1, 2004.[115] Quebec's legislation has been accepted by Canada's Privacy Commissioner as equivalent to PIPEDA, and therefore continues to govern privacy issues in Quebec even after January 1, 2004. Rather than regulating access as a function of information collection, Quebec's *Act Respecting the Protection of Personal Information in the Private Sector* gives a general right of access and rectification by the data subject to any information collected by a private entity. That entity is required to treat all information as confidential and seek specific consent for any collection or transfer, except in certain specific circumstances. Under an EU Data Protection Directive "adequacy finding," any legislation accepted as equivalent to PIPEDA will be adequate for Canadian safe harbor purposes, and the Quebec law should therefore be valid under the EU Data Protection Initiative.

In addition, Canadian common law recognizes a tort claim for invasion of privacy. The province of Manitoba has enacted a Privacy Act that creates a statutory tort of invasion of privacy giving a right to bring an action even without proof of damage against any person who substantially, unreasonably, and without claim of right violates the privacy of another person. Quebec's Charter of Human Rights and Freedoms sets a quasi-constitutional right to privacy, which is echoed in the *Civil Code of Quebec*; accordingly, a tort claim for invasion of privacy would sound in Quebec law as well.[116]

---

[115]*See* Don McGowan, "New and Upcoming Developments in Canadian Privacy Law," *Internet and E-Commerce Law in Canada,* Butterworths, Vol. 4, No. 4, June 2003 at 29.

[116]*Quebec Charter of Human Rights and Freedoms,* Articles 4 and 5, http://www. cdpdj.qc.ca/en/commun/docs/charter.pdf; *Civil Code of Quebec,* Articles 35-40, http://www.canlii.org/qc/sta/csqc/20030530/c.c.q./part1.html.

110   CHAPTER 2

b. Mexico

The Mexican Constitution,[117] in accordance with Article 12 of the Universal Declaration on Human Rights and Article 11 of the American Convention on Human Rights, acknowledges the protection of an individual's right to privacy as one of the most important fundamental rights. Furthermore, Article 16 of the Constitution establishes the basic legal framework for privacy protection with respect to persons, family, home, papers, possessions, private communications, and correspondence circulated through the postal system. The privacy of these items cannot be disturbed except by virtue of a written order by a proper authority, based on and motivated by legal proceedings. However, none of these articles provides an express protection for personal data, and, therefore, such data may not necessarily be constitutionally protected.

Although Mexico does not have a special data protection law, there are legal protections in diverse sector laws such as the Federal Consumer Protection Act,[118] the Federal Transparency and Public Governmental Information Access Act,[119] the Geographic and Statistics Information Law,[120] and the Law for Regulating Credit Information Companies.[121]

On June 8, 2000, the Mexican E-commerce Law was enacted. It is worth mentioning that this law is not a single piece of legislation; it reforms four Federal Statutes: (a) the Federal Civil Code, (b) the Federal Code of Civil Procedure, (c) the Code of Commerce, and (d) the Federal Consumer Protection Act (FCPA). The main objective of the updates was to accommodate electronic documents and digital signatures and to provide for online consumer protection within the Mexican legal framework.

The FCPA was amended in February 2004 to incorporate stronger privacy protection for e-consumers. Article 1 VIII mandates that the government "provide for the effective and real protection of consumers in transactions concluded by traditional, electronic or optic means or

---

[117]1917 Constitution of Mexico, English translation available at http://www.ilstu.edu/class/hist263/docs/1917const.html.

[118]Federal Consumer Protection Act, Mexican Official Gazette, Aug. 27, 1997, http://www.cddhcu.gob.mx/leyinfo/pdf/113.pdf (Spanish).

[119]Federal Transparency and Public Governmental Information Access Act, June 11, 2002, http://www.cddhcu.gob.mx/leyinfo/pdf/244.pdf (Spanish).

[120]Geographic and Statistics Information Law, Mexican Official Gazette, Dec. 30, 1980, amended on Dec. 12, 1983, http://www.inegi.gob.mx/difusion/espanol/fdimj.html (Spanish).

[121]Law for Regulating Credit Information Companies, Jan. 15, 2002, http://www.cddhcu.gob.mx/leyinfo/pdf/237.pdf (Spanish).

concluded by any other means, and the adequate use of the provided data" and Article 24 IX Bis gives authority to the Federal Consumer Protection Office and the Ministry of Economy to promote the use of Codes of Ethics for providers in accordance with the principles of this Act.

In addition, Article 16 establishes diverse obligations for companies and providers that use consumer information for marketing or advertising purposes. For example, these companies must (a) inform consumers or its representatives at no charge about any stored information relating to them; (b) report to consumers within 30 days of their request what data is disclosed to third parties and the identity of such third parties; (c) modify the ambiguous or incorrect consumer information according to the consumer's request within the following thirty days after its submission; and (d) inform third parties that had received the ambiguous or incorrect information of the modifications to the information. The infringement to these obligations is penalized with a fine established by Article 126.

It is also important to consider articles 17, 18 and 18 Bis that regulate spam under an opt-out regime. Article 17 grants consumers the right to request that specific providers or companies not send marketing or advertising materials to his/her address, workplace, e-mail address or use any other means to deliver such information. Likewise, consumers can demand, at any time, that his/her information not be transferred or transmitted to third parties, unless a judicial authority orders it. According to Article 126, a fine may be imposed if the obliged entities do not comply with these provisions.

Following the U.S. Do Not Call concept, under Article 18, the Federal Consumer Protection Office is authorized to manage a Public Registry for Consumers who do not want their information used for marketing or advertising purposes. Consumers can submit their registration request by traditional or electronic means and the Registry shall provide its services with no charge. Article 18 Bis expressly prohibits companies and providers from using consumer information for purposes other than authorized (marketing or advertising), and they cannot send solicitation materials to consumers who have subscribed to the Public Registry for Consumers or who have expressly notified them that they do not wish to receive such materials. Violators of this article are subject to a fine according to Article 127. It is expected that the Registry will be operating this "Robinson List" by the end of 2004.

Finally, the FCPA establishes a new chapter in Mexican law to protect the "Rights of Consumers in electronic transactions and transactions by any other means." Article 76 Bis regulates e-commerce transactions and specifically forbids the transmission of confidential consumer information if there is not an express authorization by the consumer or an order from a proper authority. It also establishes that providers must not only use technical measures to guarantee security and confidentiality to the information submitted by consumers; they must notify e-consumers about the characteristics of the system before initiating the transaction. Finally, it mandates providers not to use advertising or sales strategies that do not grant the consumer sufficient and clear information about the offered services, especially if the marketing practices are focused on a vulnerable population, such as children, elderly, ill, or disabled persons. Violators are subject to a fine under Article 128.

The Federal Transparency and Public Governmental Information Access Act guarantees the right to access information possessed by the Federal Powers and the Autonomous Entities[122] (this phrase refers to diverse government offices different from any Agency or Ministry), excluding reserved and confidential information, such as that pertaining to national security or defense. This law requires prior consent for the use and dissemination of personal data and provides a right of access and rectification. The law has created the Federal Public Information Access Institute as an entity with decision, operative, and budgetary autonomy. Officials who use or disclose personal data without the corresponding authorization are liable under administrative laws.

The Law for Regulating Credit Information Companies (LRCIC) regulates the activities of Credit Information Companies (CIC), which are obliged to operate under a special authorization from the Treasury and Public Credit Ministry to compile, process, and/or deliver credit history information from natural and legal persons contained in its databases. This information can be processed by the CIC only if the users of its services (financial entities or commercial companies) have previously obtained express consent from their clients to include their data in the corresponding databases.[123] Noncompliance with this provision is penalized as a breach of a financial secret.[124]

---

[122]These are the diverse governmental offices different from any Agency or Ministry, such as the Federal Electoral Institute, the Central Bank of Mexico, the National Human Rights Commission, the Universities, and the Autonomous Superior Studies Institutions.
[123]The Law for Regulating the Credit Information Societies, Article 28. The Act requires an opt-in from companies whose clients' or consumers' information is kept in the credit databases.
[124]The Law for Regulating the Credit Information Societies, Articles 33, 38. Diverse financial laws such as the Credit Institutions Act (Articles 17 and 18), the Values Market Law (Article 25), the Investment Partnership Act (Article 55), as well as the Popular Credit and Savings Law (Article 34) protect "financial secrets." They prohibit financial employees from providing any information related to deposits, services, or any other operation to a person other than the depositor, the debtor, the owner or the beneficiary of the account, or their legal representative, if they do not have a judicial order. The institutions that fail to comply with this duty must compensate the injured party for damages and losses generated for the unlawful disclosure of the secret, besides being subject to civil and criminal liabilities.

International Legal Framework   113

Furthermore, the special authorization to operate a CIC can be revoked, pursuant to Article 18 of LRCIC, if the CIC repeatedly violates its financial secret obligations. Under Articles 40-44, CIC´s clients (either natural or legal persons) are entitled to special proceedings to (a) compel protection of their protected data (habeas data); (b) request information possessed by the CIC; (c) obtain a detailed special credit report; or (d) make a claim for any mistake or omission regarding the person's report or credit history.

In addition to the above-mentioned Acts, diverse laws such as the Industrial Property Act,[125] the Federal Author Rights Act,[126] the Federal Telecommunications Act,[127] the Federal Employment Act,[128] the Federal Electoral Institutions and Proceedings Code,[129] and the Federal Criminal Code[130] provide an indirect protection to privacy and personal data by regulating confidential information.

---

[125]The Industrial Property Act, http://www.cddhcu.gob.mx/leyinfo/pdf/50.pdf (Spanish). The Industrial Property Act protects information with industrial or commercial application that is of a confidential nature (and kept as such by a natural or legal person), which represents an economic or competitive advantage against third parties in the performance of economic activities, and for which the confidentiality and restricted access have been guaranteed by sufficient means or systems (Art. 82). It also provides for an express prohibition to unduly reveal said information (Art. 84). The infringement of the above-mentioned obligation constitutes a criminal offence (Art. 223).
[126]The Federal Author Rights Act, http://www.cddhcu.gob.mx/leyinfo/pdf/122.pdf (Spanish). The Federal Author Rights Act (Art. 109) mandates that any access, publication, reproduction, divulgence, public communication, or transmission of private information contained in databases requires the previous authorization of the persons referred to in that database (Art. 109).
[127]Federal Telecommunications Act, http://www.cddhcu.gob.mx/leyinfo/pdf/118.pdf (Spanish). Under Article 49 of the Federal Telecommunications Act, the information transmitted by the telecommunications networks is confidential. This article is consistent with Article 1302 of the North American Free Trade Agreement.
[128]The Federal Employment Act, http://www.cddhcu.gob.mx/leyinfo/pdf/125.pdf (Spanish). Art. 47 fraction IX permits the dismissal of an employee who unduly discloses technical, commercial, industrial, or administrative secrets known by virtue of his/her job.
[129]Federal Electoral Institutions and Proceedings Code, http://www.cddhcu.gob.mx/leyinfo/pdf/5.pdf (Spanish). Pursuant to Article 135 of the Federal Electoral Institutions and Proceedings Code, citizens´ data and the information granted to the Federal Electors Registry are strictly confidential and cannot be communicated unless there is a judge's order or a proceeding before the Electoral Authorities. The violation of this confidentiality obligation is an electoral crime (Art. 405 of the Federal Criminal Code).
[130]The Federal Criminal Code, http://www.cddhcu.gob.mx/leyinfo/pdf/9.pdf (Spanish). The Federal Criminal Code provides criminal sanctions for the unlawful disclosure of reserved information or secrets known by virtue of an employee's work (Art. 210). It also punishes any person that, without authorization, unduly accesses, modifies, destroys, or provokes information losses on systems protected by any security device, including those operated by the State (Art. 211 Bis 2) or the Financial System (Art. 211 Bis 4).

114   CHAPTER 2

Because of the lack of a complete and adequate data protection regime, the Commission of Economy[131] of the Mexican House of Representatives organized a workshop[132] to analyze two preliminary draft data protection bills.[133] The first project[134] was submitted by the Democratic Revolution Party on September 2001 and is pending resolution to be sent to the Senate. The second project[135] was drafted by the Revolutionary Institutional Party (PRI), passed by the Senate last April 2002, and sent to be analyzed and voted on by the Congress during the concluded LVIII Legislature. It is worth mentioning that the Executive Power has drafted another privacy and data protection law initiative that remains largely unknown to the private sector.

By the end of 2004, it is expected that the LIX Legislature of the Mexican Congress will continue the drafting process of the new Data Protection Act, which will most likely incorporate diverse elements of the above-mentioned projects.

c. Argentina

The Argentine Constitution provides for a special judiciary remedy for the protection of personal data (known as *habeas data*), thereby establishing a fundamental right for the protection of personal data. Article 43.3 of the Constitution gives persons the right to know the content and purpose of data pertaining to them contained in public records and in private files whose purpose is to provide reports.[136]

---

[131]This is the former Commission of Trade and Industrial Promotion of the Mexican House of Representatives.

[132]Diverse entities participated in the workshop. Among the most active sectors were telecommunications and IT companies, telemarketing enterprises, public notaries, financial institutions, NGOs, chambers of commerce, associations, and academic institutions. From the public sector, participants included officers of the Public Policy Development Office of the President, the Central Bank, the Ministry of Economy, the Federal Consumer Protection Office, and the National Institute on Information, Geography and Statistics.

[133]Both drafts are influenced by the EU Data Protection Directive. The above-mentioned documents had incorporated the eight principles of said Directive, including the prohibition to transfer personal data to jurisdictions without an adequate level of security. The drafts coincide on the necessity to create a special authority to regulate data protection in Mexico. However, both documents grant insufficient faculties to the referred entity; therefore the implementation of the current proposals may cause market distortions and a negative effect for international trade.

[134]Spanish version available at http://148.243.10.8/comcome/doctos/ini%20lf%20protecc%20dat%20pers.doc

[135]Spanish version available at http://148.243.10.8/comcome/doctos/MINUTA%20DATOS%20PERSONALES.doc.

[136]*Commission Decision of 30 June 2003 pursuant to Directive 95/46/EC of the European Parliament and of the Council on the adequate protection of personal data in Argentina,* Commission of the European Communities, C(2003) 1731 final, http://europa.eu.int/comm/internal_market/privacy/docs/adequacy/decision-c2003-1731/decision-argentine_en.pdf (hereinafter "EU Argentine Data Protection Decision").

International Legal Framework 115

Argentina's Personal Data Protection Act (PDPA), also known as the "Habeas Data" law, was enacted on October 4, 2000, and took effect in December 2001.[137] As in the case of a number of central European countries, Argentina appears to have responded to the data exporting restrictions of the EU Directive (Article 25) by adopting its substance almost verbatim in many of its provisions. On June 30, 2003, the EU recognized the Argentine PDPA as being "substantially similar" to the EU Directive.[138]

The PDPA is generally applicable to personal information held by both public and private entities. Indeed, the Act creates penalties for public officials who violate its terms, which can include periods of disqualification from holding public office. These provisions are apparently designed to help combat government corruption and are similar to restrictions on public sector uses of personal information found in the laws of other countries that have emerged from formerly oppressive regimes.

Argentina defines the scope of the PDPA generally to include data relating to legal persons, such as corporations. The Act, like the EU Directive, generally requires a data subject's consent to legitimize the processing of personal information. In declaring that the law provided an "adequate level of protection for personal data," the EU Commission noted:

> The Personal Data Protection Act No. 25.326 of 4 October 2000 . . . develops and widens the Constitutional provisions. It contains provisions relating to general data protection principles, the rights of data subjects, the obligations of data controllers and data users, the supervisory authority or controlling body, sanctions, and rules of procedure in seeking "habeas data" as a judicial remedy.[139]

The Regulation that implements the PDPA supplements these provisions and clarifies areas that may be subject to differing interpretations.

Argentine data subjects must be given access to personal information. Unlike the access provisions of the EU Directive, the Argentine Act's provisions clearly define how and when access must be granted. Reports to data subjects must be in a plain-language format, regardless of how such information is stored. Access to

---

[137]Personal Data Protection Act, No. 25.326, Oct. 4, 2000, available at http://www.privacyinternational.org/countries/argentina/argentine-dpa.html (Regulation approved by Decree No. 1558/2001, Dec. 3, 2001).
[138]EU Argentine Data Protection Decision. The Commission Decision summarizes the provisions of the PDPA.
[139]*Id.* at (8).

personal information must be granted within ten calendar days of a request, and corrections (where appropriate) must be undertaken within five business days. Failure to meet either of these deadlines can trigger an action for *habeas data,* that is, a court action to compel access, correction, or "suppression" of inaccurate personal information.[140]

The notice requirements of the Act largely mirror those of the EU Directive. The Act also creates special restrictions on those who handle data at others' direction ("processors," in the parlance of the EU Directive). These restrictions include a duty to destroy personal information that has outlived the uses for which it was transferred, as contemplated in the transfer contract. This provision assumes the existence of data transfer contracts and places a burden on all businesses transferring personal information to third parties to draft such contracts carefully, to accurately describe all acceptable future uses of such information, to preserve its usefulness.

The provisions of the Act concerning information security appear to be more stringent than the EU Directive. The EU Directive establishes a flexible standard under which the security measures to protect personal data must be "appropriate to the risks . . . and the nature of the data to be protected" and under which the state of the art of information security technology and the costs of implementation are factors that may be considered. The Act, on the other hand, states without qualifications that the responsible party or user of the data files must adopt whatever technical and organizational measures are necessary both to guarantee security of personal data and to detect any intentional or unintentional alterations of the data. Furthermore, the penalty that the Act prescribes for failure to meet these standards is severe: the Act simply prohibits the recording of personal data in any system that fails to meet these requirements of technical integrity and security. It is doubtful that many systems for storing personal data could meet these standards if they were applied with literal strictness; some degree of flexibility therefore seems necessary as a practical matter.

---

[140]Paragraph 3 of Article 16 of the PDPA establishes the *habeas data* action, and it is described and guaranteed in a portion of Article 43 of the Argentine Constitution as follows: "Any person shall file this action to obtain information on the data about himself and their purpose, registered in public records or data bases, or in private ones intended to supply information; and in case of false data or discrimination, this action may be filed to request the suppression, rectification, confidentiality or updating of said data. The secret nature of the sources of journalistic information shall not be impaired." Provisions referred to as "habeas data" and by the related term amparo are found in the constitutions and laws of other Latin American countries, such as Brazil, Paraguay, and Peru. For an excellent recent survey of the subject, see A. Guadamuz, "Habeas Data: The Latin-American Response to Data Protection," *The Journal of Information, Law and Technology,* 2000, http://elj.warwick.ac.uk/jilt/00-2/guadamuz.html.

Violations of the Act carry a variety of civil and criminal penalties, including fines and imprisonment. Although the Act implements the *habeas data* private right of action, that action does not independently create an individual's right to recover damages. However, individuals may be able to bring an action for *habeas data* and then use any court findings of fact from that action as evidence supporting a second, independent suit for damages.

Certain provisions of the PDPA, however, are omnibus and apply across the nation, whereas others are left to provincial law. Omnibus provisions include the general data protection principles, rights of the data subjects, obligations of data controllers and users of data files, registers and databases, and criminal sanctions. PDPA provisions concerning the control exercised by the supervisory authority, the sanctions imposed by the supervisory authority, and the rules of procedure for the "habeas data" judicial remedy are under federal law. They apply to registers, data files, databases, or data banks that are interconnected through interprovincial, national, or international networks. Other kinds of registers, data files, databases, etc. fall within provincial law.[141]

The implementing Regulation established the National Directorate for the Protection of Personal Data.[142]

d. Paraguay

Law number 1682, which regulates Private Character Information, was passed by the Congress on December 28, 2000, and was signed into law by the President of Paraguay on January 16, 2001.[143] Its application is limited to private sector databases, and it is very restrictive. Processing of sensitive information is generally prohibited, subject to limited exceptions. Publication of information about economic status requires prior written approval of the individual concerned, unless required by law. Commercial data has to be kept updated, and must be deleted after certain periods of time. There is no central data protection authority and no requirement to register databases, as required by the EU Data Protection Directive. The Paraguayan law does not set specific penalties, but allows for sanctions and fines to be decided by the courts.

---

[141]*Id.* at (11), (12).

[142]National Directorate for the Protection of Personal Data, http://www.jus.gov.ar/minjus/DPDP/.

[143]Law No. 1682 that Regulates the Private Character Information, http://ulpiano.com/habeasdaata_paraguay_Ley.htm (Spanish); Excerpts from "Data Protection in South America 2001," Pablo A. Palazzi.

2. ASIA

Although there are no treaties or agreements dealing specifically with privacy at the Asia Pacific Economic Coordination forum (APEC) level, APEC's Electronic Commerce Steering Group conducted a mapping exercise with respect to privacy protection in June 2002; the results of this mapping exercise have been used in the preparation of this text.[144]

At the time of publication of this book, APEC's E-Commerce Steering Group has compiled draft privacy principles for its 21 Asia-Pacific member countries.[145] The U.S. has submitted a "maximizing benefits" proposal that is still under consideration. The proposal states, "Personal information should be collected, processed, held and used in a manner that both protects individual information privacy and avoids unnecessary barriers to the free flow of information both within and across borders."[146] Clearly, the U.S. is attempting to counter the EU's edge in the global privacy space by advancing a more U.S.-centric view.

a. Asian Countries with Little Privacy Protection

Although a global review of privacy legislation would not be complete without a review of Asian jurisdictions, the most striking aspect of privacy legislation in Asia is its absence. Many countries have not legislated to protect privacy at all; others have purported to regulate the government, but with large areas carved out for "law enforcement" purposes.

Some Asian countries have included a right to privacy in their constitutions:

- The Republic of the Philippines
- The Republic of China (Taiwan)
- The Kingdom of Thailand.

---

[144]"APEC Data Privacy Mapping Exercise—Submissions from Economies," APEC Electronic Commerce Steering Group, updated Mar. 19, 2003, http://www.export.gov/apececommerce/privacy/submissions_links.html (covering Australia, Canada, Chinese Taipei, Hong Kong, Japan, Korea, New Zealand, Singapore, United States). *See also* the survey maintained by Electronic Privacy and Information Center (EPIC) and Privacy International, *Privacy and Human Rights 2000: An International Survey of Privacy Laws and Developments,* http://www.privacyinternational.org/survey/phr2000/, which is one of the most cogent and comprehensive privacy resources available anywhere.

[145]*See APEC Privacy Principles (Version 9 Consultation Draft),* Feb. 27, 2004, http://www.bakercyberlawcentre.org/appcc/apec_draft_v9.htm.

[146]Murray Griffin, "APEC Privacy Policy Task Force Wrestles With U.S. Text on Preserving Data Flows," *Privacy & Security Law Report,* Bureau of National Affairs, Vol. 3, No. 12, Mar. 22, 2004 at 337.

Some of the largest jurisdictions in Asia do not have any significant privacy legislation governing the regulation of information held by the private sector. Although the following countries do recognize a civil or common law right of action for invasion of privacy, such actions are not often brought:

- Malaysia (draft legislation only)
- The Republic of the Philippines (a proposal for legislation was announced as this guide was being finalized)
- The Republic of China (Taiwan)
- The Kingdom of Thailand (a proposal for legislation was announced as this book was being finalized)
- Taiwan and Thailand also have privacy legislation governing the collection and retention of information by the government, which laws provide for the standard rights of access and rectification by the data subject.

b. People's Republic of China and Hong Kong

The constitution of the People's Republic of China (PRC) contains limited protection of privacy in an affirmation that the personal dignity of citizens is inviolable, but privacy in the PRC has been protected only on a sporadic basis. For example, the *General Principles of Civil Law (1979)* and *(1986)* provide a right to reputation and to receive mail unopened (although other laws allow postal workers to examine "non-letter postal materials"), although even these limited protections have not been consistently applied. There is no data protection law in China and very little legislation that would limit government interference with the use, collection, and disclosure of data. In fact, ISPs and proprietors of cyber cafés are required to store for sixty days and divulge upon demand the identities of any person looking at information about certain prohibited topics. Moreover, all Internet connections in the PRC must flow through certain specified government firewalls, to allow complete blocking of any unwanted information.

As for Hong Kong, the *Basic Law*, which governs Hong Kong during the "one country, two systems" period before its full reintegration into the PRC, contains certain basic rights, one of which is that freedom and privacy of communications are protected by law.[147] Hong Kong's *Personal Data (Privacy) Ordinance* (the Ordinance)[148] is

---

[147]*The Basic Law of the Hong Kong Special Administrative Region of the People's Republic of China,* http://www.info.gov.hk/basic_law/fulltext/index.htm.
[148]Personal Data (Privacy) Ordinance, Chapter 486, http://www.pco.org.hk/english/ordinance/ordfull.html.

intended to protect the privacy interests of living individuals in relation to personal data, which is any data that allows practicable identification of the data subject and is stored in such a way as to make access or processing practicable. Under the Ordinance, data can only be collected for a limited purpose and in such a way as to ensure that the data will be accurate; a private right of access and rectification is provided to the data subject.

The Ordinance provides for a Privacy Commissioner, whose powers include inspecting data storage systems and making recommendations for compliance with the Ordinance, as well as promulgating codes of practice to be applied in certain sectors. In 2002, Hong Kong issued a draft code of practice for the workplace which includes telephone, e-mail, computer usage, and closed circuit television policies. The Commissioner can also investigate and sanction breaches of the Ordinance, which can lead to fines and even jail sentences. The Ordinance also provides a private right of action for the data subject, who can seek compensation and damages for wrongful use or collection of personal data. However, the Ordinance does not apply to situations where its application might prejudice certain competing public or social interests, including security and police work, or health. The Ordinance does not apply against the governments of either Hong Kong or the PRC.

Hong Kong also has a *Code on Access to Information*,[149] which allows individuals to request information about policies, services, decisions, or other matters within the competence of a government body. However, there are large exemptions for which no information is required to be provided, including defense and security, law enforcement and legal proceedings, damage to the environment, management of the economy, and management of the public service.

c. India

India does not have a constitutional right to privacy, although the courts have found an implicit right to privacy in the constitution.[150] At present, India has no general data protection law, but has adopted some sectoral legislation at the federal level. Access to information is not provided for in the law, but the courts have found it implicit in the right to freedom of speech and expression. Indian common law does recognize the torts of invasion of privacy and defamation. At the state level, only Gujarat, Tamil Nadu, Madhya Pradesh, and Rajasthan have

---

[149]Code on Access to Information, http://www.info.gov.hk/access/code.htm.

[150]*See, e.g.*, David Bender, "Data Protection Law in India: A Change of Direction," *Privacy & Security Law Report*, Bureau of National Affairs, Vol. 3, No. 2, Jan. 12, 2004 at 45-47 (citing *Kharak Singh v. State of U.P.*, AIR 1963 SC 1295 (Supreme Court of India) (hereinafter "Bender").

any sort of privacy legislation or administrative rules, which deals only with access to information in the hands of government officials, not with protection of privacy.

The legal framework may soon change, however. India was one of the first developing countries to realize its outsourcing opportunities hinged, in part, upon the protections its legal framework could provide to data that would be processed within the country. Initially, India was determined to pass data protection legislation that was modeled after the EU Data Protection Directive. India realized the importance of an "adequate" legal framework for data protection. "Adequacy" is necessary to facilitate trade with European Member States and attract foreign direct investment (FDI). The National Association of Software and Service Companies (Nasscom) pushed the government to develop a compatible data protection law.[151] Others worried, however, that such a privacy law would be too restrictive for major flows of information coming from the U.S. After working in a cooperative fashion with the private sector, the government has now decided to back away from a comprehensive EU-style data protection law in favor of one that is modeled after the U.S. Safe Harbor principles.[152]

India's action is significant. As WTO discussions have revealed, India has emerged as a leader of developing countries in bringing their interests to the table in multinational fora. India's action may spur other developing countries around the globe to enact privacy, security, and cybercrime legislation as a means of attracting FDI and facilitating trade. Two open questions are (1) whether they will lean in the direction of the EU or the U.S. and (2) whether the EU will accept Safe Harbor-type data protection from countries other than the U.S.

d. Japan

After a couple of years of false starts, on May 23, 2003, the House of Councillors (upper house of Japan's parliament) cleared the Personal Information Protection (PIP) bill and four related bills for proclamation and immediate enforcement. The PIP law governs the collection and dissemination of personal information and reinforces privacy protections. At the same time, the House of Councillors also passed the Administrative Organizations Personal Information Protection bill, which revamps the current Law Concerning Administrative Organizations Electronic Computation Machinery and Personal

---

[151]Harbaksh Singh Nanda, "India Drafting EU-Style Data Privacy Bill: Seeks to Attract Business From Europe," *Privacy & Security Law Report,* Bureau of National Affairs, Vol. 2, No. 22, June 2, 2003 at 584.
[152]Bender at 46-47.

122   CHAPTER 2

Information Protection. The new bill protects personal information stored electronically and in print by administrative entities, such as government and affiliated organizations.[153]

On December 4, 2003, Prime Minister Koizumi's cabinet approved a resolution for the full implementation of the law in April 2005. The PIP law, which has only been implemented in the public sector, will place restrictions on businesses that handle personal information and requires them to notify and obtain the consent of the individual if the information is to be provided to third parties. The law provides for some limited small business exemptions.[154] Companies must also take security measures to prevent disclosure of the information. Violators can be fined up to 500,000 yen (about US$4,000) or be imprisoned for up to one year.

Following the enactment of PIP and the related legislation, each ministry will begin drafting sector-specific laws, including amendments to existing laws, in such areas as medical and pharmaceutical, education, financial, telecommunications, etc. These areas with "sensitive information" will be given careful attention to protect privacy in these areas.[155] The Cabinet Offices's "Basic Guideline on Personal Information Protection," (Guideline) directs government agencies to coordinate in preparing "special measures" for data protection in the medical, pharmaceutical, financial services, credit, and information and communication sectors. The Guideline suggests private sector companies develop privacy policies and name a Personal Information Protection Management Officer prior to the April 1, 2005 implementation date.[156]

The Japanese government has already given clear indication that it takes privacy protections seriously. A Japanese court ordered the Japanese Self-Defense Agency to pay $1,000 in damages to a plaintiff after finding that the Agency had violated the PIP when it internally distributed a list of names of persons who were seeking information under a public disclosure law.[157] Additionally, the Ministry of Justice

---

[153]"Japanese Parliament Enacts Bills On Personal Information Protection," *Privacy & Security Law Report,* Bureau of National Affairs, Vol. 2, No. 22, June 2, 2003 at 584 (hereinafter "Japanese Parliament"); *see also* David E. Case, "The New Japanese Personal Information Protection Law," *Privacy & Security Law Report,* Bureau of National Affairs, Vol. 2, No. 23, June 9, 2003 at 633-35 (hereinafter "Case").

[154]"Japan Sets Out Policy for Private Sector Application of Personal Data Protection Law," *Privacy & Security Law* Report, Bureau of National Affairs, Vol. 2, No. 48, Dec. 8, 2003 at 1378-79.

[155]Japanese Parliament at 584; Case at 633-35.

[156]"Japan Releases Privacy Protection Guidelines for Medical, Financial, Credit, Consumer Information," *Privacy & Security Law Report,* Bureau of National Affairs, Vol. 3, No. 10 at 281-82.

[157]"Japanese Court Rules Government Agency Breached Privacy Under Personal Info Law," *Privacy & Security Law Report,* Bureau of National Affairs, Vol. 3, No. 8 at 211.

has announced that it will revise its rules effective April 1, 2004 in response to privacy violations on the Internet, disclosure of personal information, and other incidents that resulted in potential human rights violations. The Ministry had attempted to modify its rules in 2003 but failed to gain the support of the coalition government.[158] Even though PIP is not binding on the private sector until April 2005, the Japanese government has already sent a warning shot to industry regarding its intention to strictly enforce privacy protections. Following the loss of millions of pieces of personal information by Yahoo Japan, the Ministry of Public Management, Home Affairs, Posts, and Telecommunications announced they would reinforce the Guidelines regarding privacy responsibilities of telecom carriers.[159]

e. Republic of Korea (South Korea)

Article 17 of South Korea's Constitution simply states that "The privacy of no citizen may be infringed."[160] Korea also has comprehensive and sectoral privacy legislation.[161] The Act on the Protection of Personal Information Managed by Public Agencies of 1994 governs the management of computer-based personal information held by government agencies. It is based on the OECD Privacy Guidelines. The Act requires government agencies to limit the amount of data collected, provide access to such data, ensure the data's accuracy, keep a public register of data collected, ensure the security of the data, and limit the data's use to the purposes for which they were collected. The Act is enforced by the Minister of Government Administration.[162]

Korea's sectoral legislation covers such sectors as medical information, telecommunications, and e-commerce. South Korea also has laws that purport to require people to use their real name and identity in financial transactions and when posting on Internet bulletin boards. South Korea has become known as one of the world's hotbeds of unsolicited e-mail, and as this guide was being finalized, the

---

[158]"Japan's Justice Ministry Moves to Speed Resolution of Privacy, Human Rights Cases," *Privacy & Security Law Report*, Bureau of National Affairs, Vol. 3, No. 13 at 369-70.
[159]"Japan to Stiffen Internet Security Code In Wake of Massive Customer Data Breach," *Privacy & Security Law Report*, Bureau of National Affairs, Vol. 3, No. 12, Mar. 22, 2004 at 342.
[160]South Korea—Constitution, Article 17, July 17, 1948, http://www.oefre.unibe.ch/law/icl/ks00000_.html.
[161]*See* "Personal Data Protection in Korea," Korea Information Security Agency, Secretariat of Personal Information Dispute Mediation Committee, Aug. 2002, www.cyberprivacy.or.kr/per01.doc (hereinafter "Personal Data Protection in Korea"); *see also Privacy and Human Rights 2000: An International Survey of Privacy Laws and Developments,* "Country Reports," "Republic of Korea (South Korea)," http://www.privacyinternational.org/survey/phr2000 (hereinafter "EPIC/ PI Korea Country Report").
[162]EPIC/PI Korea Country Report.

government had begun cracking down on this, threatening criminal pursuit of egregious violators.

In an attempt to consolidate and create an umbrella privacy law, the Ministry of Information and Communications (MIC) is expected to forward a bill to the National Assembly in June 2004 entitled the "Law on the Protection of Personal Information" (Law on PPI). Privacy advocates have been urging MIC to draft comprehensive legislation that would consolidate privacy protections that are currently scattered throughout several laws. It is anticipated that the Law on PPI will regulate transborder flows of data and create a national agency to establish government-wide privacy policies. In the meantime, the Ministry of Finance and Economy has sponsored a bill that would regulate online banking and financial services, however, it has yet to be enacted.[163]

To protect privacy, South Korea has developed its ePrivacy Mark, awarded by the Korea Association of Information and Telecommunication to online businesses and Internet sites that respect data protection. It has also created a Personal Information Dispute Mediation Committee to allow data subjects and service providers the opportunity to settle disputes out of court either before or in lieu of judicial proceedings.[164]

The MIC has established a Cyber Privacy Center and issued privacy guidelines in May 2000. Under the guidelines, consent is necessary before "sensitive information" (race, medical, religion, beliefs, sexual orientation, etc.) and information from minors under the age of 14 can be shared.[165]

f. Singapore

Singapore's constitution contains no right to privacy.[166] Moreover, the constitution gives the government broad powers to preserve public order. Therefore, any privacy protections that may exist in the common law should be understood as being subordinated to the government's desire to preserve the social order.

Singapore has not enacted any legislation directly creating rights to privacy, and it has no omnibus data protection laws, relying instead on the traditional common law protections and individual provisions in

---

[163]James Lim, "South Korea Slates June Introduction of Sweeping Data Privacy Legislation," *Privacy & Security Law Report*, Bureau of National Affairs, Vol 3, No. 11, Mar. 15, 2004.

[164]Personal Data Protection in Korea at 9.

[165]EPIC/PI Korea Country Report.

[166]The laws of Singapore are available online, but the site at which they are most accessible does not permit deep linking. *See* the table of contents at http://statutes.agc.gov.sg.

individual statutes. The *Application of English Law Act* states that the English common law as it was known before November 12, 1993, continues to apply in Singapore unless expressly repealed, and therefore any tort remedies that would be known to the common law, including invasion of privacy and defamation (in their U.K. and not U.S. applications), continue to govern. In practice, Singapore relies extensively on self-regulation and industry codes.

Singapore's *Electronic Transactions Act* gives private individuals the right to use public key encryption to preserve the integrity of their digital signatures, but imposes upon them the duty to keep their private keys confidential to ensure the reliability of digital signatures. In response to an incident in May 1999, when an ISP scanned 200,000 customers' computers for viruses and Trojan horses, the Infocomm Development Authority of Singapore developed "Guidelines for Internet Access Service Providers (IASPs) on Scanning of Subscribers' Computers," pursuant to which an ISP is required to obtain affirmative consent from a customer before engaging in such scanning or other activities that might involve the ISP's accessing a customer's computer. However, the Computer Misuse Act makes it an offense to refuse access to the police at any time to any decryption information even without a warrant, as long as the police action is authorized by the Public Prosecutor, which suggests that privacy issues may take a back seat to law enforcement concerns.[167]

g. Australia

Neither the Australian federal constitution nor the constitutions of its six states contain any express privacy protection. In 1988, the Australian commonwealth government passed its *Privacy Act* (the Act), which regulates most federal public sector agencies.[168] A broad series of amendments to the Act were brought into force in 2001 to extend its scope and ambit to cover the private sector as well. Coverage for health care providers was added in 2001, although some small businesses (with annual revenue turnover of less than A$3 million) are exempt from the application of the Act.

The Act is based upon a set of National Privacy Principles that limit the collection of data to only that information necessary for the activities of the organization, with an effort to be made to collect data directly from the data subject wherever possible. Information must be kept as accurate as possible, and data subjects have a right of access and of rectification. Interestingly, one of the ten National Privacy Principles

---

[167]*Computer Misuse Act*, Cap. 50A, s. 15, available via http://statutes.agc.gov.sg.
[168]Privacy Act 1988, http://www.austlii.edu.au/au/legis/cth/consol_act/pa1988108/index.html#longtitle.

under the Act sets forth the position that, wherever it is lawful and practicable, individuals must have the option of not identifying themselves when transacting with an organization; that is, anonymity is one of the ten Principles. The Act also requires the establishment of clearly explained formal e-mail use policies in the workplace.

Although the Act is based in part upon the OECD Guidelines, the Act has not yet been recognized as providing an "adequate" degree of legal protection by the EU Commission, which raises an inference that the Commission does not deem the Act to meet the requirements of the EU Data Protection Directive.[169]

Australia's federal Privacy Commissioner investigates complaints brought under the Act and conducts audits of agencies and organizations that are subject to the audit provisions of the Act. The Privacy Commissioner has the authority to approve private sector codes that have obligations at least equivalent to those set forth in the Act. If the Privacy Commissioner approves a private code, then that code has the force of law against the organization which developed the code, and violations are treated as violations of the Act. The Commissioner also investigates circumstances where information about criminal records is disclosed in violation of the *Crimes Act 1914.*

Australia also has specific legislation prohibiting the unlawful use or disclosure of tax file numbers, and the *Data-matching Program (Assistance and Tax) Act 1990* regulates the use of the tax file number to link tax information to the records of social service agencies.

Under the *Telecommunications Act 1997*, ISPs are prohibited from disclosing information or documents that come into their possession as a result of their business as an ISP, except where reasonably necessary for the enforcement of criminal law or protection of the public revenue. ISPs can be forced to provide information to assist with ongoing criminal investigations, and the 2001 Cybercrime Act allows law enforcement agencies to force a specified person with knowledge of a specific computer to provide them with information about that system and its workings.[170]

Australian State/Territory Legislation

Legislation of privacy issues at the state and territory level in Australia predates the federal legislation, going as far back as 1969, when

---

[169]*See* "EU Reservations on Australian Privacy Law," EU Working Party on Data Privacy, Apr. 23, 2001, http://www.qlinks.net/items/qlitem10338.htm. (The EU Working Party on Data Privacy determined that data transfers to Australia should have certain safeguards put in place before the Australian Act should be deemed appropriate.)
[170]*Privacy and Human Rights 2000: An International Survey of Privacy Laws and Developments*, "Country Reports," "Australia," http://www.privacyinternational.org/survey/phr2000/countriesag.html#Heading2.

International Legal Framework 127

listening device legislation was passed in New South Wales and Victoria. From the late 1970s to the 1990s, the various states and territories passed a series of privacy laws. Today, the majority of states and territories have regulated surveillance devices, health information, and privacy of personal information. Some states have passed comprehensive privacy legislation similar in form and content to those of the federal laws governing those areas within their legislative competence, and New South Wales has a Privacy Commissioner.[171]

h. New Zealand

New Zealand's *Privacy Act 1993* (the Act)[172] sets forth a broad privacy regime based upon twelve fundamental principles. The Act requires that, wherever possible, information is to be collected directly from the data subject, and for a specific purpose that is identified to the subject. The data subject has a right of access and rectification of the data, and there are limits on both the use and the disclosure of personal information. Significantly, the Act addresses information that is kept in "public registers" like the land titles register and prohibits the accumulation for sale of information from several public registers.

New Zealand has an active Privacy Commissioner, who has the power to develop codes of practice covering specific agencies and activities, as well as to investigate complaints of interference with privacy by agencies.[173] The Act also places a positive requirement upon any agency (which includes government departments and private companies) to have a privacy officer, and the Commissioner is to contact that person when a complaint is received. If the Commissioner is unable to mediate a settlement between the complainant and the agency's privacy officer, the Commissioner refers the complaint to the Proceedings Commissioner, who can bring the matter before the Complaints Review Tribunal. The Complaints Review Tribunal can render an order of damages or compensation, as well as injunctive relief.

3. MIDDLE EAST AND AFRICA

a. Israel

Israeli law treats the right of privacy as a basic right. Israel's *Protection of Privacy Law* (the Law) requires that owners of databases with more

---

[171]"Office of the New South Wales Privacy Commissioner," http://www.lawlink.nsw.gov.au/pc.nsf/pages/index.
[172]"Meet the Privacy Act, the Commissioner, & the Office," http://www.privacy.org.nz/recept/rectop.html.
[173]"Privacy Commissioner," http://www.privacy.org.nz/top.html.

128   CHAPTER 2

than 10,000 names must register with the Registrar of Databases, who has the authority to investigate violations of the Law. The Law prohibits certain activities and limits the use of information in databases to the purpose for which the data were collected. Israel also has a *Freedom of Information Law* to allow citizens to exercise their fundamental right to obtain information from the government.[174]

b. Republic of South Africa

The South African constitution contains a right to privacy and a right of access to information held by the state. South Africa has begun to draft a general privacy law; until such a law is passed, privacy issues are dealt with only sectorally, especially in telecommunications, where service providers are required to collect information about customers and pass it on to law enforcement officials when requested. South Africa recognizes the tort of invasion of privacy.[175]

c. Republic of Turkey

The 1982 Turkish Constitution contains rights to privacy and to secrecy of communication.[176] A person whose rights have been violated has a cause of action and can seek injunctive relief. Turkey does not have a general data protection law. It is a member of the Council of Europe and has signed the *Convention for the Protection of Human Rights and Fundamental Freedoms*, but has not signed the Council of Europe Cybercrime Convention.[177] It has also signed the CoE *Convention for the Protection of Individuals with Regard to Automatic Processing of Personal Data* but has not ratified it.

D. Extraterritorial Application of Law

1. UNITED STATES

Although no U.S. privacy law explicitly purports to have extraterritorial effect, these effects have nonetheless been felt with

---

[174]This legislation is unavailable online. *See Privacy and Human Rights 2000: An International Survey of Privacy Laws and Developments,* "Country Reports," "State of Israel," http://www.privacyinternational.org/survey/phr2000/countrieshp.html#Heading5.

[175]This legislation is unavailable online. *See Privacy and Human Rights 2000: An International Survey of Privacy Laws and Developments,* "Country Reports," "Republic of South Africa," http://www.privacyinternational.org/survey/phr2000/countriesru.html#Heading7.

[176]Turkish legislation is unavailable online, although its Constitution can be found at: http://www.tbmm.gov.tr/anayasa/constitution.htm.

[177]*See also Privacy and Human Rights 2000: An International Survey of Privacy Laws and Developments,* "Country Reports," "Republic of Turkey," http://www.privacy international.org/survey/phr2000/countriesru.html#Heading13.

respect to the application of certain laws. The Children's Online Privacy Protection Act (COPPA) is intended to prohibit the online collection of personal information from children under the age of 13 without prior "verifiable parental consent." COPPA does not explicitly purport to apply to website operators based outside the United States, but exists to protect underage U.S. consumers. To that end, the Federal Trade Commission (which enforces COPPA) has indicated that it expects any website targeted at U.S. children will comply with COPPA. Although the FTC does not have jurisdiction to enforce COPPA against non-U.S. website operators, such operators who also have or who may wish to establish U.S. operations may find that noncompliance with COPPA could result in complications for those businesses.[178]

The same principle is true across a range of other U.S. sectoral privacy laws. As an example, the GLBA does not explicitly apply to companies based outside the United States, but because such laws apply to U.S.-based operations and for the benefit of U.S.-based consumers, these laws can produce extraterritorial effects. For instance, a U.S.-based financial institution with individual customers located both inside and outside the United States will likely be expected to distribute privacy notices (pursuant to GLBA) to all customers, including such non-U.S.-based individuals. Conversely, a non-U.S.-based financial institution doing business with individual customers in the United States will be expected to comply with the terms of GLBA with respect to its U.S. customers. These effects are, however, perhaps more indicative of the complexities of doing business globally than of any intended extraterritorial application of U.S. law.

2. EUROPEAN UNION

The EU Data Protection Directive, and the national laws promulgated thereunder, have had a strong extraterritorial effect. The EU Directive's prohibition on the export of personal information from the EU to jurisdictions lacking "adequate" legal protections for privacy (as determined by EU data protection regulators) has, in effect, created a barrier to trade for any country that has not adopted a substantially similar legal regime. This has had the effect, around the world, of causing countries to pass EU-style privacy laws to protect their trade with Europe. Examples include Argentina, Canada, Hong Kong, New

---

[178]See "Children's Privacy: The Children's Online Privacy Protection Act," Federal Trade Commission, http://www.ftc.gov/privacy/privacyinitiatives/childrens.html; "Children's Privacy: Laws & Rules," Federal Trade Commission, http://www.ftc.gov/privacy/privacyinitiatives/childrens_lr.html; "Children's Privacy: Enforcement," Federal Trade Commission, http://www.ftc.gov/privacy/ privacyinitiatives/childrens_enf.html.

Zealand, and numerous eastern European countries that are slated for eventual admission into the EU. By turn, most of these countries included provisions in their laws that also limit the export of personal information to countries whose laws are not substantially similar, thus creating additional pressure on those countries that have not yet adopted EU-style laws.

The notable exception to the trend of adopting the EU model is the United States. Because of its significant economic leverage and its tradition of enacting privacy laws by industry sector, the United States has been unwilling to adopt a sweeping omnibus privacy law in response to the threat of interrupted trade with Europe. However, the acceptance of the EU/U.S. Safe Harbor arrangement, and the agreement by the U.S. government to enforce noncompliance with the arrangement against U.S. companies operating in the United States, represents a significant concession by the United States to the pressures created by the EU Directive.

E. Conclusion

The international legal framework appears to be leaning toward the omnibus privacy approach taken by the EU Data Protection Directive. The EU approach is consistent with that taken by the OECD and the CoE. The EU's "adequate" level of protection requirement for data going out of the EU has had a significant global impact. Numerous countries, including those in line for accession into the EU, have drafted laws that are intended to afford "adequate" levels of protection to ensure their cross-border data flows will not be interrupted. The Safe Harbor agreement that was negotiated between the United States and the EU has offered participating U.S. companies the same assurance regarding cross-border data transfers. The EU model contractual clauses are controversial, however, and are indicative of the degree to which the international privacy legal framework remains unsettled. Additionally, the data retention requirements set forth in the EU Electronic Communications Directive undercut some of the privacy provisions of the Data Protection Directive.

Even though Canada's PIPEDA is an omnibus privacy law, its deference to provincial laws can make international business difficult. The privacy laws in Latin American countries, such as Mexico and Argentina, are relatively strong, with the EU having recently deemed Argentina's law as "adequate" per the Data Protection Directive. With the exception of Japan and South Korea, Asian countries have few privacy laws. Recognizing that the ability to transfer European data into a country depends on whether it affords the data "adequate" protection has clearly driven some developing countries toward EU-style data protection regimes. India, however, has reversed its course and appears to be moving more toward a compromise approach mimicking that of the U.S. Safe Harbor principles. Whether other developing countries follow suit remains to be seen.

The extraterritorial application of privacy laws and the looming question of "adequacy" as data moves from country to country highlights the need for increased international agreement regarding privacy of data and cross-border data flows.

CHAPTER ❖ 3

Privacy Programs: Plans, Policies & Procedures

A. Overview

Maintaining privacy in today's electronically operated world is much more difficult than in the days when a secretary held the key to the file cabinet and privacy was viewed as in the control of one or a few persons. Every company has private information. Some information that is private is protected "personally identifiable information" (PII) or "personal information" (hereinafter referred to as personal information),[1] other information must be kept private due to contractual obligations, nondisclosure agreements, or legal/regulatory

---

[1]Personal information is a very wide concept, with various definitions depending upon the context. However, in a recent consent order agreement with the United States Federal Trade Commission, personal information was defined as:

[I]nformation from or about an individual including, but not limited to: (a) a first and last name; (b) a home or other physical address, including street name and name of city or town; (c) an email address or other online contact information, such as an instant messaging user identifier or a screen name that reveals an individual's email address; (d) a telephone number; (e) a Social Security Number; (f) a persistent identifier, such as a customer number held in a "cookie" or processor serial number, that is combined with other available data that identifies an individual; or (g) any information that is combined with any of (a) through (f) above.

See In the Matter of Microsoft Corporation, File No. 012 3240, Agreement Containing Consent Order, http://www.ftc.gov/os/2002/08/microsoftagree.pdf (Consent order accorded final approval on December 20, 2002) (hereinafter "Microsoft Consent Order"). Within the context of the U.S. Safe Harbor Privacy Principles, PII is defined as "[D]ata about an identified or identifiable individual that are within the scope of the [Directive 95/46/EC of the European Parliament], that is received by a U.S. organization from the European Union, and recorded in any form."

requirements (such as those required by the Gramm-Leach-Bliley Act (GLBA) and the Health Insurance Portability and Accountability Act (HIPAA)). Yet additional information that is critical to the business's bottom line, such as supply sources, pricing and customer lists, strategic documents, and intellectual property should also be kept confidential for business and competitive reasons.

Today, every business should have a privacy program that addresses the collection, use, disclosure, and safeguarding of information, because information is a key corporate asset. Privacy considerations determine what a company can or cannot do with that asset—or should or should not do—without incurring legal liabilities and unwanted risk. Therefore, privacy is a strategic business issue that necessitates the careful attention of the enterprise from the boardroom to the loading dock. As a consequence, "[p]rivacy management needs to be comprehensive and enterprise wide"; it involves all aspects of the extended enterprise, including customer service, sales and marketing, communications, human resources, information technology, security (of information and physical facilities), operations, legal, internal audit, and enterprise partners (for example, agents, contractors, suppliers, etc.).[2] The goal of the privacy program should be to

> Avoid costly lawsuits and embarrassing public relations incidents that may result from revealing information that is protected by law, that management has determined could be detrimental to the enterprise if known by competitors or the public, or that customers [and employees] feel should be kept private.[3]

Given the potential impact of privacy on a company's business, a well-thought-out privacy program that is endorsed by senior management and adopted by the organization is critical.[4]

See the full text of the Safe Harbor Principles (and associated materials), available at http://www.export.gov/safeharbor/sh_documents.html (hereinafter "Safe Harbor Principles"). The EU Directive defines "personal data as:

> [A]ny information relating to an identified or identifiable natural person ('data subject'); an identifiable person is one who can be identified, directly or indirectly, in particular by reference to an identification number or to one or more factors specific to his physical, physiological, mental, economic, cultural or social identity.

See Directive 95/46/EC of the European Parliament and of the Council of 24 October 1995 on the protection of individuals with regard to the processing of personal data and on the free movement of such data, Official Journal L 281/31, Nov. 23, 1995, http://europa. eu.int/smartapi/cgi/sga_doc?smartapi!celexapi!prod!CELEXnumdoc&lg=EN&numdoc =31995L0046&model=guichett (hereinafter "EU Data Protection Directive").

[2]Michael Erbschloe and John Vacca, *Net Privacy,* McGraw-Hill, 2001 at xvii.

[3]*Id.*

[4]Rena Mears, Eileen MacNeil, and Kenneth DeJarnette, "A Matter of Trust: Vital trust requires a delicate balance between security and privacy," *Optimize,* March 2003 at 60, http://www.optimizemag.com/issue/017/ethics.htm (hereinafter "A Matter of Trust").

1. THE PRIVACY PROGRAM

The privacy program represents the entity's executable strategy for addressing privacy. *In general, the privacy program comprises a privacy plan, policies, and procedures.* A privacy plan is the overall strategic document that serves as the "business plan" for controlling personal information usage and safeguarding that information. It encompasses a myriad of considerations and drives the development of the policies and procedures. For medium- to large-sized operations, the overall privacy plan may have several components that correspond to business units, locations, or systems. The plan—or each component thereof—will have corresponding security policies and procedures.

Most privacy plans are "risk based." In other words, as a component of their privacy plan, companies conduct a privacy risk assessment by comparing their privacy requirements (corporate and legal) against their information collection, use, storage, sharing and distribution, retention, and destruction practices. *Only after this task is accomplished* can the appropriate privacy policies and procedures be designed and implemented for the organization or existing policies be evaluated and revised. To avoid deceptive practice allegations (which can have significant liability and reputational impacts), it is critical that the policies and procedures accurately reflect what the company can and is doing from an operational perspective.

Privacy policies and procedures are sub-components of the privacy plan. Privacy policies define how the organization obtains and handles information and how that information is to be safeguarded. Therefore, privacy policies should be high-level, relatively static, formal statements that (a) provide a framework of expected and mandated behavior for employees, contractors, agents, partners, technology and processes and (b) define the privacy "rights" granted customers and employees with regard to personal information.[5]

Privacy procedures move the policies into action through the organization's people and processes. For example, for a medical entity, the *privacy plan* may require enhanced privacy controls for certain medical records, setting forth use restrictions, and using authorization, authentication, and encryption software to safeguard that information. The *privacy policy* corresponding to that plan might state that certain medical records (1) can only be used for particular purposes; (2) can only be accessed or processed by authorized personnel whose identify has been authenticated; (3) can only be accessed from a particular location; and (4) that certain personal information in those records must be encrypted. The *privacy procedures*, which make up the next level, would

---

[5]*See* Michael Rasmussen, "The Difference Between Information Security Policy, Guidelines, Procedures and Standards, *Ideabyte,* Sept. 3, 2001 (hereinafter "Rasmussen Difference Between").

136   CHAPTER 3

set forth (1) which personnel would be authorized; (2) what security technology would be used for authorization (for example, password, biometric identifier, smart card, etc.); (3) which specific fields must be encrypted and how; (4) restrictions on disclosing those data to any person or entity other than those specifically specified; and (5) how to report unauthorized access or suspicious behavior.

2. THE RELATIONSHIP BETWEEN PRIVACY AND SECURITY

As shown by the above example, privacy and security are interrelated. Security involves the protection of information, applications and operating systems, networks, and hardware and supporting equipment. If networks can be breached, information can be accessed; if applications or operating systems can be manipulated, data can be sabotaged or compromised; if information controls can be broken, then information can be stolen, disclosed, or compromised. In part, security is about protecting information from loss, misuse, unauthorized access, disclosure, alteration, and destruction.[6]

Privacy programs deal with *protecting* information; security programs deal with *securing* networks, software, and information. Without security, there is no privacy. Thus, privacy programs and plans are concerned with both the acquisition and handling of information *and the safeguards (or security) protecting that information.*[7] Thus, all privacy programs, plans, and procedures should dovetail with (and, to an extent, be incorporated into) the entity's security program. Indeed, the financial consumer privacy requirements that were mandated by the Financial Services Modernization Act of 1999 (commonly known as the Gramm-Leach-Bliley Act) have both a privacy and a safeguard component.[8] The Health Insurance Portability

---

[6]AICPA/CICA, *Privacy Framework Exposure Draft,* American Institute of Certified Public Accountants and Canadian Institute of Chartered Accountants, June 2003, www.aicpa.org/innovation/baas/ewp/2003_06_ed_execsumm.asp.

[7]*See Fair Information Practices,* Organisation for Economic Cooperation and Development, http://privacilla.org/business/oecdguidelines.html; *see also* Financial Services Modernization Act of 1999, Pub. Law 106-102, Nov. 12, 1999, 15 U.S.C. Section 6801(b) (safeguarding requirements), 15 U.S.C. Sections 6802 and 6803 (use restrictions), http://thomas.loc.gov/cgi-bin/bdquery/z?d106:SN00900:| (hereinafter "Gramm-Leach-Bliley Act" or "GLBA").

[8]GBLA, 15 U.S.C. Section 6801(a), http://www4.law.cornell.edu/uscode/15/6801.html ("each financial institution has an affirmative and continuing obligation to respect the privacy of its customers and to protect the security and confidentiality of those customers' nonpublic personal information"); *see* "Financial Privacy: The Gramm-Leach Bliley Act," http://www.ftc.gov/privacy/glbact/; Privacy of Consumer Financial Information, 65 *Federal Register* 33646-89, May 24, 2000 (codified at 16 C.F.R. Part 313), http://www.ftc.gov/os/2000/05/65fr33645.pdf; Standards for Safeguarding Customer Information, 67 *Federal Register* 36484-94, May 23, 2000 (codified at 16 C.F.R. Part 314), http://www.ftc.gov/os/2002/05/67fr36585.pdf.

and Accountability Act (HIPAA) has both a privacy rule (which contains a "mini-security" rule) and a security rule.[9]

Many entities tend to "stovepipe" privacy and security, but a lack of coordination between the security and privacy plans can be disastrous: the privacy program might mischaracterize the entity's security program,[10] or the security program may threaten the privacy rights granted to employees or customers of the entity (for example, through employee monitoring, intrusion detection, logging, and monitoring programs) or leave data unsecured because of a lack of awareness of privacy requirements. Because a privacy program should include a safeguarding element, significant portions of a privacy plan may be comprised of security components.

Increasingly, courts and regulators are defining the adequacy of a privacy and/or security program in the United States in regulatory actions covering the safeguarding of personal information.[11] Conversely, industry-recognized security standards and guidelines are beginning to include data privacy requirements that, without coordination, may lead security professionals to devise privacy safeguards that contradict or conflict with the entity's privacy program.[12] It is just as important that those responsible for developing and implementing the privacy and security programs should work as a team to develop a common taxonomy, since the terminology in the two fields can be confusing.[13]

---

[9]Health Insurance Portability and Accountability Act of 1996, Pub. Law 104-191, http://aspe.hhs.gov/admnsimp/pl104191.htm (hereinafter "HIPAA"); Individually Identifiable Health Information, 45 C.F.R. Parts 160, 164, http://www.hhs.gov/ocr/hipaa/finalreg.html; Health Insurance Reform: Security Standards, 68 Federal Register 8333-81, Feb. 20, 2003 (codified at 45 C.F.R. Parts 160, 162, 164), http://www.wedi.org/snip/public/articles/HIPAA_Security_Final_Rule_official_version.pdf.

[10]See In re Eli Lilly and Co., File No. 012 3214, Docket No. C-4047, http://www.ftc.gov/os/2002/01/lillycmp.pdf (hereinafter "Lilly Complaint"); In re Eli Lilly and Co., Agreement Containing Consent Order, FTC No. 0123214, Jan 18, 2002, http://www.ftc.gov/os/2002/01/lillyagree.pdf (consent order accorded final approval on May 10, 2002) (hereinafter "Lilly Consent Order"). In the Matter of Microsoft Corporation, File No. 012 3240, Docket No. C-4069, http://www.ftc.gov/os/2002/12/microsoftcomplaint.pdf; Microsoft Consent Order.

[11]See id.; see also Marilou King, "Lessons from the Eli Lilly Case," Privacy Officers Advisor, Vol. 2, No. 11, Aug. 2002 at 1-3; http://www.privacyassociation.org/docs/POA0802.pdf (hereinafter "Marilou King").

[12]See International Standards Organization, ISO 17799, Section 4.10, http://www.iso.org; ISO/IEC 17799:2000.

[13]For instance, the term "access" can have different meanings, depending upon the context. In the Safe Harbor Privacy Principles, "access" refers to the following:

Individuals must have access to personal information about them that an organization holds and be able to correct, amend, or delete that information where it is inaccurate, except where the burden or expense of providing access would be disproportionate to the risks to the individual's privacy in the case in question, or where the rights of persons other than the individual would be violated.

138   CHAPTER 3

3. THE IMPACT OF LAWS, REGULATIONS, PRINCIPLES, STANDARDS, AND GUIDELINES

Privacy laws, regulations, principles, standards, and guidelines can be thought of as a set of controls or requirements "placed upon organizations over the uses of . . . information in their custody or control."[14] As such, these sources of requirements have a profound impact on an entity's privacy plan or program. Although many principles, standards, and guidelines may not have the "force of law," in this emerging field they may form the basis by which courts or administrative agencies and regulatory bodies judge plans or programs for reasonableness.

The relevant privacy laws, regulations, standards, and guidelines are found in a bewildering number of places and can vary widely by subject matter and context. They can affect industry-specific information, such as financial and health data, or cut across industry sectors, as with direct marketing information. They can also pertain to all businesses, such as the EU Data Protection Directive,[15] thereby affecting cross-border data flows. Last, they can define cyber criminal conduct and prescribe penalties. However, many laws, regulations, standards, and guidelines are based on a common set of principles, known as fair information practices.[16] In the context of the Safe Harbor Privacy Principles, fair information practices include choice, notice, onward transfer, security, data integrity, access, and enforcement provisions.[17]

Corporate privacy programs should be based on fair information practices, which, in many instances, will cover the majority of an entity's requirements. However, the complexity of privacy laws and regulations that apply to an organization is dependent upon many

---

Safe Harbor Principles, http://www.export.gov/safeharbor/sh_documents.html.

Within the security context, access is multifaceted. It can refer to user access, network access, operating system access, and application access (all types of logical access) as well as physical access. *see* ISO/IEC 17799:2000, "Information Technology—Code of Practice for Information Security Management," Section 7, "Physical and Environmental Security" and Section 9 "Access Control."

[14] *See* "The Security-Privacy Paradox: Issues, Misconceptions, and Strategies," A Joint Report by The Information and Privacy Commissioner, Ontario and Deloitte & Touche, August 2003 at 2, http://www.deloitte.com/dtt/cda/doc/content/dtt_financial services_securityprivacyparadox_030829.pdf (hereinafter "Security-Privacy Paradox").

[15] EU Data Protection Directive, http://europa.eu.int/smartapi/cgi/sga_doc?smartapi! celexapi!prod!CELEXnumdoc&lg=EN&numdoc=31995L0046&model=guichett.

[16] Ann Cavoukian and Tyler J. Hamilton, *The Privacy Payoff: How Successful Business Build Customer Trust*, McGraw-Hill Ryerson Inc., 2002 at xx.

[17] "Safe Harbor Overview," U.S. Department of Commerce, Export Portal, http://www.export.gov/safeharbor/sh_overview.html.

factors, including the location of its customers and employees,[18] the method of information collection,[19] the type of information collected,[20] particular characteristics of its customers,[21] where the information is located,[22] and the company's characterization.[23]

4. THE IMPORTANCE OF A COMPREHENSIVE, ENTERPRISE-WIDE PRIVACY APPROACH

Although privacy is a fairly new concern for many companies and there are relatively few reported cases concerning privacy programs, the fundamental lesson of this short history is that the privacy program must make certain that the company's policy is aligned with its people, processes, and technology. A privacy policy designed in a vacuum, taken from "boiler plate," and based on either purely legal advice or technical analysis may be designed for operational failure, and the risk of liability is increased. Given the ambiguity of most U.S. privacy laws and regulations, companies have an opportunity to define many key elements of their policy and align them with their business model requirements and their system architecture (both operational processes and technology).

In the FTC case against Eli Lilly,[24] the FTC found that (1) the company possessed appropriate written policies, and (2) the privacy breaches alleged in the complaint (and discussed in Chapter One) could have been avoided.[25] Although Eli Lilly had adopted

---

[18]For example, a U.S. corporation with offices or customers in Europe has two quite inconsistent bodies of privacy law that affect its operations and privacy program: the EU Data Protection Directive as implemented in the Member States where the company is doing business, and the more liberal U.S. legal framework.

[19]For example, the U.S. Children's Online Privacy Protection Act restricts the collection of information from minors under thirteen years of age.

[20]For example, the collection of information pertaining to health is considered "sensitive information" in the EU and a growing number of jurisdictions around the globe, subjecting this information to more stringent privacy requirements.

[21]Financial institutions, for example, have to comply with GLBA consumer financial requirements as well as money laundering rules that require reporting suspicious transactions, which are usually adduced from financial information obtained by the institution.

[22]For example, a corporation should know where its employee and customer PII is located to understand whether it has to comply with more restrictive privacy and data flow requirements (such as those mandated by the EU Data Protection Directive and other laws that mirror it). Location considerations can also apply to whether data are simply viewed or accessed. If one views data that resides in Europe, but does not actually download it and cause a transborder flow, then the EU laws arguably would not apply.

[23]For example, entities deemed "financial institutions" under GLBA or within the scope of HIPAA have added privacy requirements.

[24]Lilly Complaint, http://www.ftc.gov/os/2002/01/lillycmp.pdf; Lilly Consent Order, http://www.ftc.gov/ os/2002/01/lillyagree.pdf.

[25]Id.; see also Marilou King at 2 (interview of FTC supervising counsels in the Eli Lilly case).

140   CHAPTER 3

appropriate policies, the investigation showed that the policies were
not part of an enterprise privacy program:

> Our investigation revealed that this disclosure, while
> unintentional on the part of Lilly and its employee, resulted
> from a failure by the company to maintain or implement
> appropriate internal security measures to protect sensitive
> consumer information. Specifically, Lilly did not provide
> oversight or assistance for the inexperienced employee who
> sent the e-mail to the subscriber list, and did not review the
> computer program used to send the e-mail or the e-mail itself
> before it was transmitted to the subscriber list. The
> investigation showed us that this privacy breach could have
> been prevented by reasonable measures on Lilly's part,
> particularly with respect to employee training and restrictions
> on internal access to consumer data. In fact, Lilly had certain
> written policies in place that may have helped to prevent the
> breach, but those policies were not followed.[26]

The order agreed to by Eli Lilly requires the company to establish
and maintain reasonable and appropriate administrative, technical,
and physical safeguards to protect consumer personal information
against "reasonably foreseeable internal and external risks to the
security, confidentiality, and integrity of personal information."[27] The
details of the program were left to the company "in terms of what
works best for them,"[28] but the FTC Order specified that the four-part
framework had to include:

1. Designating personnel to coordinate and oversee the program
2. Identifying reasonably foreseeable risks, including any such
   risks posed by lack of training (such as unauthorized access)
   and addressing these risks in each relevant area of its operations
   (including management and training, information systems, and
   prevention and response to incidents, including unauthorized
   access)
3. Conducting annual reviews of the program's effectiveness
4. Adjusting the program in response to any finding and
   recommendations resulting from reviews or ongoing
   monitoring.[29]

What appears clear from the *Eli Lilly* case is that a privacy program must
take a holistic, enterprise approach to be successful and cannot rely upon
the mere development or adoption of privacy compliance policies.

---

[26]Marilou King at 2.
[27]Lilly Consent Order at 4.
[28]Marilou King at 2.
[29]Lilly Consent Order at 4; *see also id.*

Privacy Programs: Plans, Policies & Procedures   141

The importance of a comprehensive privacy program cannot be overstated. The lack of an enterprise privacy program with corresponding laws, policies, and procedures that links the technology, operational, and legal considerations with the people is all too frequently the reason why organizations suffer privacy breaches, reputational damage, and face potential liabilities.

B. Development of a Privacy Plan

Developing a privacy plan is the initial step in the development of a privacy program. The privacy plan is an enterprise document and, therefore, should be consistent with (a) the business operations and legal compliance requirements, (b) management goals and the culture of the organization, and (c) the company's technology infrastructure (including system and application architecture). While the basic components of an enterprise privacy plan can follow a generic skeleton, each privacy plan is unique to that organization's specific business model, operations and culture, information life cycle, contractual obligations, legal compliance requirements, and technology. Privacy plans, policies, and procedures that are out of step with these factors often cause more problems than they solve.

At a minimum, the enterprise privacy plan must address how the company will:

- Govern privacy matters (including issues of accountability and ownership);
- Determine its privacy requirements (including its brand, contractual, regulatory, and existing policy requirements);
- Determine how it will handle information (including the acquisition, use, storage, sharing and distribution, retention, and destruction of information);[30]
- Adopt an appropriate taxonomy for the company (the definition of personal and sensitive information, the meaning of secondary usage or access within the context of the company's operations);
- Develop appropriate policies and procedures that are aligned with its culture, people, processes, and technology;
- Implement its privacy plan (including appropriate policies, procedures, training, standards, and guidelines that ensure value adoption); and
- Monitor, evaluate, and adjust that plan on an ongoing basis, based on changes to brand, contractual and regulatory requirements, processes, technologies and information systems,

---

[30]T. D. Wilson, "Information Management," University of Sheffield, United Kingdom, http://informationr.net/tdw/publ/papers/encyclopedia_entry.html (also known as the information life cycle, based on records management principles).

142   CHAPTER 3

geographies and markets served, and business arrangements, such as mergers and acquisitions, alliances, joint ventures, and outsourcing arrangements.

The enterprise privacy plan articulates the privacy program goals and the process for achieving those goals.

1. GOVERNANCE STRUCTURE

Enterprise privacy plans must be developed as an enterprise effort, with three levels of activity: (1) senior management and boards of directors, (2) internal management team, and (3) staff. Each has separate roles and responsibilities.

a. Directors and Senior Management

Senior management and boards of directors must take the lead by providing oversight and guidance, setting corporate tone and policy, and conducting annual audits and reviews. Up to now, most privacy plans, policies, and procedures were developed by legal or regulatory compliance personnel reporting to either a general counsel or chief compliance officer.

Recently enacted laws and regulations impose specific privacy/security compliance requirements on targeted industry sectors. For example, in the United States, the Health Insurance Portability and Accountability Act[31] and Gramm-Leach-Bliley Act[32] each impose specific requirements pertaining to oversight by senior management. For instance, under the Gramm-Leach-Bliley Act many entities are required to:

Involve the Board of Directors. Your board of directors or an appropriate committee of the board shall:

1. Approve your written information security program; and
2. Oversee the development, implementation, and maintenance of your information security program, including assigning specific responsibility for its implementation and reviewing reports from management.[33]

Failure to take prudent steps to enact and oversee a reasonable privacy program may result in liability for directors and officers,

---

[31]HIPAA, http://aspe.hhs.gov/admnsimp/pl104191.htm.

[32]GLBA, http://thomas.loc.gov/cgi-bin/bdquery/z?d106:SN00900:|.

[33]"Interagency Guidelines Establishing Standards for Safeguarding Customer Information and Rescission of Year 2000 Standards for Safety and Soundness," Final Rule, 12 C.F.R. Part 30 *et al* (hereinafter "Interagency Guidelines for Safeguarding").

Privacy Programs: Plans, Policies & Procedures 143

because privacy can affect their fiduciary duty and may include legal risk management issues. Because personal information is a key corporate asset, it logically follows that oversight of a privacy program falls within the duty owed by officers and directors in overseeing the operations of a corporation.

In the United States, two rules govern the duty of directors and officers. The majority of cases follow the business judgment rule that the standard of care is that which a reasonably prudent director of a similar corporation would have used. Other jurisdictions have adopted a higher standard of care requiring the diligence, care, and skill that would be exercised by a prudent person in similar circumstances in their own personal business. To date, no shareholder suit has been brought against officers or directors for failure to take necessary steps to protect personal information; however, shareholders may in the future rely on such a theory as a basis for such derivative suits.[34]

The recent Delaware *Caremark International Inc. Derivative Litigation* case noted that officer/director liability can arise in two contexts: (1) from losses arising out of ill-advised or negligent board decisions (which are broadly protected by the business judgment rule as long as the decision was reached out of a process that was rational or employed in a good-faith effort) and (2) from circumstances where the board failed to act in circumstances where "due attention" would have prevented the loss. In the latter situation, the *Caremark* court noted that:

> [I]t would, in my opinion, be a mistake to conclude that . . . corporate boards may satisfy their obligation to be reasonably informed concerning the corporation, without assuring themselves that information and reporting systems exist in the organization that are reasonably designed to provide to senior management and to the board itself timely, accurate information sufficient to allow management and the board, each within its scope, to reach informed judgments concerning both the corporation's compliance with law and its business performance. . . .
>
> Obviously the level of detail that is appropriate for such an information system is a question of business judgment. . . But it is important that the board exercise a good faith judgment that the corporation's information and reporting system is in concept and design adequate to assure the board that appropriate information will come to its attention in a timely

---

[34]Jody R. Westby, "Protection of Trade Secrets and Confidential Information: How to Guard Against Security Breaches and Economic Espionage," *Intellectual Property Counselor*, (Jan. 2000) at 4-5 (hereinafter "Westby Trade Secrets").

144   CHAPTER 3

manner as a matter of ordinary operations, so that it may satisfy its responsibility.[35]

The *Caremark* case could provide a basis for a shareholder suit against officers and directors for failure to implement an information and reporting system on its privacy program such that it could (1) determine it is adequately meeting statutory, regulatory, or contractual obligations to protect certain data from theft, disclosure or inappropriate use and (2) be assured that the data critical to normal business operations and market share are protected.[36]

Securities laws and regulations also require public corporations to adequately disclose in public filings and public communications relevant risks to the corporation and its assets. The *Independent Director* put this in the context of information systems by reporting that:

> Management of information risk is central to the success of any organization operating today. For Directors, this means that Board performance is increasingly being judged by how well their company measures up to internationally-accepted codes and guidelines on preferred Information Assurance practice.[37]

Additionally, when a company is a victim of an attack on its information systems, whether from an insider or an outside bad actor, previous studies have shown that this can result in a lack of confidence in the company and even a drop in the company stock price.[38] Consequently, shareholders may also initiate a derivative suit for loss to stock price or market share caused by inadequate attention by officers and directors to privacy issues. Clearly, directors and officers need to undertake a certain level of involvement and oversight in ensuring that the organization is properly protected against a privacy breach to protect against shareholder derivative suits.

---

[35]*Caremark International Inc. Derivative Litigation,* 698 A.2d 959 (Del. Ch. 1996).

[36]*See, e.g., id.;* For a general discussion on corporate liability related to board and officer responsibilities to ensure adequate information and control systems are in place, *see* Steven G. Schulman and U. Seth Ottensoser, "Duties and Liabilities of Outside Directors to Ensure That Adequate Information and Control Systems are in Place—A Study in Delaware Law and The Private Securities Litigation Reform Act of 1995," Professional Liability Underwriting Society, 2002 D&O Symposium, Feb. 6-7, 2002, http://www. plusweb.org/ Events/Do/materials/2002/Source/Duties%20and%20Liabilities.pdf.

[37]*Id.* (citing Dr. Andrew Rathmell, Chairman of the Information Assurance Advisory Council, "Information Assurance: Protecting your Key Asset," http://www.iaac.ac.uk).

[38]A. Marshall Acuff, Jr., "Information Security Impacting Securities Valuations: Information Technology and the Internet Changing the Face of Business," Salomon Smith Barney, 2000, at 3-4, http://www.theiia.org/itaudit/index.cfm?fuseaction= forum&fid=143.

Privacy Programs: Plans, Policies & Procedures 145

In line with rules like the Interagency Guidelines (for GLBA),[39] the board of directors or a board-level committee should be tasked with the oversight of the development and implementation, and maintenance of an information security program, including protection of information subject to privacy requirements. In light of today's sensitivity to conflicts of interest and given laws like Sarbanes-Oxley, the audit committee may not be the best committee to assume these responsibilities because, for U.S. corporations, the audit committee now has a responsibility to conduct annual security audits that will include the privacy and security programs. A risk management or security committee that is responsible for corporate risk management may be the better choice.

In exercising oversight of the privacy plan, senior officers and directors should consider the following:

Assessment

- Is the organization an intensive user of technology? Are the systems using state-of-the-art technologies? Are the systems being kept up to date, in terms of both software and hardware?
- What digital functions are outsourced? Have steps been taken to ensure the outsourced vendor systems meet the organization's privacy and security requirements? Is the company's data stored separately from the vendor's other client data? Does the contract require the outsource vendor to notify the company in the event of a security breach of its system?
- Is the company using any Application Service Providers? Have steps been taken to ensure the security of their operations and the organization's data? Are there contractual provisions requiring notification in the event of a privacy or security breach of their system?
- Does the company share system functions with business partners, vendors, distributors, or customers or allow collaborative computing? What privacy and security requirements are imposed? What reviews and monitoring are conducted?
- What privacy incidents has the organization had in the past year? How many were internal? External? What were the causes? Did any involve law enforcement or the press? What was the associated economic loss? Did they affect stock price or market share?
- Has a privacy and vulnerability assessment been conducted by an outside entity? Was it conducted under the protection of attorney work product? How was the report handled?

---

[39]Interagency Guidelines for Safeguarding.

146   CHAPTER 3

- How does the organization determine acceptable levels of risk?
- Does the company have adequate insurance coverage to protect against privacy and security breaches?

Privacy Program

- Does the organization have a comprehensive privacy (and security) plan? If so, when was it last reviewed? Is it adhered to?
- Are there policies and procedures that support the privacy plan? (A wide range of policies and procedures are necessary, including e-mail, monitoring, customer information, human resources information.)[40] Are they monitored for compliance and is there a procedure for enforcement?
- Has personal information (and corporate digital assets) been through a classification process? Have those assets central to the core business functions and competitiveness been identified?
- What is the annual expenditure on privacy and security programs? How is return on investment measured? How is performance measured? Are the privacy and security solutions cost effective? Is the privacy and security program adequately funded? How does the company's privacy and security program compare against other companies' programs?

Internal Controls

- Does the company have the proper line management to assume responsibility for the management of these issues, for example, a chief privacy officer, chief security officer, and/or chief information officer?
- Does the company have an internal management team that communicates and coordinates across the organization on these issues? Does it comprise business unit managers and human resources, security, technical, legal, and public affairs representatives?
- Is there a procedure for reporting and investigating privacy incidents, including unauthorized access and usage? Who are the corporate personnel involved? How are incidents that may involve law enforcement handled (like unauthorized access under the California Unauthorized Disclosure Law)?[41]
- What internal controls and systems are in place to alert personnel, line managers, and officers and board members of both privacy and security incidents and compliance information?

---

[40]Policies should consider the sensitivity of current and former employee and retiree information. This includes information provided when references are given or even information provided by applicants for employment.

[41]Cal. Civ. Code Section 1798.82.

Implementation

- Is there an awareness and training program for personnel on privacy and security and the policies and procedures applicable to their positions and responsibilities?

Compliance

- Does the company conduct an internal and external annual audit? If so, who performs these functions?
- Is the organization in compliance with the privacy and security laws and regulations where it does business? Have inconsistencies in laws been taken into account?[42]

With regard to senior management, the role of a chief privacy officer or executive is relatively new in the United States. Many large multinationals such as IBM, General Electric, Citicorp, American Express, Hewlett-Packard, and Microsoft have privacy officers who head a staffed office. Because privacy involves all aspects of the entity, a privacy officer needs to possess a variety of skills, including:

- People, negotiation, and management skills
- Ability to work with consumer and employee groups
- Ability to maintain external relationships with the media and regulators
- Ability to manage task forces and large projects
- The ability to serve as an "ambassador and champion" of privacy
- The ability to understand complex privacy trends and their impact on the success of their business
- The ability to handle complaints and manage dispute resolution systems
- An awareness of emerging legislative and regulatory agency issues with privacy implications for privacy officers who actively lobby on behalf of their companies
- The ability to understand legal issues and materials
- An understanding of computer and information systems and their applications
- An understanding of auditing and compliance processes.[43]

---

[42]Pat Carbine, "Questions for Board Members to Ask About Information Security," Presentation at the White House, Apr. 18, 2000; Jody R. Westby, "Protection of Trade Secrets and Confidential Information: How to Guard Against Security Breaches and Economic Espionage," *Intellectual Property Counselor*, (Jan. 2000) at 4-5; Dan Verton, "Disaster recovery planning still lags," *Computerworld,* Apr. 1, 2002, http://www.computerworld.com/securitytopics/security/story/0,10801,69705,00.html (citing Ernst & Young for "Aligning Security With Your Business: 10 Questions to Ask").

[43]*The Selection and Evaluation of CPOs: A Guide to Companies,* Privacy & American Business, 2003 at 5, http://www.pandab.org/conf2k3materials.pdf.

Ensuring proper board and senior management oversight of the privacy program increases the likelihood that the privacy program will align with business objectives and the organization's culture and be adopted and adequately supported by the organization and modified and enhanced to meet operational and environmental change.

b. Cross-Organizational Privacy Team

Director and senior management oversight necessarily only goes so far; the actual development of a privacy plan and the day-to-day operational risk considerations are best delegated to a privacy management team. Privacy issues should not be "stovepiped" within divisions or left to legal personnel. It is important that the organization establish an internal team of personnel who regularly meet and discuss privacy risk management issues and work together to develop/review the privacy plan, policies, and procedures.

The participants of this team should include business unit managers and representatives from human resources, legal, technical, security, and public relations. Generally, this structure will include the chief privacy officer, chief security officer, and chief counsel, or their representatives. Of course, one person assumes the lead, usually the privacy officer or person in charge of risk management.

When developing this structure, in addition to determining who will be involved, it is important to determine the roles and responsibilities each person will have, and the time commitment that will be required throughout the various stages of the privacy program. Once the privacy program is in place, this team should meet no less than once per quarter to discuss compliance, reviews, audits, new issues, incidents, investigations, remedial measures, etc. The responsibilities and time commitments should be documented and incorporated into the privacy plan to demonstrate each participant's commitment to the privacy initiatives.

The privacy management team's responsibilities should include:

- Development of an ongoing privacy risk assessment and gap analysis program that covers data uses/flows and laws and regulations that affect them;
- Development of an ongoing sequential privacy program to bring the organization into cost-effective privacy compliance and administration based on the risk assessment and gap analysis;
- Development of a common language to discuss privacy within the operational context of the company's business;
- Development of privacy roles and responsibilities throughout the organization;
- Development of a privacy monitoring and evaluation program; and

- Development of a periodic privacy reporting program that keeps senior management and directors up to date on the privacy programs progress and needs.[44]

While many of the foregoing tasks may seem obvious, the *Eli Lilly* case demonstrates that failure to (a) address privacy programmatically, (b) identify reasonably foreseeable risks, (c) assign qualified oversight personnel, and (d) implement comprehensive programs that address people, processes, technology, and operational issues can lead to significant consequences.

c. Personnel

A privacy plan comes to life through the employees and other personnel who implement the policies and procedures. From the receptionist to the executive suites, all personnel should be viewed as an invaluable part of the development of the privacy plan, policies, and procedures. Operational personnel who use personal information in their day-to-day activities should not be viewed as an afterthought They are the ones who know the business needs and processes best, who understand what works and what does not, who know where vulnerabilities are, and who can provide valuable input into the privacy planning process. Moreover, consulting employees[45] in this process yields a valuable return: they appreciate being consulted and considered part of the process, and, in return, they are more likely to support the privacy program and understand that privacy is an important part of their job and that management takes privacy seriously.

2. PRIVACY RISK ASSESSMENT AND GAP ANALYSIS

Risk assessments and gap analysis are critical components of the privacy program process because they identify the greatest risks that must be addressed. The risk analysis process (a) analyzes the environment (both regulatory and operational), (b) identifies risks and vulnerabilities associated with usage and safeguarding of personal information, (c) assesses the potential for the undesired event, and (d) identifies appropriate countermeasures. Governments and certain industry sectors, such as financial, must adhere to assessment guidelines to ensure proper risk assessment.[46]

---

[44]*See generally id.* (discussing roles of privacy officers).

[45]For purposes of this discussion, "employee" is intended to mean employees, contractors, vendors, agents, business partners, consultants, temporary staff, or any other person who has access to the data, systems, or network.

[46]*See, e.g.,* Federal Information Security Management Act, Title III of E-Government Act of 2002, Pub. Law 107-347, http://csrc.nist.gov/policies/FISMA-final.pdf; Marianne Swanson, *Security Self-Assessment Guide for Information Technology Systems,* NIST Special Publication, 800-26, Nov. 2001, http:csrc.nist.gov/publications/nistpubs/; Gary Stoneburner, Alice Goguen, and Alexis Feringa, *Risk Management Guide for Information*

150   CHAPTER 3

Ideally, determination of acceptable and unacceptable risks is made at the senior management and board level. This decision is a key driver of the privacy plan for the organization. Every industry and each individual organization is unique in the risk it faces (for example, how it collects personal information, its cross-border data flows, its systems and applications). How much risk is acceptable depends on industry standards, the value of the information, the culture of the organization, and the willingness of management to accept risks.[47] Additionally, each organization needs to factor in the risk of potential legal liability, civil and/or criminal penalties, and downstream consequences such as unfavorable publicity, damage to reputation, loss of business partners or market share, or drop in share price. Each organization needs to decide what level of risk is appropriate for the business unit, process, or system and manage it accordingly.[48] There are four possible responses to any risk:

- Avoid the risk—Involves making the appropriate business decisions in which the risk is not taken. This may involve declining to take a position or an action regarding a new system or relationship. Not acting also has risks.
- Mitigate/reduce the risk—Through the implementation of privacy and security controls, risks can be reduced to an acceptable level. The key is to achieve a level of "acceptable" privacy and security, not the elimination of risk.
- Accept the risk—There is always the option to accept the risk as a cost of doing business. Some risks need to be taken and cannot be effectively mitigated or transferred.
- Transfer/insure the risk—Establishing some sort of insurance or agreement that transfers the risk to a third entity. Insurance cannot always be effective, since it may not always cover all losses. A cyber insurance policy may cover certain damages, but it cannot restore the loss of customer confidence or damage to a reputation.[49]

Technology Systems, NIST Draft Special Publication 800-30 Rev A, Jan. 21, 2001, http://csrc.nist.gov/publications/drafts.html; *IT Examination Handbook,* Federal Financial Institutions Examination Council, Dec. 2002, http://wbln0018.worldbank.org/html/FinancialSectorWeb.nsf/SearchGeneral?openform&E-Security/E-Finance&Policies+&+Guidelines; *Technology Risk Management Guidelines for Financial Institutions,* Monetary Authority of Singapore, Draft Nov. 11, 2002, http://www.mas.gov.sg/display.cfm?id=94D063CD-5EB6-4636-82B5A725F9F6E9F5.

[47] Michael Rasmussen, "Creating a Road Map for an Information Protection Program," RPA-062002-00026, Giga Information Group, June 25, 2002.

[48] Carol A. Siegel, Ty R. Sagalow, and Paul Serritella, "Cyber-Risk Management: Technical and Insurance Controls for Enterprise-level Security, CRC Press, Mar. 2002, http://www.aignetadvantage.com/content/netad/CyberRisk_Article_043002.pdf.

[49] Michael Rasmussen, "Four Responses to Risk," RIB-092002-00209, Sept. 26, 2002.

Privacy Programs: Plans, Policies & Procedures   151

In general, the privacy risk assessment and gap analysis process involves the following steps:

- Identification of regulatory, contractual, existing policy, and brand privacy requirements
- Rationalization of these requirements, taking into consideration the entity's business model (for example, online business or direct marketing) and infrastructure (distributive versus centralized architecture) and dividing them into logical areas (for example, notice, choice, data transfers, storage, etc.)
- Creation of a requirements framework from the rationalization process
- Determination of personal information life-cycle data flow within the entity (including the classes of data, such as sensitive and nonsensitive personal information) and the acquisition, storage, location, distribution and sharing (including third parties), and retention and destruction of personal information)
- Determination of usage practices (by class) for personal information at each stage of the information data life cycle
- Determination of the safeguarding measures present at each stage of the information life cycle
- Assessment of the information gathered against the privacy requirements framework
- Analysis of the usage and safeguarding practices against the requirements framework to identify risks and mitigating controls
- Categorization and prioritization of risks
- Creation of plans to mitigate risks (or accept risks) in a programmatic fashion
- Periodic repetition of the process.[50]

To perform a privacy risk assessment and gap analysis, the organization must remember that an information life cycle analysis includes more than just tracking the information in the company's central systems and applications (for example, paper files, offsite storage, and local information systems). In fact, most privacy risks arguably involve information legitimately accessed from central systems and applications and processed or used in end-user computing applications.

A company should also consider developing or acquiring a tool to gather and maintain the information the organization collects and its requirements. This tool can be as simple as a questionnaire, which is either completed through an interview with members of the business unit or independently completed and submitted to the privacy project

---

[50]*See generally A Matter of Trust.*

152   CHAPTER 3

team. The key is to develop a repeatable process, to create an information baseline of and periodically update the requirements, assessment, and risk mitigation plans.

3. LEGAL CONSIDERATIONS AND RISKS

Determining privacy risk is a complicated area. Because of the interconnected global network, companies ranging from small enterprises to the largest multinationals all have to consider a wide range of factors, including (a) compliance requirements with laws, regulations, and standards; (b) jurisdictional differences in laws and regulations; (c) contract and nondisclosure agreement requirements; (d) confidential and proprietary information and due diligence; and (e) political expectations. Practically speaking, it is impossible for most companies to meet all of their compliance requirements. As a consequence, companies must assess their risks, prioritize them, and implement safeguards based on their assessment of those risks.

a. Compliance Requirements with Laws, Regulations, and Standards

Personal information can be protected by constitutions, laws, regulations, case law (for common law jurisdictions), and contracts between parties. There are numerous categories of information protected by laws and regulations around the globe. In the United States, state laws commonly protect arrest records and criminal justice data, bank records, cable television subscriber data, credit information, employment data, insurance information, mailing lists, medical and health data, polygraph results, school records, social security numbers, tax records, and telephone service and solicitation records. Federal laws protect all of the foregoing (except arrest records) plus government data banks and wiretap information.[51] In addition, the U.S. Electronic Communications Privacy Act[52] protects certain personal information from disclosure in the absence of compliance with specified procedures.

The European Union's 1995 Data Protection Directive[53] protects personal data, and its extraterritorial application has had an impact around the globe. The Directive essentially precludes the flow of personal information outside the EU unless it is provided equivalent privacy protections. Additional privacy protections were included in

---

[51]*Privacy Laws by State* (excerpted from *Compilation of State and Federal Privacy Laws*, 1997, ed., by Robert Ellis Smith and *Privacy Journal*), http://www.epic.org/privacy/consumer/states.html.

[52]Electronic Communications Privacy Act, 18 U.S.C. Section 2701 *et seq.*

[53]EU Data Protection Directive, http://europa.eu.int/smartapi/cgi/sga_doc?smartapi!celexapi!prod!CELEXnumdoc&lg=EN&numdoc=31995L0046&model=guichett.

the 1997 Telecommunications Privacy Directive which added protections for telephone, digital television, and mobile and telecommunication systems.[54] The 1997 Directive is intended to protect personal data from misuse and requires the immediate deletion of all personal identifying information following the termination of a communication that is not needed for billing and other limited purposes. Subsequent amendments to the EU Directive have replaced the 1997 Directive and extended its scope to encompass the Internet (electronic communications).[55]

Since September 11, 2001, numerous countries have enacted laws directed at countering terrorism, which have broken down some privacy protections by giving governments greater access to records, enhancing search and seizure capabilities, increasing intra- and intergovernmental information sharing, and introducing new profiling and tracking systems. On the other hand, the effect of these measures has aroused privacy advocates around the globe and has spurred the enactment of some new privacy legislation, including workplace protections, in some countries. Additionally, Eastern European countries planning to join the European Union have enacted new privacy provisions to bring their legal frameworks into compliance with EU directives.[56] The result of this activity is that the global legal framework is more unsettled than ever in the privacy arena, which significantly affects compliance requirements and security plans, policies, and procedures.

Another legal compliance consideration concerns the collection, use, and sharing of data. For example, organizations may be prohibited from collecting certain data in the course of business and from sharing it with another entity, even a subsidiary company.[57] National, state, and municipal regulatory agencies may also impose privacy and

---

[54]Electronic Privacy Information Center and Privacy International, *Privacy and Human Rights 2002: An International Survey of Privacy Laws and Developments*, 2002 at 10-11, http://www.privacyinternational.org/survey/phr2002/phr2002-part1.pdf (hereinafter "Privacy and Human Rights 2002").

[55]*Directive 2002/58/EC of the European Parliament and of the Council of 12 July 2002 concerning the processing of personal data and the protection of privacy in the electronic communications sector (Directive on privacy and electronic communications)*, Official Journal L 201/37, July 31, 2002, at 37-47 (replacing EU Directive 97/66/EC), http:// europa.eu.int/smartapi/cgi/sga_doc?smartapi!celexapi!prod!CELEXnumdoc&lg=en& numdoc=32002L0058&model=guichett (hereinafter "EU Electronic Communications Directive"); *see also* http://europa.eu.int/eur-lex/pri/en/oj/dat/2002/l_201/l_201200 20731en00370047.pdf.

[56]Privacy and Human Rights 2002 at iii-iv.

[57]*See, e.g.*, M. Maureen Murphy, "Financial Privacy Laws Affecting Sharing of Customer Information Among Affiliated Institutions," *CRS Report for Congress*, RS21427, Feb. 27, 2003, http://www.epic.org/privacy/fcra/RS21427.pdf. One should also be mindful of trade control laws so that visitors from abroad and holders of certain types of visas are not granted access to certain systems, especially those being developed under federal government contract.

154   CHAPTER 3

security requirements on data. Many of these are industry specific or
spill over into several sectors. For example, the U.S. Health Insurance
Portability and Accountability Act (HIPAA)[58] imposes extensive
privacy and security regulations on health and medical information
and affects health care providers, claims processors, insurance
companies, and businesses. The Gramm-Leach-Bliley Act[59] requires
privacy of consumer credit information and governs disclosure and
security of personal information held by financial institutions. Other
industry sectors frequently subject to privacy and security regulations
are insurance, communications providers, and government
contractors. Many other countries have similar privacy regulations.[60]
Professional ethics rules and codes of conduct also subject certain
categories of professionals to privacy or security requirements. For
example, attorneys, accountants, and physicians are required by
professional rules to safeguard client information and protect it from
unauthorized access or disclosure.

b. Jurisdictional Differences

Inconsistencies in legal frameworks can pose serious privacy and security
dilemmas for organizations and make their privacy plans quite complex.
The communications industry sector has faced increasing difficulties with
subpoenas for customer records that are protected in the provider's
jurisdiction but not in the jurisdiction of the court seeking the
information. The U.S. Electronic Communications Privacy Act, for
instance, protects certain personal information from disclosure in the
absence of compliance with specified procedures. Therefore, requests
from courts and law enforcement for protected data are often challenged,
sometimes by communications providers who fear liability if they
disclose the information.[61] The cross-border transfer of information can
also be especially problematic if one jurisdiction protects the data and the
other does not. Frequently data move through several locations in there
life cycle. Therefore, it is important to track the origin of the information
and determine whether privacy protections, such as those required by the
EU, travel with the data.

---

[58]HIPAA, http://www.hipaadvisory.com/regs/law/index.htm; Information on
HIPAA privacy, security, and electronic transaction regulations can be found at
http://www. hipaadvisory.com/regs/index.htm.
[59]GLBA, http://thomas.loc.gov/cgi-bin/bdquery/z?d106:SN00900:1.
[60]For an extensive discussion of global privacy requirements and country-by-country
reports, *see* Privacy and Human Rights 2002 at 10-11, http://www.privacy
international.org/survey/phr2002/phr2002-part1.pdf.
[61]Jody R. Westby, ed., *International Guide to Combating Cybercrime*, American Bar
Association, Section of Science & Technology Law, Privacy & Computer Crime
Committee, ABA Publishing, 2003 at 58, http://www.abanet.org/abapubs/books/
cybercrime/ (hereinafter "Cybercrime Guide").

Data retention is another issue that can vary among jurisdictions and has enormous privacy considerations.[62] For example, the United States does not generally impose a data retention requirement on communication providers, although it can ask a provider to begin retaining specific account information on a case-by-case basis to meet law enforcement or other legal requirements.[63] On July 25, 2002, the EU adopted a Directive on privacy and electronic communications allowing Member States to require communications providers to retain traffic and location data of all communications taking place over mobile and land telephones, faxes, e-mails, chat rooms, the Internet, or any other communications device.[64] Therefore, depending upon EU Member State implementations, privacy and security programs may now have to provide for adequate retention of these data and ensure privacy protections while they are being retained.[65]

c. Contracts and Nondisclosure Agreements

Contractual provisions protecting certain personal information are often obscure and known to only a few people. Likewise, nondisclosure agreements often place strict confidentiality and security requirements upon personal information, but these requirements seldom trickle down to technical staff. Moreover, there is a tendency to treat the data of another organization with less care than one's own—even though contractual provisions require equal or greater protections.

To prosecute unauthorized access and disclosure of information, companies must have privacy and security policies and procedures that will meet the evidentiary requirements of the cybercrime laws in that jurisdiction.[66] For example, most countries' laws require "unauthorized" access. Therefore, information that is open to anyone on the system would not meet this threshold.

d. Confidential and Proprietary Information and Due Diligence

Privacy programs must protect confidential and proprietary information in a manner that meets the legal thresholds of trade secret

---

[62]*See, e.g.,* Daniel J. Solove and Marc Rotenberg, *Information Privacy Law,* Aspen Publishers, 2003 at 721-24.

[63]Cybercrime Guide at 59.

[64]*EU Electronic Communications Directive,* http://europa.eu.int/smartapi/cgi/sga_doc? smartapi!celexapi!prod!CELEXnumdoc&lg=en&numdoc=32002L0058&model=guichett, *see also* http://europa.eu.int/eur-lex/pri/en/oj/dat/2002/l_201/l_20120020731en 00370047.pdf.

[65]One should be mindful that a well-considered data retention policy is necessary, especially one that does not run afoul of data retention rules in anticipation of litigation.

[66]*See* Cybercrime Guide for a full discussion of this issue in the Cybercrime Laws chapter.

laws and the civil and criminal laws that would permit prosecution and monetary damages in the jurisdictions where the organization does business. The legal threshold of the U.S. Economic Espionage Act is discussed in Chapter One of this book. These requirements must be met for all intellectual property, trade secrets, or confidential/ proprietary or sensitive information. Special care must also be taken to safeguard protected information during due diligence for mergers and acquisitions. Increasingly, electronic documents are reviewed in the due diligence process instead of paper ones, and document production procedures must take special care to safeguard protected information.

e. Political and Cultural Expectations

There are instances where there are no laws or regulations regarding the privacy or security of certain information; however, there is a public perception that disclosure of this type of data is not acceptable. Lawmakers tend to watch these situations closely, and it behooves companies to put special protections into their security programs for this type of data, even though they are not mandated to do so under law. Voluntary protection is always less costly to business than mandated compliance. For example, over the past couple of years, in the United States there have been several disclosures of driver's license information. Eventually, state legislators were convinced that this data would not be properly protected without a legal mandate, and now several states have passed laws protecting this information.[67]

In addition, cultural distinctions abound. In the United States

> [T]he prevailing concept in the privacy sector is that once an individual provides personal information to an organization, the organization is the data owner, as well as the data user. U.S. firms often consider that the data they collect becomes their property and that they have a right, barring any sector-specific privacy legislation, to determine the use of it.[68]

In contrast, in European "privacy regimes, the individual is usually referred to as the data subject . . . [and] retains certain rights . . . the data user has the responsibilities for of a custodian . . . ."[69] Thus, if cultural distinctions are not understood, companies can underestimate the risks they confront.

---

[67]Dibya Sarkar, "Cybersecurity Laws Spread," *Federal Computer Week*, July 23, 2003, http://www.fcw.com/geb/articles/2003/0721/web-ncs-07-23-03.asp.
[68]Security-Privacy Paradox at 1-2.
[69]*Id.*

4. DATA CLASSIFICATION

One of the most important steps in the development of any privacy and security program is the classification of its information and systems, including personal information. Frequently, this is the most ignored step. Organizations all too often focus on the system requirements or an operational aspect without considering whether the information (personal or nonpersonal), system, or network is central to their core mission, critical to their competitiveness, central to their reputation or business relationships, or a key component of their business strategy. For example, unauthorized disclosure of sensitive personal data (for example, medical information) may result in steep civil fines, criminal penalties, lawsuits, and/or embarrassing publicity that could adversely affect the organization.[70]

Classification priorities are determined only after managers step back and look at the "big picture" of their organization, analyze the business operations and legal risks, and identify the organization's information assets. In the context of privacy, classifications must take into consideration regulatory distinctions (sensitive versus nonsensitive information), contractual obligations, and brand requirements (potentially embarrassing or information representing a competitive advantage). For instance, under the U.S. Safe Harbor Privacy Principles, sensitive information is defined as:

> [P]ersonal information specifying medical or health conditions, racial or ethnic origin, political opinions, religious or philosophical beliefs, trade union membership or information specifying the sex life of the individual.[71]

An entity may wish to implement added safeguards to protect this sensitive information. However, to do so, it must first identify it, apply a common data classification to it, and determine the appropriate safeguards to accompany that data (for example, data protection standards associated with the data classification at each phase of its movement through the organization).

Data classification includes not only information in the form of a data file or database; it also encompasses the associated system and user documentation, operational and support procedures, training materials, and continuity and disaster recovery plans.[72] Some information security experts view data classification as "the embodiment of management's tolerance of information risk."[73] Data

---

[70]*See generally* Westby Trade Secrets at 5.
[71]*See* Safe Harbor Privacy Principles, "Choice."
[72]ISO-17799, Section 5.1.1 "Inventory of assets," at 8.
[73]Christopher M. King, Curtis E. Dalton, and T. Ertem Osmanoglu, *Security Architecture Design, Deployment & Operations*, McGraw-Hill, 2001 at 42.

158   CHAPTER 3

classification systems are also indicative of the organization's commitment to safeguarding valuable or protected information.[74]

The classification of data is not a rigid process based on costly analysis; it is classified according to requirements for confidentiality, availability, and integrity. Other considerations in the classification of information involve whether the data is intellectual property or proprietary, whether it is a legally protected category of information (either through laws, regulations, case law, or contractual agreement, such as a nondisclosure agreement), and whether the data is critical to business continuity.[75] Various pieces of information may be categorized, so that all information within that group is similarly protected. There is no one right way to develop a classification scheme, but because of the need for widespread adoption within an organization, any classification system that is developed needs to be simple to apply and relatively intuitive.[76]

Numerous categories of protection can be created, although some experts find it useful to model data classification levels after national security classification schemes of top secret, secret, confidential, and unclassified:

- Top Secret—Applies to the most sensitive information, which is only for internal use. Disclosure of this information could have very significant consequences for the organization, stockholders, business partners, customers, and/or third parties. An example might be social security numbers, credit card and associated pin numbers, sexual orientation, or medical history.
- Secret—Applies to less sensitive information that is still for internal use. Unauthorized disclosure could negatively affect the organization, stockholders, business partners, customers, and/or third parties.
- Confidential—Applies to personal information intended for use within the organization. Unauthorized disclosure could negatively affect it and/or its employees.

---

[74]Ronald L. Krutz and Russell Dean Vines, *The CISSP Prep Guide: Mastering the Ten Domains of Computer Security*, John Wiley & Sons, Inc., 2001 at 6 (hereinafter "CISSP Prep Guide").

[75]Jody R. Westby, "Digital Corporate Governance," May 5, 2003 at 3.

[76]For excellent guidance in this area, *see* William C. Boeher, *Volume 1: Guide for Mapping Types of Information and Information Systems to Security Categories*, NIST Special Publication 800-60, Draft Version 2.0, http://csrc.nist.gov/publications/drafts/800-60vlf.pdf; William C. Barker and Annabelle Lee, Volume II: Appendices to Guide for Mapping Types of Information and Information Systems to Security Categories, NIST Special Publication 800-60, Draft Version 2.0, http://csrc.nist.gov/publications/drafts/sp800-60V2f.pdf (hereinafter "NIST Categorization Guide").

- Unclassified—Applies to information not within the above categories. Disclosure would not be expected to seriously affect the organization.[77]

An alternative approach would be to classify all information into one of four categories:

- Public (or Unclassified)—Nonsensitive information available for public disclosure (for example, press releases, information on public portions of company websites).
- Internal—Information belonging to the organization and not for disclosure to the public or external parties (that is, generally available to employees and authorized third parties), where unauthorized disclosure would likely cause limited harm to the organization (for example, company e-mail or telephone directories).
- Confidential—Information that is sensitive or confidential with the organization and intended for business use by those with a need to know, where unauthorized disclosure would likely cause significant legal, financial, competitive, or reputational harm (for example, individually identifiable customer information, social security numbers, legally privileged information).
- Restricted—Information that is extremely sensitive or private, of highest value to the organization, and intended for use only by named individuals, where unauthorized disclosure would likely cause severe legal, financial, competitive, or reputational harm (for example, merger-related information, major trade secrets, individually identifiable medical records, files containing unencrypted passwords, or other confidential personal identifiers).

Within an organization, virtually anyone may create, access, use, modify, or store data through the information's life cycle; this includes the owner of the information, custodian, users, security personnel, and processing personnel (internal, outsourced, or application service provider). The location (server, hard drive, disk, on site, off premises) of the data can be very important. Access to the data may also be restricted through the use of authorization and authentication technologies. In addition, the information may be encrypted and controls may restrict whether the data can be accessed or modified and limit access to specific locations (on site or remote).[78] A data

---

[77]Ben Rothke, "Security Management Practices," http://www.cccure.org/modules.php ?name=Download&d_op=viewdownload&cid=45 (hereinafter "Rothke").

[78]Christian F. Byrnes and Dale Kutnick, *Securing Business Information: Strategies to Protect the Enterprise and Its Network,* Intel Press, 2002 at 31-50 (hereinafter "Byrnes and Kutnick").

classification matrix is a common method of charting data into categories and indicating specific treatment of that information regarding:

- Dataset
- Owner
- Custodian
- Technical location (server, disk, tape, Internet, etc.)
- Geographic location
- Users (persons/entities)
- Usage (choice and/or preference requirements)
- Protection (encryption, authentication, authorization, passwords, malware protections, etc.)
- Backup and recovery.[79]

As set forth earlier, there may be distinctions between privacy and security requirements. In the case of classification, usage is an important element in classification schemes. For instance, under the Safe Harbor Privacy Principles, a person must be "given affirmative or explicit (opt-in) choice if sensitive information is to be disclosed to a third party or used for a purpose other than those for which it was originally collected or subsequently authorized by the individual through the exercise of opt-in choice."[80] Not only must the appropriate safeguard protections be applied to the information, *but the individual's choice must follow the information through the information life cycle.*

Recognizing the linkage between risk and classification, the U.S. National Institute of Standards and Technology (NIST) has released a draft Federal Information Processing Standard (FIPS) 199 to be used by government agencies to categorize information and information systems and to provide appropriate levels of information security according to a range of risk levels.[81]

C. Privacy Policies and Procedures

Once a workable and achievable Privacy Plan has been developed, the tools to communicate, implement, and maintain it must be constructed, that is, privacy policies and procedures. Policies are high-level statements that provide a framework of expected and mandated

---

[79]*See, e.g.,* Byrnes and Kutnick, at 31-109; CISSP Prep Guide at 4-15.

[80]*See* Safe Harbor Privacy Principles, "Choice."

[81]*Standards for Security Categorization of Federal Information and Information Systems,* National Institute of Standards and Technology, Computer Security Division, Federal Information Processing Standards Publication FIPS PUB 199, Feb. 2004, http://csrc.nist.gov/publications/fips/fips199/FIPS-PUB-199-final.pdf; *see also* NIST Categorization Guide.

behavior for workers, management, technology, and processes.[82] They state the organization's objectives, expectations, and measurement requirements. They must be based on a company's operating structure, any regulatory and legal requirements (from industry-specific ones such as GLBA or HIPAA to contractual obligations and EU personal information protections), and the system architecture. They must also be easily integrated into an organization's training regimen.

The term "Privacy Policy" can take on different meanings in different companies. A Privacy Policy may be as simple as a company's Statement of Principles regarding privacy, or it may be so broad as to include an organization's internal privacy policies, procedures, and safeguards as well as include external privacy notices sent to a company's customers or posted on the company's website. The Privacy Policy will often be the public expression of a company's policies, procedures, and commitment to privacy. For the purpose of this section, a Privacy Policy is meant to be the main embodiment of an organization's official, documented internal and external position on customer privacy in support of the overall privacy plan. It is important to note that a company can have many different privacy policies associated with the privacy plan, with each policy supporting a part of the plan and specific information.

1. MAIN POLICY ELEMENTS

a. Internal Policies

The expression of a company's commitment to privacy must start from within. An internal privacy policy, if well communicated and integrated into business operations, establishes a base principle that can be enforced and reinforced and carried virtually throughout the culture of the corporation and employee work habits.

An internal privacy policy should start from the very top of an organization with a strong but succinct Statement of Principles that provides the framework for more specific operating guidelines within a company's departments or business units. Some companies may receive and handle very little information that requires protection, whereas others may be required to collect, handle, or retain extensive levels of PII and sensitive information, corporate confidential and proprietary information, or intellectual property. Depending on the level of information gathered, the Statement of Principles can be tailored to provide the right frame of reference for a company's

---

[82]Rasmussen—Differences Between.

operating environment. It can be the equivalent of the "Ten Commandments" on privacy or a more general organizational philosophy about privacy. In either case, the Statement of Principles creates the framework from which the remaining internal procedures and guidelines can be created and serves as a reference point for creating an external privacy policy. Establishing the level of an organization's commitment to privacy will start with its Statement of Principles.

Once the Statement of Principles has been adopted (whether simply by senior management or perhaps a company's Board of Directors) it can be used to create the internal operational or functional privacy policies needed at various levels of a company. These internal operating privacy policies will support the development of privacy procedures. Internal privacy policies will form the basis of both new employee orientation and training and ongoing privacy compliance and monitoring. The internal operating privacy policies must reflect the actual handling and safeguarding of private information. For years, companies have often included provisions and materials in their employee manuals that have addressed proprietary and confidential company information. These same principles must be expanded and adapted to support the privacy plan and desired goals and objectives.[83]

b. External Privacy Policies

An external privacy statement may take on different forms (and purposes), depending on the mission of an organization or the industry and customer base of a particular company, but it must support the privacy plan and internal privacy policies. Certainly for U.S. financial institutions, the external privacy statement is now a mandated "Privacy Notice" or "Privacy Disclosure" that must conform to the requirements of Gramm-Leach-Bliley and/or HIPAA as well as evolving interpretations and regulations covering the banking and insurance industries and medical provider communities. To a certain extent, the guidelines published by the various bank and insurance regulatory bodies during 2000 and 2001 have aided in the creation of industry-specific privacy notices. Virtually everyone with a U.S. bank account or insurance policy may recall the onslaught of "Privacy Notices" and "Privacy Policies" included in bank statements, insurance policies, and various other mailings from their financial institutions in the spring of 2001 (and ongoing today) announcing the companies' privacy practices.

---

[83]Christopher Sloan, Liberty Mutual Group, Privacy Compliance Practices Working Files, April 2002 (on file with the author).

Privacy Programs: Plans, Policies & Procedures   163

Irrespective of whether an external privacy policy is mandated for specific industry sectors or all customers, it is imperative that it be consistent with internal operations and adhered to. The U.S. Federal Trade Commission has instigated a series of enforcements against companies whose corporate operations were not in compliance with their own external privacy policies.[84] Mandated privacy policies have raised awareness about privacy considerations and, in many instances, served as models for other corporations who voluntarily wanted to issue privacy statements. Certain high-profile news stories about breaches of personal information have also heightened public interest in external privacy policies. One example of this trend may be found online with the growing number of privacy statements, policies, or notices (however termed) now posted on websites, especially those that gather any sort of personal information as part of a consumer transaction or inquiry.

The components of an external privacy notice will obviously differ for each organization, depending on its industry sector, jurisdictions in which it is operating or dealing with customers, its operational requirements, and the extent of protected information that is collected, handled, or retained. As a general guideline these notices should at the very least include:

- A description of the personal information collected by the organization, from websites and third parties;
- A description of how the information is used and a list of parties with whom it may be shared;
- A list of the options available regarding the collection, use, sharing, and distribution of the information;
- A description of how inaccuracies can be corrected;
- A list of the websites that are linked to the organization's site and a disclaimer that the organization is not responsible for the privacy practices of other sites; and
- A description of how the information is safeguarded (both physically and electronically) against loss, misuse, and alteration once it is collected by the organization.[85]

---

[84]*See, e.g.,* "Enforcing Privacy Promises: Section 5 of the FTC Act," Federal Trade Commission, http://www.ftc.gov/privacy/privacyinitiatives/promises.html; "Enforcing Privacy Promises: Enforcement, Federal Trade Commission, http://www.ftc.gov/privacy/privacyinitiatives/promises_enf.html.

[85]"A Matter of Policy: Model Privacy Statement," *CIO,* Apr. 1, 2000 at 198, http://www.cio.com/archive/040100/privacypol.html. Since it is often overlooked by all but the hackers, the information in log files should also be considered.

164   CHAPTER 3

The Federal Trade Commission's website on the Privacy Initiative[86] provides a good starting point for several aspects of external privacy statements, from their necessity in certain cases, to their wording and proper distribution.

c. Practical Tips for Policies

The following is a list of practical tips compiled from various privacy and security experts:

- Obtain senior management support
- Policies should be easy to understand and as brief as possible
- Make it fit: with culture, job function, real operating environment
- Policies must be reasonable and enable the company to meet its business objectives
- Policies must be enforceable
- State what must be done in positive terms (*shall, will, must*); avoid *never*
- Address all forms of information, equipment, and networks
- Have normal policies: make policies fit in with other organizational policies
- State what is to be protected and scope (where within an organization it applies)
- State when the policy takes effect
- List to whom it applies
- State the reason for the policy and who developed it
- State how compliance will be monitored
- State how it will be enforced, who is responsible for enforcement, and what action will be taken for noncompliance
- State any deviations that are allowed
- State when policy is reviewed and who has the authority to revise it
- Indicate the date of last revision and whether there is an archive of policy past to present
- Policies that use the term *electronic* can apply to electronic functions; policies that do not use the term *electronic* can refer to personal information regardless of technology or medium[87]
- Identify points of contact for incidents, suspicious behavior, and anomalies

---

[86]*See* "Privacy Initiatives: Introduction," Federal Trade Commission, http://www.ftc.gov/privacy/index.html.
[87]Harold F. Tipton and Micki Krause, eds., *The Information Security Handbook*, 4th ed., Vol. 2, CRC Press LLC, 2001 at 224, 237 (hereinafter "Tipton and Krause").

Privacy Programs: Plans, Policies & Procedures 165

- Balance level of control with level of productivity
- Make the policy fit the size of the organization
- Make trust a key component of policy
- Cross-reference to the record retention policy.[88]

2. PROCEDURES

Procedures take the policies down to the operational level and explain how the policy is implemented in daily operations. Compliance with policies is largely dependent upon how complete the procedures are and how well they describe or define the tasks to be undertaken to meet the security requirements.[89] For example, procedures for a hospital policy regarding protection of medical information would identify the personnel who should have access to diagnostic records, specify what authentication and authorization process is required, state what physical security is required (for example, do not leave papers open on desk), how the diagnosis information is to be entered and what encryption algorithm is to be used, identify who they are allowed to provide information to, and suggest how to avoid common mistakes, etc.

D. Reviewing and Updating Privacy Plan, Policies, and Procedures

1. REVIEWS

Privacy regulations, requirements, and threats continually evolve. It is critical that regular reviews of privacy plans, policies, and procedures be conducted at least annually. If a particular operational area is one afforded high sensitivity (for example, credit card processing), more frequent reviews may be warranted. In large measure, the frequency of review will depend upon many factors, including

- The nature of the data involved
- The technology involved
- The success or failure of the current privacy plan
- The nature of the industry or mission of the organization
- The frequency of changes to laws and regulations and whether reviews are mandated
- The expansion of the company into other geographic areas where privacy concerns may be greater
- Expectations of the persons whose privacy is being protected.

---

[88]Guel at 3, 9, 11.
[89]Tipton and Krause at 238.

Internal and external audits are another means of reviewing privacy programs and correcting areas of vulnerability and deficiencies.[90] A legal review is also necessary to ensure the privacy program meets any new legal or regulatory requirements for the jurisdictions in which the organization is operating.

Technology upgrades and system architecture configuration changes can significantly affect the privacy plan, especially the functional, computing, and baseline policies and corresponding procedures. Changes in business operations and shifts in management or culture can affect all levels of policy and procedures.

2. CHANGE MANAGEMENT

Privacy continually introduces new dynamics into an organization; however, when change is coupled with technology, organizations must contend with a "dynamic duo." Change management "defines a systematic way to introduce change into a complex system of any kind."[91] As noted by the *Handbook of Information Security Management*, "The most easily sidestepped control is change control."[92] Every organization undergoes changes in business processes, including the following: people decide to perform a task in a different way; information comes into the company in a different format or from a new source; technology upgrades change operating procedures; new laws/regulations impose different compliance requirements; management shifts alter the culture of the organization; and shifts in office locations introduce new privacy considerations. Therefore, every company must have a policy regarding accommodating changes to ensure that the entire privacy program is not upended because of quiet changes that randomly take place without consideration for the entire privacy plan or result in unintended consequences.

For these reasons, privacy plans and policies and procedures should undergo regular review and modification. To manage the changes required, general procedures must be in place for (1) introducing the change, (2) cataloging the change, (3) scheduling the change, (4) implementing the change, and (5) reporting changes to management. For each component of the privacy plan, one person must be assigned to manage changes through the associated policies

---

[90] A fuller discussion of audits appears in Chapter 4.

[91] Mike Chapple, Debra Shinder, and Ed Tittle, *TICSA Certification: Information Security Basics*, Que, 2003, http://www.examcram2.com/title/0789727838.

[92] Micki Krause and Harold Tipton, "Change Management Controls," *Handbook of Information Security Management*, CRC Press LLC, 2001, http://www.cccure.org/Documents/HISM/670-672.html.

and procedures.[93] This is important for creating an audit trail, tracking changes through a documentation procedure to trace back problems, ensuring information confidentiality and integrity, and detecting unauthorized changes.[94] Change control systems should apply to all technical (hardware, software, and network) and operational changes that affect the privacy plan.[95]

Changing policies and procedures raises several legal considerations. Policies that apply to customers, business partners, vendors, and the like may be more difficult to change if it is perceived that the original policy established an implied contract between the company and the affected party.[96] Likewise, changes in office locations and major shifts in business operations can usher in new legal considerations, depending on the jurisdiction involved and whether the operational changes would make the organization subject to laws and regulations not previously considered.

It is always wise to include a provision within the privacy policy stating that the company reserves the right to change the policy at any time and that the policy does not establish any relationship or implied contract between the company and the customer or user. This does not, however, insulate companies that do change their privacy policies from the rage of customers. In March 2002, Yahoo! was in the news regarding two changes to its privacy policy. The first change involved a change in Yahoo!'s privacy policy to allow marketing offers, cold calls, and spam to reach all of Yahoo!'s subscribers. Thus, the change in privacy policy also changed all Yahoo!'s user account preferences. The outcry from subscribers damaged Yahoo!'s reputation in the press.[97] The second change involved a revision to the policy to more clearly note how personal data will be treated in certain circumstances. The new policy stated that Yahoo! would cooperate with law enforcement authorities regarding illegal activity such as fraud, violations of the terms of its service agreement, and the use of its service for potential threats. In part, this change was a response to a new provision in the USA PATRIOT Act and the September 11 terrorist attacks. The change, however, caused privacy and consumer advocates great concern.

---

[93]Rothke, http://www.cccure.org/modules.php?name=Downloads&d_op=viewdown load&cid=45.

[94]Roberta Bragg, "CISSP Security Management and Practices," Dec. 20, 2002 (hereinafter "Bragg").

[95]Id.

[96]See, e.g., David Holtzman, "The privacy imbroglio," News.com, Mar. 21, 2002, http://news.com.com/2010-1075-865409.html.

[97]See, e.g., Michelle Delio, "Yahoo's 'Opt-Out' Angers Users," Wired.com, Apr. 2, 2002, http://www.wired.com/news/privacy/0,1848,51461,00.html; Andrew Orlowski, "Yahoo! Rips! Up! Privacy! Policy!" The Register, Mar. 4, 2002, http://www. theregister.co.uk/content /6/24683.html.

Online Privacy Group's executive director, Will Doherty, noted that the privacy policy change had been a "public relations disaster for Yahoo!"[98]

E. Conclusion

Privacy programs, consisting of privacy plans, policies, and procedures, are multifaceted and require the full horizontal and vertical involvement of an organization. Most corporate assets today are digital, yet many companies have not developed a comprehensive, enterprise-wide privacy program. In addition, they have not linked their privacy program with their security program. The FTC action in the *Lilly* case, as well as subsequent cases, clearly links privacy and security and requires an enterprise-wide approach that dovetails administrative, legal, technical, and physical safeguards. Laws like GLBA and HIPAA have imposed privacy and security requirements on corporate operations, and these requirements are beginning to be emulated in other regulations and looked to by enforcement agencies, such as the FTC.

The development of a privacy plan requires the involvement of the board of directors and senior management, the line managers, and an active cross-organizational team. It also requires the involvement of the staff that handles the data as part of their job responsibilities. It must also take into consideration the culture of the organization. Privacy risk assessments and gap analysis should be performed, where feasible, as attorney work product to help protect this type of sensitive information from being disclosed in litigation. An analysis of an organization's legal requirements (including compliance with laws/regulations, varying jurisdictional requirements, contractual obligations, and the protection of confidential and proprietary information) is necessary to ensure compliance measures and appropriate safeguards are included in the privacy program. Classification of data is an essential step.

Privacy policies (both internal and external) should be well thought out by senior management. They should be high-level, relatively static statements that set the tone for corporate operations, mandate certain behavior, set levels of measurement, and require compliance. Although brief, privacy policies set the framework laid

---

[98]"Yahoo Web Portal Changes Privacy Policy, Opt-In Policy for Unsolicited Advertisements," *Privacy & Security Law Report*, Bureau of National Affairs, Vol. 1, No. 14, Apr. 8, 2002; *see also* Jim Hu, "Yahoo revises privacy policy," *News.com*, Mar. 28, 2003, http://news.com.com/2100-1023-870270.html.

out in the privacy plan. Procedures guide the daily operational steps. Their effectiveness is dependent upon employee acceptance and "buy-in." Thus, employee involvement throughout the organization is essential. An effective change management system is critical.

Regular reviews and updates are an essential component of any privacy program.

CHAPTER ❖ 4

Implementation and Science & Technology

A. Overview

The goal of any privacy program is to *manage risks* associated with the use of information. This includes managing privacy risks, security breaches, insider and unauthorized activities, theft and sabotage, public relations consequences, employee morale, and *avoiding* liabilities, civil and criminal penalties, loss of market share, drop in stock price, and financial loss. The privacy program, consisting of an overall privacy plan and corresponding policies and procedures, should have been developed by addressing the considerations set forth in the preceding chapters of this book, including the type of information to be protected, the legal framework considerations, and best practices, guidance, and relevant standards. A solid privacy plan with well-designed policies and procedures, however, is of little use and affords little risk protection if the policies are not implemented. The privacy program should be viewed as the foundation upon which business operations can base the use of information.

Risks cannot be managed and institutional assets protected if a privacy plan is implemented only through documentation and privacy management software. A privacy program must be brought to life through the people in an organization and seen as the responsibility of all. In particular, privacy must be viewed as an integral part of the responsibility of all levels of line management, rather than as a set of legal or technical requirements emanating from the chief privacy officer or legal counsel. Chapter Three discussed the need for enterprise-wide privacy plans, policies, and procedures that combine

171

172   CHAPTER 4

business operational, legal, and technical considerations. Similarly, implementation of the privacy plan, policies, and procedures requires coverage of all three areas as well.

The U.S. Federal Trade Commission's action against Eli Lilly & Co.[1] (*Lilly*) (discussed extensively in Chapters One and Three) brought global attention to the importance of the implementation step. After an employee mistakenly sent subscriber information on Prozac (a well-know antidepressant) to consumers via a string e-mail instead of a listserv (thereby revealing all 669 subscriber names), the FTC brought an action against Eli Lilly, alleging its privacy practices were unfair and deceptive because Eli Lilly had promised these subscribers privacy and confidentiality, but in fact had disclosed identifying information. Through the *Lilly* case, the agency made it clear it would investigate privacy breaches—even those that were inadvertent-that occurred because of a lack of implementation of commonly accepted privacy practices.

Today, the *Lilly* case clearly shows why companies must do more than develop privacy policies: they must *implement* those policies through corresponding procedures, train their employees, and provide appropriate oversight and assistance to inexperienced employees. A clear point drawn from the *Lilly* case is that privacy policies and procedures need to be embedded with internal checks and controls on the processes. The FTC also required Lilly to establish and maintain a four-stage information privacy and security program that would safeguard consumers' personal information against any reasonably anticipated threats or hazards to its security, confidentiality, or integrity, and to protect such information against unauthorized access, use, or disclosure.[2]

The company was to designate appropriate personnel to coordinate and oversee the program. It had to be ready to identify reasonably foreseeable internal and external risks to the security, confidentiality, and integrity of personal information, including any such risks posed by lack of training, and to address these risks in each relevant area of its operations, whether performed by employees or agents, including (a) management and training of personnel; (b) information systems for the processing, storage, transmission, or disposal of personal information; and (c) prevention and response to attacks, intrusions, unauthorized access, or other information systems failures. The program also had to include an annual written review by qualified persons, within ninety days after the date of service of the

---

[1]*In the Matter of Eli Lilly and Company,* FTC Docket No. C-4047 (2002), http://www.ftc.gov/os/2002/01/lillycmp.pdf.
[2]*Id.* at 7.

order and yearly thereafter, to monitor and document compliance with the program, evaluate the program's effectiveness, and recommend changes to it. The security program was then to be adjusted in light of any findings and recommendations resulting from reviews or ongoing monitoring, and in light of any material changes to Lilly's operations that might affect the program.[3]

Lilly involved the inadvertent disclosure of sensitive information by a company. The FTC action in *In the Matter of Guess?, Inc. and Guess.com*[4] highlighted the "hand-in-glove" relationship between privacy and security. The *Guess?* case involved the disclosure of personal information, including credit card numbers, through a security breach. The FTC, in issuing its complaint, reasoned that this type of security breach was well known and documented and, Guess? had failed to properly safeguard this information and, therefore, had breached its external privacy policy that it used reasonable and appropriate measures to protect its consumers' information.[5] As in *Lilly*, the consent order mandated specific security remedies that would safeguard the information it gathered from its consumers, including bi-annual risk assessments.[6]

The *Microsoft Passport* case was another implementation example. Although there had been no security breach or information disclosure, the FTC alleged that Microsoft failed to employ reasonable and appropriate measures to protect the personal information collected in connection with these services because it failed to (1) implement procedures needed to prevent or detect unauthorized access; (2) monitor the system for potential vulnerabilities; and (3) perform appropriate security audits or investigations. The consent order required Microsoft to implement an information privacy/security program similar to that required under the FTC's Gramm-Leach-Bliley Safeguards Rule.

The *Lilly* case also highlights the role of management in the privacy/security process. Eli Lilly & Co. received some very negative publicity arising out of the case, which was due in part to the fact that

---

[3]*Id.; see also* Alan Charles Raul, Frank R. Volpe, and Edward R. McNicholas, "Eli Lilly—FTC Consent Order Is a Good Road Map for Corporate Data Protection," *Electronic Commerce & Law Report,* Bureau of National Affairs, Vol. 7, No. 6, Feb. 6, 2002; "Eli Lilly's Unintentional Online Disclosure of Consumer Data Leads to FTC Settlement, *Electronic Commerce & Law Report,* Bureau of National Affairs, Vol. 7, No. 4, Jan. 23, 2002.

[4]*In the Matter of Guess?, Inc. and Guess.com,* File No. 022 3260, Docket No. 0223260, http://www.ftc.gov/os/2003/06/guesscmp.pdf.

[5]*Id.*

[6]*In the Matter of Guess?, Inc. and Guess.com,* File No. 022 3260, Agreement Containing Consent Order, http://www.ftc.gov/os/2003/06/guessagree.pdf (consent agreement placed on public record on June 18, 2003).

174   CHAPTER 4

the particular personal information released was very sensitive. Senior executives of an organization should regard privacy and information security as a management responsibility rather than a technical problem. In addition to their fiduciary duty to shareholders and their obligation to safeguard corporate assets, market share, and capitalization, senior management is now faced with Sarbanes-Oxley provisions requiring both management and external auditors to attest to the effectiveness of internal controls. The "internal measures" referenced in the FTC Complaint are easily identifiable with the "internal controls" referenced in Sarbanes-Oxley that require management's assessment and attestation that they are adequate.[7]

Management has the responsibility to promote and ensure a culture that respects and protects privacy. Therefore, top management is responsible for vetting the institutional privacy plan and overseeing its implementation and review. The privacy plan should contain the overall privacy vision and strategy that shapes and directs privacy and security within the organization. The privacy policies are the formal, relatively static, high-level statements that support the privacy plan. The privacy procedures are the individualized steps that are taken in the course of day-to-day operations that implement the security policies and plan.[8]

B. Implementation: What Is Required

The implementation of a privacy program has three clear components: (1) training, (2) compliance, and (3) enforcement. The review/evaluation process that should occur on a regular basis is discussed in Chapter Three on Privacy Plans, Policies, and Procedures.[9] Because this publication is a companion to the *International Guide to Cyber Security*, it will try to parallel the related chapter in that document.

---

[7]Sarbanes-Oxley Act of 2002, Pub. Law 107-204, Sections 302, 404, http://news.findlaw.com/hdocs/docs/gwbush/sarbanesoxley072302.pdf.

[8]Thomas A. Longstaff, James T. Ellis, Shawn V. Hernan, Howard F. Lipson, Robert D. McMillan, Linda Hutz Pesante, and Derek Simmel, "Security of the Internet," *The Froehlich/Kent Encyclopedia of Telecommunications*, Vol. 15, Marcel Dekker, 1997 at 231-55, http://www.cert.org/encyc_article/tocencyc.html (hereinafter "Security of the Internet"). One should beware not to inadvertently put forth the privacy policy as a binding contract (or one that could imply it is a binding contract) between the company and its business partners or the company and its employees. In fact, good privacy policy enforcement is the responsibility of all of the employees of the company.

[9]*In re Eli Lilly and Co.*, Agreement Containing Consent Order, Section II, FTC No. 0123214, Jan 18, 2002, http://www.ftc.gov/os/2002/01/lillyagree.pdf.

1. TRAINING

For a privacy program to be effective, its policies and procedures must be communicated. Personnel cannot be held accountable if they were never aware of what was expected of them. As one noted privacy expert stated:

> An effective information protection program is one that actively and continually communicates policies. A concept promoted by one vendor, is the "Human Firewall." This concept involves ensuring that individuals know what is expected of them and how they are to go about complying with these expectations. The majority of attacks involve an insider to the organization—often naively. Insiders who know how to appropriately manage and protect the information they come in contact with provide the best defense for an organization.[10]

It is essential to understand that privacy is a *people* and a *process* problem in which technology plays only a small part.[11] A recent survey by the Computing Technology Industry Association (CompTIA) revealed that most security breaches are caused by human error and that "80% of respondents believe human error was caused by lack of security knowledge, training or failure to follow security procedures."[12] The objective of IT training and awareness efforts is to ensure that personnel[13] are using technology effectively and are aware of the risks and responsibilities associated with their use of technology. This means training should occur at several levels and be given to various audiences, with differing goals.

Privacy training should consider targeting the following audiences:[14]

- *All employees* should attend privacy awareness and ethics training The basic concept of confidentiality, integrity, and availability of

---

[10]Michael Rasmussen, "Information Protection: Assuring Stakeholder Value in a Digital Age," Giga Information Group, Inc., Special ForSITE Report 2002 at 15.

[11]Michael Rasmussen, "Enterprise Security Architectures—Organizational Pressures on Information Protection," Sept. 24, 2002 at 1 (hereinafter "Rasmussen—Enterprise Security Architectures").

[12]"Committing to Security: A CompTIA Analysis of IT Security and the Workforce," Mar. 2003, http://www.comptia.org/research/files/summaries/securitysummary031703.pdf.

[13]The term "personnel" or "employee" in the context of this discussion is intended to encompass employees, consultants, agents, contractors, temporary personnel, distributors, vendors, business partners, or any other person who has access to and use of information, the system, or the network.

[14]Of course a company should consider its size, its core business, its exposure, and its budget when implementing privacy plans.

information is at the core of this training, and it is essential to creating a security culture. Information security is a part of everyone's job description, from the receptionist to the CEO. An organization may build a technical fortress between itself and the Internet, but if the information is leaking out through individuals who do not understand their obligation in protecting information, then both privacy and security plans have failed.[15] This training may vary, depending upon the operations and specific privacy/security requirements. For example, operations dealing with sensitive information, handling or developing intellectual property, or subject to national security considerations will have a heightened information security awareness versus employees in a general operational area with routine business data. The ethical conduct in the use of Information and Communication Technology (ICTs) and associated privacy practices are an important element of overall information security training.

- *Technical employees* will require training on the use and maintenance of the software and equipment they use in the performance of their responsibilities. This will require an understanding of how the particular technologies fit in with the entire system architecture and the privacy program. For example, training regarding change management is a critical component of technical personnel training. For these employees to adopt a "privacy culture" mentality, they need to understand how their piece of the system fits in the privacy program and learn the specific information security responsibilities expected of them. It is also important that they understand how the technical aspects dovetail with the legal, managerial, and operational aspects of the privacy program.

- *System administrators and Computer Security Incident Response Teams (CSIRTs)* will require specialized training in handling incidents, avoiding pretext scenarios, analyzing events, improving security, and—two critical areas—disaster recovery and business continuity. Giga Information Group estimates that only one out of four intrusion detection deployments are even remotely successful. The high rate of failure is due to organizations focusing on products as opposed to the process behind them. Technology alone does not solve the incident response problem; it is a process that requires people, policies, and education along with

---

[15]Michael Rasmussen, "Common Mistakes in Information Security," June 14, 2002 at 1 (hereinafter "Rasmussen—Common Mistakes").

technology.[16] The integrity of the privacy program is directly linked to an organization's capability to detect and respond to intrusion detections and to maintain the desired privacy in emergency situations requiring disaster recovery or business contingency/continuity response capabilities.

- *Boards and senior-level management* need to understand not only the corporate privacy obligations, but how to be "privacy smart" in their own company. This includes understanding their role in setting policies and exercising oversight of the privacy and security programs. They also need periodic briefings on new developments (legal, organizational, and technical) that will affect their operations and business plan. Senior management must have training regarding how to handle the data they require for their jobs and how to protect sensitive corporate data that is at risk through personal digital assistants (PDAs), laptops, cell phones, and other wireless devices.

- *Line and middle-level managers* need training regarding their responsibilities in creating a privacy culture and ensuring the privacy program is implemented and complied with. They need to understand their role in implementing the program, including monitoring compliance and handling enforcement issues. This includes understanding the data classification process and the specific privacy controls on information in their area of responsibility. Like senior management, they also require training regarding (1) how to securely and appropriately use the technology they require for their jobs, such as personal device assistants (PDAs), laptops, cell phones, and other wireless devices, and (2) periodic briefings on new developments (legal, organizational, and technical) that will affect their operations and business plan.

- *Operational personnel* require additional training regarding the privacy policies and procedures that apply to their responsibilities. They need to understand the privacy plan and how the work they do on a daily basis is part of the privacy and security culture and important to the operations of the company overall. Users should be aware of information security threats and the correct use of IT facilities to minimize security risks, the specific privacy responsibilities they have, and how to handle anomalies, suspicious incidents, or suspected wrongdoing.

---

[16]Rasmussen—Common Mistakes at 1. For information on education and training of Computer Security Incident Response Teams (CSIRTs), *see* http://www.cert.org/csirts/more.html; for guidance on best practices in handling security incidents *see* Tim Grance, Karen Kent, and Brian Kim, *Computer Security Incident Handling Guide*, National Institute of Standards and Technology, Special Publication 800-61, Jan. 2004, http://csrc.nist.gov/publications/nistpubs/.

178   CHAPTER 4

In the interest of managing human resources, a motivated and competent workforce is a key objective. The underlying premise is that a key resource in ICT operations is people. Training and awareness are critical to the development and maintenance of this key resource, but so are flexibility and an appreciation for the corporate culture.

A comprehensive training plan will accommodate new training technologies and methods and the development of a knowledge base. It will invite feedback and input as an important driver in the development and maintenance of the overall security program. Training requirements should be developed and maintained continuously. Training alternatives should also be investigated, such as internal or external location, in-house trainers or third-party trainers, etc. To fulfill specific needs, trainers should be retained and training sessions organized. A skills inventory should be maintained and personnel productivity should be tracked.

A written policy should state that employees will be provided with orientation upon hiring and ongoing training to maintain their knowledge, skills, abilities, and privacy/security awareness to the level required to perform effectively. The objective of training and awareness programs is to raise the technical and management skill levels of personnel and to ensure compliance with the privacy program. The policy should be reviewed regularly along with the privacy and security programs in place.

Change management also plays an important role in training. Organizations and technologies evolve, and the threats to an organization's information assets change rapidly. Training and awareness programs should change with the circumstances of the organization and changing threats. Some of the changes that may affect training and education include legislative and regulatory changes, technology upgrades, changes in business operations and system architecture, and changes in contractual restrictions and obligations. It is imperative that as these elements are worked into the security program, the training is changed to accommodate them, and that such changes are implemented under a controlled change management process.

A maturity model for training and awareness is included in the CobiT standard,[17] which indicates an organization's level of

---

[17]See CobiT, *Control Objectives*, 3rd ed., July 2000, "Delivery and Support—Education and Training" (DS7), "Planning & Organization—Manage Human Resources" (PO7), "IT Governance Management Guideline," http://www.usmd.edu/Leadership/USMOffice/AdminFinance/IAO/is/cobit-management-guidelines.pdf; CobiT, *Management Guidelines*, 3rd ed., July 2000, http://www.isaca.org/cobit.htm; *see also* ISO/IEC 17799:2000, "Information Technology—Code of Practice for Information Security Management."

achievement from "nonexistent" to "optimized." In an "optimized" organization, training and awareness efforts result in an improvement of individual performance. They are fully integrated into employee career paths, and sufficient budgets, resources, facilities, and instructors are provided for training and education programs. There is continuous improvement in business processes taking advantage of best external practices and maturity modeling with other organizations. Problems are resolved with root-cause analysis, and organization response is efficient and fast. Employees have a positive attitude toward ethical conduct and system security principles. Automated tools and other education technologies are used extensively and integrated into training and education programs. External trainers are used as needed.

Key Performance Indicators (KPI) can be used to measure the performance of training and awareness programs and to assess the achievement of goals. Such indicators may include the percentage of employees trained, the age of employee training curricula, the time lag between identification of training need and the delivery of the training, the number of training alternatives available to employees from in-house and third-party sources, the percentage of employees trained in ethical conduct requirements and security practices, and the number of identified employee ethical violations and security incidents related to employees.

Critical success factors (CSFs) have been identified to facilitate the achievement of objectives. The factors are:

- The existence of a comprehensive education and awareness program focused on individual and corporate needs;
- Education and awareness programs that are supported by budgets, resources, facilities, and trainers;
- Training and awareness are considered critical components of the employee career path;
- Employees and managers identify and document training needs;
- Needed training is provided in a timely manner;
- Senior management support the performance of staff functions in an ethical and secure manner;
- There is management acceptance that training costs are investments in lowering the total costs of technology ownership;
- Corporate policy requires that all employees receive a basic training program covering ethical conduct, privacy practices, and permitted use of IT resources; and
- Employees receive training in privacy practices and the availability, confidentiality, and integrity of information.

180   CHAPTER 4

2. MONITORING

It is important to ensure privacy policies and procedures are being complied with and that there is a process in place to enforce the policy. Personnel may be held responsible for complying with the organization's privacy policy. This responsibility can only result, however, if they are given orientation training followed by subsequent training and awareness campaigns. The organization's personnel cannot be held responsible for their actions unless it can be demonstrated that they were aware of the policy before any enforcement attempts. As the *Lilly* case demonstrates, simply drafting policies and putting them in a manual or exposing people to a policy is not sufficient. Thorough training coupled with performance metrics is the best way to demonstrate that people are truly aware of the policies and procedures associated with their responsibilities or use of technology.

Increasingly, organizations are turning to electronic policies that require the user of a computer to take specific steps. Personnel are shown a "pop-up" screen and are required to affirmatively click an acknowledgment of the policy and agree to its terms before access to information, applications, or networks. While not feasible for all policies, use of such technology ensures employee awareness regarding those activities that are associated with high risk, liabilities, or penalties, such as Internet usage, e-mail policies, and access to protected information. All statements in a privacy policy should also be documented in a central resource manual or handbook. It may be appropriate to follow training on specific policies with formal testing. As organizational policies change, the changes should be communicated to employees. Therefore, education and testing should be updated frequently. Classes and testing are recommended at a frequency of at least three times per year.[18]

Employee monitoring of ICT usage is one of the easiest ways to monitor compliance with privacy/security policies and procedures, but it is an area increasingly fraught with legal liability. At the outset, there are wide inconsistencies in the global legal framework in this area. Under U.S. law (and in most developing countries),[19] private sector employees are afforded virtually no expectation of privacy in the

---

[18]Dale McNulty, "Management's Role in Information Security—The 7 Top Mistakes," Nov. 4, 2002, www.surrex.com/changing_it_landscape/2002_11_04.html.
[19]"Workplace Privacy," Electronic Privacy Information Center, http://www.epic.org/privacy/workplace/.

workplace[20] and are not protected by a constitutional right to privacy.[21] A few states have laws protecting privacy in the workplace; however, a notice to employees that there is no expectation of privacy often removes their effect.[22] According to a review of case law by the U.S. General Accounting Office (GAO), "Courts have consistently held, however, that privacy rights in such communications do not extend to employees using company-owned computer systems, even in situations where employees have password-protected accounts."[23] Public sector employees, however, are afforded the Constitutional right to privacy.[24] The Tenth Circuit Court of Appeals has found government employees' expectation to privacy to depend on "whether the claim to privacy from government intrusion is reasonable in light of all the surrounding circumstances."[25] Following this line, a Kansas U.S. District Court recently found that a Kansas state government staff attorney had a reasonable expectation to privacy of private files

---

[20]*See, e.g.*, Patti Waldmeir, "US employees find no right to privacy in cyberspace," *The Financial Times,* Aug. 13, 2001 at 12; Allison R. Michael and Scott M. Lidman, "Monitoring of Employees Still Growing: Employers Seek Greater Productivity and Avoidance of Harassment Liability; Most Workers Have Lost on Privacy Claims," *The National Law Journal,* Jan. 29, 2001 at B9, B15, B17-18. Some U.S. state constitutions do contain express protections of privacy; however, this does not guarantee a right to privacy. *See, e.g.,* "Computer Use Policy, Widespread Monitoring Doom Claim of Privacy in Company Computer," *Electronic Commerce & Law Report,* Bureau of National Affairs, Vol. 7, No. 10, Mar. 6, 2002 at 217 (hereinafter "Computer Use Policy").

[21]Cheryl Blackwell Bryson and Michelle Day, "Workplace Surveillance Poses Legal, Ethical Issues," *The National Law Journal,* Jan. 11, 1999 at B8 (hereinafter "Workplace Surveillance").

[22]A small number of states have statutes that may restrict monitoring of employees. The strength of these protections varies. For example, Connecticut's statute essentially prohibits bosses from operating "any electronic surveillance device or system, including but not limited to the recording of sound or voice or a closed circuit television system, or any combination thereof, for the purpose of recording or monitoring the activities of his employees in areas designed for the health or personal comfort of the employees or for safeguarding of their possessions, such as rest rooms, locker rooms or lounges." *See* Connecticut General Statutes Annotated Section 31-48b (2003). Delaware laws, by contrast, are largely limited to requiring employers to provide "an electronic notice of such monitoring or intercepting policies or activities to the employee." *See* Delaware Code Title XIX, Section 705 (2003).

[23]*Employee Privacy: Computer-Use Monitoring Practices and Policies of Selected Companies,* Report to the Ranking Minority Member, Subcommittee on 21st Century Competitiveness, Committee on Education and the Workforce, U.S. House of Representatives, GAO-020717, Sept. 2002 at 6, http://www.gao.gov/new.items/d02717.pdf.

[24]"Workplace Privacy," Electronic Privacy Information Center, http://www.epic.org/privacy/workplace/.

[25]*United States vs. Angevine,* 281 F.3d 1130 (10th Cir. 2001).

contained on his workplace computer despite a policy to the contrary.[26] U.S. common law tort theories also provide employees with remedies for invasion of privacy.[27] Although the U.S. Congress considered legislation in 1999 to require employers to give employees notice of electronic monitoring, the bill stalled and was dropped.[28]

The European Union, however, affords much greater privacy to both information and employees in the workplace due to its comprehensive data protection laws,[29] and the EU approach is starting to be followed globally.[30] *Thus, companies should take care to ensure that their employee monitoring policy is in compliance with all jurisdictions where they have employees.*

Employee monitoring can take the form of Internet monitoring and filtering, e-mail monitoring, instant message monitoring, telephone monitoring, location monitoring, and keystroke logging.[31] In the United States, the Electronic Communications Privacy Act of 1996[32] is the only federal law that provides employee communications privacy protections in the workplace. Although the ECPA does allow employee monitoring for business purposes,[33] such as telephone calls and e-mail, employers may not listen in on purely personal calls. An employer may intercept communications if there is actual or implied consent. If the employer gives notice of monitoring, however, courts have found this equal to consent from the employee.[34]

---

[26]*Haynes v. Kline,* D. Kan., No. 03-42-9-RDR, Dec. 23, 2003; *see* "Computer Policy Did Not Dispel Employee's Expectation of Privacy in State Employment," *Privacy & Security Law Report,* Bureau of National Affairs, Vol. 3, No. 6, Feb. 9, 2004 at 144-45.
[27]Workplace Surveillance at B8.
[28]Philip L. Gordon, "Federal Judge's Victory Just the First Shot in the Battle Over Workplace Monitoring," Sept. 20, 2001, http://www.privacyfoundation.org/workplace/law/law_show.asp?ed=75&action=0.
[29]"Workplace Privacy," Electronic Privacy Information Center, http://www.epic.org/privacy/workplace/; *see also,* Ellen Temperton and Ana-Marie Norbury, "Workplace Monitoring Standards in Europe," *Privacy & Security Law Report,* Bureau of National Affairs, Vol. 3, No. 7, Feb. 16, 2004 at 190-91.
[30]"As Data Privacy Laws Evolve Globally Many Nations Consider European Model," *Privacy & Security Law Report,* Bureau of National Affairs, Vol. 2, No. 16, Apr. 21, 2003 at 425-28; "European Data Protection Law Seen as Spilling into Latin America," *Privacy & Security Law Report,* Bureau of National Affairs, Vol. 2, No. 16, Apr. 21, 2003 at 428-30.
[31]"Workplace Privacy," Electronic Privacy Information Center, http://www.epic.org/privacy/workplace/; *see also* "Privacy Rights Clearinghouse," Consumer//www.consumeraction.org/English/library/privacy_rights/1996_FS07_EmployeeMonitoring. php.
[32]*Electronic Communications Privacy Act,* 18 U.S.C. 2701 *et seq.,* http://www4.law.cornell.edu/uscode/18/2701.html.
[33]Electronic Communications Privacy Act, 18 U.S.C. Section 2510(5)(a)(i).
[34]"Workplace Privacy," Electronic Privacy Information Center, http://www.epic.org/privacy/workplace/; *see also* "Employee Monitoring: Is There Privacy in the Workplace?" Privacy Rights Clearinghouse, Sept. 2002, http://www.privacyrights.org/fs/fs7-work.htm.

Implementation and Science & Technology   183

According to the American Management Association, in 2001, 75 percent of major U.S. firms monitored, recorded, and reviewed employee communications by telephone, e-mail, Internet, and computer files to (1) demonstrate compliance with regulations, (2) demonstrate due diligence, (3) reduce potential workplace liabilities, (4) conduct performance reviews, (5) make productivity measures, and (6) protect trade secrets and confidential information.[35] The U.S. General Accounting Office (GAO) recently conducted a review of research and literature, consulted with privacy experts, and interviewed officials from fourteen Fortune 1,000 companies to determine the extent of employee monitoring by a diverse group of U.S. companies. All fourteen companies stored employees' electronic transactions, information on Internet sites visited, and computer file activity.

Some issues to consider when developing and implementing an employee monitoring policy include the following:

1. **Reserve the right to review and monitor employee communications.** Employers can (inadvertently or otherwise) create a reasonable expectation of privacy with respect to certain employee communications if such privacy is promised or implied in applicable corporate policies or guidelines. Such an expectation could serve as the foundation of an invasion of privacy claim if the expectation is breached through monitoring activities.

   Employees should be notified in writing (that is, as part of the employee handbook, which might also include an acknowledgment form to be signed and returned by the employee) that the employer will treat all messages sent, received, or stored in the e-mail system as nonpersonal business correspondence, which the company is entitled to review, monitor, and disclose. The company should expressly notify employees that if they make use of the e-mail system to transmit personal messages, such messages will not be treated differently from other messages, and will be subject to the same monitoring policies.

   The policy should state explicitly that employees should not use company e-mail to send or to receive any messages that they wish to remain private. Employers should notify employees that even though their files may be protected by passwords, such passwords do not prevent system administrators and other

---

[35]Computer Use Policy at 217; *see also* "Electronic Surveillance in the Workplace," *USA Today*, Oct. 18, 2001, http://www.usatoday.com/tech/columnist/2001/10/18/sinrod.htm.

184   CHAPTER 4

authorized employees from accessing messages for business purposes. Furthermore, employers may want to restrict the individual use of nonsanctioned cryptographic tools by employees, as such steganography or other tools that could subvert the effectiveness of monitoring policies.

2. **Limit the use of company property to business purposes only.** Employees should be notified that all company-owned technology, including hardware, e-mail, and Internet access, is provided by the company to assist employees in advancing the business interests of the company. Organizations may want to consider explicitly stating that use of company property (including e-mail, telephones, and Internet access) for personal use is in violation of company policy and will subject the offending employee to disciplinary action. If employers allow employees to designate certain messages as personal, private, or personal/confidential, then they should indicate that such messages are also subject to the same monitoring policy. Failing to do so may create a protected privacy interest in those communications and lead to liability if they are monitored, intentionally or inadvertently.

3. **Include notice and consent language.** Include in the policy language a statement that makes it clear that by using the company's systems, the employee acknowledges he or she is aware of and consents to be covered by the policy. In addition, make clear that by using the e-mail system, the employee expressly consents to the company's review and monitoring of e-mail messages as outlined in the policy.[36]

3. COMPLIANCE AND AUDITS

a. Compliance

Compliance with privacy policies and procedures—and therefore the privacy plan—requires an examination of both (1) the technical architecture and how the system is functioning and (2) the business processes and how the information is being accessed, handled, stored, and disseminated by personnel. For example, it is quite common for security professionals to find unauthorized modems and applications on systems and data critical to operations stored on hard drives instead of a server. Unauthorized modems provide an unauthorized

---

[36]Kathleen M. Porter, David Wilson, and Jacqueline Scheib, "Work Station or purgatory? Steps Toward a Company Policy on E-Mail and Using the Net," *Business Law Today*, July/Aug. 2002 at 59-62.

"window" into the system, thereby jeopardizing the security of the information held by the company. Data stored on hard drives are not subject to the information backups and privacy protections that are built into the system architecture. In essence, such data "bypass" the privacy plan. It is also common to observe personnel taking "short cuts" in the performance of their jobs that have unintended consequences. Privacy plans are developed by a cross-organizational team based upon a myriad of considerations. They must be observed and complied with until they are changed through the agreed-upon process.

To validate that an information protection program is working according to adopted standards and governing regulations, it is necessary to measure compliance with those standards on a consistent basis. With increasing legal, insurance, and regulatory pressures, validating ongoing compliance will become a regular process for many organizations. Organizations will have to prove to others that their information is secure. To manage this process, organizations need to adopt processes, technologies, and services that will regularly measure the compliance of the privacy program.[37]

The ability to prove a level of diligence in security within an organization will be measured by validating compliance to standards[38] and regulations. Consider the following:

- If an organization desires a cyber insurance policy, validating compliance with information protection standards is used to measure premiums.
- In a civil litigation case, where a system was compromised and used to attack another party, the ability to show that standards were adopted and applied consistently to protect information can assist in validating due diligence or a standard of care.
- For the organization looking to attract investors, proving compliance with industry or regulatory standards (such as in the health industry) goes a long way in ensuring future stakeholder value in our digital age.
- To illustrate to business partners that the organization is effectively managing security, demonstrating adherence to

---

[37]Michael Rasmussen, "Creating a Road Map for an Information Protection Program," June 25, 2002 (hereinafter "Rasmussen—Road Map").

[38]The defining standard for the architecture of an information protection program is the ISO 17799 standard, which is under revision in 2003. Other standards and methodologies can be used in conjunction with or independently of ISO 17700, such as CobiT, OCTAVE, and AICPA SysTrust. Other technical standards and baselines are available from NIST, SANS, CASPR, and Internet Security Alliance. Rasmussen—Enterprise Security Architectures at 5.

privacy and security standards can give business partners an increased level of confidence.[39]

Organizations have two countervailing means by which to measure compliance with the privacy plan and laws/regulations: internal and external audits. While some organizations will manage and certify themselves as compliant internally, others look for external validation. Either way, it starts with internal compliance efforts. A well-documented information protection program that conducts self-audits and responds to gaps in compliance will have a much easier time getting external validation of its security program.[40]

b. Annual Audit

Internal audits play a key role in information privacy and security. They provide an independent measure of risk, an analysis of the competence of internal controls, and an examination of the level of compliance with standards and laws.[41] The mission of a privacy audit is to evaluate the adequacy and effectiveness of the privacy controls and checks built into the system, while proactively working with management to identify new risks and develop strategies for addressing those risks.[42] Moreover, audits can be multifaceted; for example, they can be designed to look at the security of particular data sets, or to assess the adequacy of training programs, or determine whether intrusion detection and access controls are actually effective. These are just some examples of the types and scope of audits that can be used to enhance baseline information security.

Frequency

Entities should conduct these internal audits regularly so that system enhancements do not compromise security once secure systems are installed.[43] The initial design of the network may be entirely secure, but it is likely that over time certain deficiencies and security gaps will

---

[39]Rasmussen—Enterprise Security Architectures at 5.

[40]*Id.*

[41]"Comments Regarding the President's Critical Infrastructure Protection Board's Exposure Draft of *The National Strategy to Secure Cyberspace*," Letter to Richard A. Clarke, President's Critical Infrastructure Board, from Barbara Hafer, President, National Association of State Auditors, Comptrollers and Treasurers, Nov. 18, 2002 at 1, http://www.nasact.org/techupdates/downloads/CRC/LOC/11_02-Cyberspace.pdf (hereinafter "NASACT Comments").

[42]Allan R. Paliotta, "A Personal View of a World Class IT Auditing Function," Information Systems Audit and Control Association, *InfoBytes*, June 1999 at 1, http://isaca.org/art11.htm (hereinafter "Paliotta").

[43]NASACT Comments at 1.

emerge as a result of underlying system enhancements, architecture modifications, or security requirement changes. Therefore, networks are not secure without regular, periodic audits.[44]

The frequency and extent of internal audits should be determined by simple common sense: the higher the risk and value of a system, the more frequently it should be audited. The National Association of State Auditors, Comptrollers and Treasurers (NASACT) recommends that an entity should assess risks at least annually and then develop an audit plan based on that assessment.[45] In many instances, critical systems can be built with automated audit and compliance systems that allow for immediate notification of any deviation from a standard or accepted practice. Where feasible, automated compliance procedures should be considered.

Method

As noted above, automated assessment tools can be a great help in conducting ongoing privacy assessments and remedial efforts. The President's *National Strategy to Secure Cyberspace* recommends the expanded use of such tools as a means for verifying the effectiveness of security controls and for providing a continuous understanding of the current risks to systems.[46] Because of the linkage between privacy and security, this is equally applicable in the privacy context.

However, it is also essential for companies to conduct an annual privacy audit with trained privacy and security staff.[47] This is true even when companies employ automated assessment tools and application services. While automated tools can assess processes, best practices, physical security, and other components of an entity's overall privacy program, an overall assessment can involve additional issues that require the involvement of appropriate, skilled personnel to fully assess the entire privacy process within an enterprise.[48]

Scope

In particular, companies and local governments often overlook the personnel aspects of security in an internal audit.[49] The first and most

---

[44]Sayana, "Benefits of IS Audit," at 1, http://isaca.org/ (hereinafter "Sayana").

[45]NASACT Comments at 1.

[46]*The National Strategy to Secure Cyberspace,* Feb. 14, 2003 at xi, http://www.dhs.gov/interweb/assetlibrary/National_Cyberspace_Strategy.pdf (hereinafter "U.S. National Cyberspace Strategy").

[47]Deborah Radcliff, "The Annual Checkup," *ComputerWorld,* Sept. 9, 2002, http://www.computerworld.com/printthis/2002/0,4814,73993,00.html (hereinafter "Radcliff").

[48]*Id.*

[49]NASACT Comments at 1.

important determination is whether the entity has established responsibility and accountability for the security of the information assets.[50] Another component of this personnel aspect is the need for security clearances and background checks for people in sensitive positions.[51]

The auditing staff should consider the following factors as components of an internal audit program:

- Existence of physical and cyber privacy policies
- Accountability for the enforcement of the policy
- Robust risk assessment processes, especially for key assets
- Account management and access control policy compliance
- Authentication
- Change management
- Session controls
- Network security policies
- Internet access policies
- Cryptographic technologies for transmission and storage
- Remote network access policies
- Clear system administration processes and procedures
- Incident response and reporting
- Auditing
- Viruses and malware prevention and mitigation capabilities
- Backups
- Maintenance
- Information identification and management
- Media sanitizing and disposal
- Physical security
- Training and awareness[52]
- Compliance with applicable standards and laws[53]
- Business Continuity and Emergency Management.[54]

c. Internal and external audits

External Audits

External audits provide a good check and balance of the strengths and weaknesses of the privacy program. For example, companies are

---

[50] Paliotta at 1.
[51] NASACT Comments at 1.
[52] Radcliff.
[53] NASACT Comments at 1.
[54] Paliotta at 1.

constantly striving to increase efficiencies and reduce costs. Often this means re-engineering processes to reduce the human work force and increase automation. The remaining people manage larger workloads. An external auditor can effectively assess the information systems controls that have replaced the human controls.[55] However, involvement of external auditors creates additional privacy risks that must be considered.

External auditors need to build a relationship with the internal cross-organizational privacy team. The external auditors have an educational role so that internal staff are able to properly assess and control information security risks when the organization decides to implement new technology or make changes in the operational processes.[56] However, engaging an outside auditor requires the chief privacy and security officers to be completely confident in the information security capabilities of the external auditor. Thus, it is important to ensure that an "audit of the auditor" has been completed so as to protect the confidential and potentially critical nature of information that will be used, stored, and maintained within the systems of the auditor. Documented security breaches can create roadmaps for malevolent actors, and thus it is critical to ensure that the output of any audit, but specifically the output generated by an external auditor, is maintained in a secure environment. These security enhancements should also be discussed and considered if government authorities engage an entity in discussions regarding an external audit. While compliance with a government-mandated audit is a necessary part of doing business, it is important for a company to be able to certify that its sensitive network and digital information is protected, even when provided to government authorities.

Internal Audits

For internal auditing, NASACT recommends stressing routine exercises.[57] According to NASACT, these exercises are extremely important for three reasons:

- Emphasizing the importance of effective controls
- Ensuring the establishment of priorities
- Making certain trained personnel are in place to deal with privacy and security incidents of varying levels of severity.

---

[55]Sayana.
[56]Paliotta at 1.
[57]NASACT Comments at 1.

An important consideration for internal auditing is that the auditing staff must constantly work to keep itself informed of the latest technologies, best practices, and developments in the legal framework, emerging standards, and privacy issues. Because privacy and security are constantly evolving subjects, periodic staff training is absolutely necessary.[58]

Reporting Requirements (Internal, External, Legal)

Documentation of a privacy audit provides a record of the auditing work performed and outlines the evidence that supports the auditor's findings, recommendations, and conclusions.[59] The Information Systems Audit and Control Association (ISACA) lists several potential uses for such documentation:

- To show what measures the auditor has employed
- To assist with planning, performance, and review of audits
- To facilitate third-party review, if necessary
- To evaluate the auditor's quality assurance program
- To provide support in case of insurance claims, fraud cases, and lawsuits
- To assist with professional development of staff.[60]

Application Audits

An effective cyber security auditor will audit each application to ensure that the application is secure.[61] Given that applications often are products licensed from software vendors, there often are vulnerabilities that are beyond the organization's control. This task contains four main components:

- Provide input to make certain that the application is consistent with all business policies
- Enforce the policies though preventative controls
- Point out departure from the policies in reports
- Recommend complementary business procedures around the application.[62]

Accordingly, when implementing an application audit policy, the auditor must not only consider the "key components" listed above, but

---

[58]Paliotta at 1.

[59]"Audit Documentation," Information Systems Audit and Control Association, IS Auditing Guideline, May 1, 1999, http://www.isaca.org/standard/guide12.pdf.

[60]Id.

[61]Sayana.

[62]Id.

Implementation and Science & Technology   191

must also take into consideration the application's life cycle and management of security issues related to the product itself.

Replacement Controls

External auditors can evaluate the information systems controls that replace the human controls. The auditor should counsel the entity about the adequacy and efficacy of such replacement or automated controls.[63]

Privacy Policy

Another reporting function of auditors is to certify that an up-to-date privacy policy is maintained and to verify compliance with the policy.[64] In the audit report, the auditor should

- Note the level of compliance with the policy
- Offer suggestions to improve compliance
- Suggest updates to the policy
- Note systems or situations not adequately addressed in the policy and offer guidance.[65]

Format

While computer auditing processes continue to evolve, inconsistencies exist regarding format and content of audits at this time. However, ISACA gives helpful suggestions as to the format of audit documentation. According to ISACA, the report should contain a record of

- The planning and preparation of the audit scope and objectives
- The audit program
- The audit steps performed and evidence gathered
- The audit findings, conclusions, and recommendations
- A supervisory review.[66]

Awareness

A successful auditor also uses the audit report as a means of increasing privacy awareness among IT users, corporate boards, corporate management, and system administrators.[67] A lack of such awareness is

---

[63] *Id.*
[64] *Id.*
[65] *Id.*
[66] Information Systems Audit and Control Association, "Audit Documentation," IS Auditing Guideline, May 1, 1999, http://www.isaca.org/standard/guide12.pdf.
[67] Sayana; U.S. National Cyberspace Strategy at xi.

the root cause of many cyber vulnerabilities.[68] Privacy and security awareness helps to deter information security breaches and motivates security officers and systems administrators to perform at a higher level.[69] Increased awareness can also sensitize corporate executives to the importance of reporting cybercrimes. Repeated prosecution of hackers or insider wrongdoing will ultimately increase awareness about the penalties associated with computer crime and serve as a deterrent, which ultimately benefits corporate entities.

It is also important to increase awareness because new technology brings risks as well as rewards.[70] Management needs to be aware that new technology often has inherent vulnerabilities or incompatibilities with existing technologies. A successful awareness or "post-audit briefing" will assist executives in avoiding technologies that will put the organization in an unacceptable cyber security risk position or be more amenable to rigorous security testing or processes that address new technology vulnerabilities or incompatibilities. If an aware management does decide to implement new technology, a strong "awareness" initiative will ensure that proper controls are in place to handle information security issues.[71]

Strategic Objectives

Auditors can also add value to their services by adding a strategic element to the information in their reports. The best auditors ensure information security and controls while staying focused on business objectives.[72]

Use of Attorney-Client Privilege and Work Product in Audits

i. Work Product Privilege

Attorneys play an important role in advising clients about their audits. The attorney work product privilege *may* provide some degree of protection from disclosure of certain audit information, when specific conditions are met.[73] Generally, the attorney work product

---

[68]U.S. National Cyberspace Strategy at xi.

[69]Sayana.

[70]Paliotta at 1.

[71]*Id.*

[72]Sayana.

[73]Attorney work product privilege may also apply to risk assessments and vulnerability testing. Corporate counsel should note that, as corporate employees, their work might be discoverable and these privileges do not apply to them in the same manner as they would to outside counsel, if at all.

privilege established in *Hickman v. Taylor*[74] protects from disclosure materials prepared by attorneys "in anticipation of litigation." Such work product includes an attorney's thoughts, litigation plan or strategy, evaluation of facts and evidence, and legal theories relevant to his client's case.[75] However, a significant limitation is placed on this privilege: the work product must be prepared in anticipation of or during litigation.[76] In other words, "at the very least, some articulable claim, likely to lead to litigation, must have arisen."[77]

The work product privilege may not provide blanket protection for internal audit reports. In *Coastal States Gas Corporation*, the court found "[t]o argue that every audit is potentially the subject of litigation is to go too far" and that "the documents must at least have been prepared with a specific claim supported by concrete facts which would likely lead to litigation in mind . . . ."[78] Even under the broad test established by the court in *Kent Corp. v. NLRB*,[79] where the court found reports were protected under the work product privilege notwithstanding that they were prepared before it was determined that a charge had substance, the Fifth Circuit found there had been some previous claims making the prospect of litigation more likely and the privilege justifiable. These limitations must be kept in mind by counsel when audit information is concerned.

ii. Attorney-Client Privilege

Generally, the attorney-client privilege, established in *Upjohn Co. v. United States*,[80] protects confidential communication between attorneys and their clients where the client is seeking legal advice.[81] Importantly, the protection of the privilege extends only to confidential

---

[74]*Hickman v. Taylor*, 329 U.S. 495 (1947) (codified as Federal Rules of Civil Procedure Rule 26(b)(3)).

[75]*Id.* at 510.

[76]*Coastal States Gas Corp. v. Dept. of Energy*, 199 U.S. App. D.C. 272; 617 F.2d 854, 864 (1980) (hereinafter "Coastal States"). State law, however, may differ on this rule. For example, under California Civil Procedure Code 2018, there is not mention of the "anticipation of litigation" requirement, and California courts have ruled according to this statute that the privilege also applies to the work product of an attorney when he acts as counselor in a nonlitigation capacity. *See Casualty & Surety Co. v. Superior Ct*, 153 Cal. App. 3d 467, 478-479 (1984); *Rumac, Inc. v. Bottomley*, 143 Cal. App. 3d 810, 815-16 (1983).

[77]Coastal States at 864.

[78]*Id.* at 864.

[79]*Kent Corp. v. NLRB*, 530 F.2d 612 (1976).

[80]*Upjohn Co. v. United States*, 449 U.S 383 (1981).

[81]*Id.* at 389.

communications and not objective facts.[82] Furthermore, the privilege is not limited only to communications made in anticipation of litigation or a specific dispute; rather it extends to all circumstances in which an attorney's advice is sought on a legal matter.[83] A fundamental prerequisite to the assertion of the privilege, however, is confidentiality both at the time of the communication and maintained since.[84]

With respect to audit reports, the attorney-client privilege may not provide a blanket protection from disclosure. In *Coastal States Gas Corporation*, the plaintiff sought memoranda from the Department of Energy's legal counsel to the agency's auditor regarding unpublished interpretations of the agency's regulations. The court noted, "[r]ather than 'counseling,' intended to assist the agency in protecting its interest, the memoranda seem to be neutral, objective of agency regulations."[85] The burden is on the client to demonstrate that confidentiality is expected and that the information is such that is it necessary to protect it from disclosure.

4. ENFORCEMENT AND REPORTING

Enforcement is the next logical step to follow training, monitoring, and compliance. Policies and procedures are often drafted and implemented without thought to enforcement. Enforcement of privacy policies and procedures is critical. Policies that have no consequences for violations will not be followed by personnel and may introduce liability concerns, since they can set an obligation of due diligence for the organization to live by.[86] In fact, "organizations that adopt policies but never implement nor enforce them may find these same policies to be a liability."[87]

Consequences for breach of privacy policies and procedures need to be well thought out beforehand. This can range from a conversation with the person who violated the policy to termination and even to instigating charges against the person. It does not make sense for an organization to develop an information protection program, prepare and communicate policies, and deploy security technologies if privacy and security violations are ignored. Moreover, if an organization continually ignores violations, it is difficult for that organization to respond to a future

---

[82]*Id.* at 395 (discussing that a client cannot be forced to answer "What did you say or write to the attorney?" but may be required to disclose any relevant fact even if incorporated into his communication with his attorney).

[83]*Coastal States Gas Corp.* at 862 (noting that the privilege applies not only to disclosures made by a client to an attorney but also communications from an attorney to a client).

[84]*Id.* at 863.

[85]*Id.*

[86]Rasmussen—Common Mistakes.

[87]Michael Rasmussen, "Adopted But Not Implemented Security Policies May Be Your Liability," *Ideabyte,* Apr. 9, 2002.

incident. Internal employees can become lax in their adherence to policies if they know management is not enforcing them. This makes it easy for malicious attackers to use this to their advantage, as the organization's guard is let down over time. To combat this, regular monitoring of the information protection policies and technical controls needs to be in place, and security incidents must be responded to.[88]

There is also a need to have a process in place for enforcing the provisions of privacy and security laws within and across national boundaries when illegal activities affect the organization. The fact that so many different types of computer- or systems-related intrusions actually originate through activities conducted in countries with weak legal and enforcement regimes for electronic security makes it essential that a broad international approach be taken in developing enforcement procedures. In particular, a specific set of steps is needed. First, a process should be a process that is established from the executive offices through the operational level to report incidents, analyze them, and determine what course of action to take and whether to involve law enforcement. Clearly, this is not a decision to be put solely upon the shoulders of the chief information officer or security officer, but should involve senior management and, perhaps, the board of directors, depending on the circumstances.

In many countries, cybercrime laws are either nonexistent or carry minimal civil or criminal penalties.[89] Therefore, a determination must be made whether the mechanisms for international cooperation in cyber security investigations will result in anything more for the company than negative publicity.

Mandated reporting is quickly becoming one of the hottest issues in the privacy area. At the state level, California enacted the Security Breach Information Act (SB 1386), a law that requires any state agency, person, or business that conducts business in California to notify the owner or licensee of information of any security breach of unencrypted personal information of any resident of California.[90] Although California is ahead of the curve, the trend is clearly toward legislation requiring mandatory reporting of computer security breaches. Indeed, U.S. Senator Dianne Feinstein has introduced Senate Bill (SB) 1350, The

---

[88]Rasmussen—Road Map.

[89]*See* Jody R. Westby, ed., *International Guide to Combating Cybercrime*, American Bar Association, Section of Science & Technology Law, Privacy & Computer Crime Committee, ABA Publishing, 2003, http://www.abanet.org/abapubs/books/cybercrime/.

[90]Security Breach Information Act (SB 1386), Feb. 12, 2002, http://info. sen.ca.gov/pub/01-02/bill/sen/sb_1351-1400/sb_1386_bill_20020926_chaptered.html; Devon Hewitt, "New California privacy law has nationwide ripple," *Washington Technology*, July 7, 2003 at 12; Keith Poulsen, "California disclosure law has national reach," *SecurityFocus Online*, Jan. 6, 2003, http://online.securityfocus.com/news/1984.

Notification of Risk to Personal Data Act, modeled after the California reporting law. The Senator stated: "I strongly believe individuals have a right to be notified when their most sensitive information is compromised—because it is truly their information."[91]

C. Technological Considerations

The relationship between privacy and security in today's enterprise is complex, and some security tools can cause privacy violations and problems for companies. On the one hand, a multilevel security program is absolutely critical to providing data privacy to any set of data subjects. However, the core mechanisms and controls integral to a robust security strategy often stand in direct opposition to privacy-centric principles such as minimization of data collection, anonymity/pseudonymity, and the like. If the wings of security are clipped too close, privacy will be vulnerable to unauthorized data access. If security measures are rolled out without privacy interests being taken into consideration, the resulting surveillance, logging, and data retention policies can render privacy principles moot or even violate laws. *Thus, while effective security is a prerequisite to data privacy, its application must be considered and circumspect, designed to support the privacy plan's requirements, yet restrained from overpowering the privacy plan in favor of the most comprehensive audit trail available.*

As the market for privacy-enhancing and privacy-compliance technologies matures, an increasing number of sophisticated and useful tools are becoming available to enhance organizational privacy posture. However, as renowned cryptographer and security expert Brice Schneier has stated:

> Security is never black and white, and context matters more than technology.... A system might be secure against an average criminal, or a certain type of industrial spy, or a national intelligence agency with a certain skill set. A system might be secure as long as certain mathematical advances don't occur, or for a certain period of time, against certain types of attacks."[92]

However, given the inherent tensions between privacy and security interests and a legal and regulatory landscape that appears to be changing in real time, evaluating and deploying enterprise privacy tools in a manner that effectively maximizes their value while responsibly leveraging risk presents unique challenges.

---

[91]"Senator Feinstein Seeks to Ensure Individuals are Notified when Personal Information is Stolen from Databases," U.S. Senator Dianne Feinstein, June 26, 2003, http://feinstein.senate.gov/03Releases/datasecurityrelease.htm.
[92]Bruce Schneier, *Secrets and Lies: Digital Security in a Networked World,* John Wiley and Sons, Inc., 2000 at 12-13.

Only after a comprehensive privacy risk assessment has been conducted, and information assets have been catalogued and identified with respect to relative sensitivity, can one realistically assess the value of technological offerings in securing such assets.

1. ENCRYPTION

Encryption is generally acknowledged as a critical component of any data-centric information security strategy. However, organizations should be careful to avoid the common misperception that sophisticated encryption schemes are "silver-bullet" technologies. Instead, encryption should be understood as one core technological component of a robust security process. The process implementation is far more critical to information security and the privacy of data subjects than the crypto-system used.

In assessing cryptographic technology, one should opt for tools that implement algorithms that have been subject to wide peer review. For example, the Advanced Encryption Standard (AES) algorithm Rijndael was selected by the National Institute of Standards and Technology (NIST) after extended and informed competition among a number of promising encryption algorithms. This algorithm is available royalty-free worldwide, which will likely lead to widespread implementation in a number of privately branded encryption products. The public disclosure and analysis of the algorithm bolster the likelihood that it is genuinely secure (at least given current technology and the state of cryptanalysis), and its widespread use would likely lead to expedited discovery of vulnerabilities and accelerated efforts to resolve potential weaknesses.

The benefits of encryption are accompanied by risks: (1) encryption tools must be used in a manner that does not compromise the strength of the procedure, and (2) the organization must maintain the security of and access to its cryptographic keys needed to decrypt information.[93] There are only six basic types of cryptographic tools:

1. *Symmetric Key Encryption.*[94] The same secret key is used to encrypt and decrypt the data. These cyphers can execute at high

---

[93] *See, e.g.,* "OMB Guidance to Federal Agencies on Data Availability and Encryption," http://csrc.nist.gov/policies/ombencryption-guidance.pdf.

[94] *Announcing the Advanced Encryption Standard (AES),* National Institute of Standards and Technology, Computer Security Division, Federal Information Processing Standards Publication 197, http://csrc.nist.gov/publications/fips/fips197/fips-197.pdf (announcing AES as the new standard for symmetric encryption); *see also* "The Next Generation of Cryptography: Public Key Sizes for AES," *Code & Cipher,* Certicom, http://www.certicom.com/index.php?action=res,cc_1_1&article=1-nextgen ("AES succeeds DES and Triple-DES . . . . To date, AES remains the only symmetric encryption algorithm providing at least 128 bits of security that is approved for use by U.S. government organizations to protect sensitive, unclassified information.").

speed and efficiency. Their associated difficulty (the "Key Distribution Problem") is the secure exchange of the unique secret keys between the communicating parties over the network.[95]

2. *Asymmetric (Public/Private) Key Encryption.* Asymmetric key systems avoid the key distribution problem through the use of different encryption and decryption keys, one public and the other private. These systems rely on the difficulty of a mathematical problem for their security.[96] The development of public key cryptography[97] in 1975 and the subsequent evolution[98] of that approach have put strong cryptography in the hands of private enterprises and the general public.

3. *One-Way Hash Functions.* One-way hash functions are mathematical algorithms that transform an arbitrarily long input message into one of fixed length. To be useful and secure the algorithm should be computationally efficient and collision-free,[99] and it should be provably impossible to compute the inverse of the hash function.

---

[95]"The Key Distribution Problem . . . . is very complex. Entire systems have been built solely to perform this function. The 'Kerberos' 98 system developed by MIT, based upon the work of Needham and Schroeder, dedicates entire servers simply to the task of being trusted third parties for distribution of secret keys. In many cases, the need for a key distribution system such as Kerberos entirely can be avoided through the use of asymmetric key encryption." Thomas Glaessner, Tom Kellermann, and Valerie McNevin, *Electronic Security: Risk Mitigation in Financial Transactions—Public Policy Issues,* The World Bank, June 2002, http://wwwl.worldbank.org/finance/assets/images/Global_Dialogue_2002-final3.pdf (hereinafter "Glaessner, Kellermann, and McNevin").

[96]The theoretical strength of an encryption system is measured by the amount of time required by a computer to break the coding algorithm.

[97]Whitfield Diffie and M.E. Hellman, "New Directions in Cryptography," *IEEE, Transactions on Information Theory,* Vol. IT-22, Nov. 1976 at 644-54. The best known (though not the strongest) public key system is the RSA algorithm based on factorization of large integers. R. L. Rivest, A. Shamir, and L. M. Adleman, "A method for obtaining digital signatures and public-key cryptosystems," *Communications of the ACM,* Vol. 21, Feb. 1978 at 120-26.

[98]"Today, only three types of systems should be considered both secure and efficient. The systems, classified according to the mathematical problem on which they are based, are: the Integer Factorization systems (of which RSA is the best known example), the Discrete Logarithm systems (such as the U.S. government's DSA), and the Elliptic Curve Cryptosystem (also defined as the Elliptic curve Discrete Logarithm System)." "The Elliptic Curve Cryptosystem," *Certicom,* July 2000 at 3.

[99]A hash function is collision-free if it is computationally infeasible to find two input messages that produce the same hash output. Modern hash algorithms produce hash values of 128 bits and higher.

4. *Message Authentication Codes (MACs).* MACs are data blocks appended to messages to protect the authentication and integrity of messages, that is, to ensure that the content of the message has not been modified in any way. MACs typically depend on the use of one-way hash functions.
5. *Digital Signatures.* (discussed below)
6. *Random Number Generators.* Many cryptographic tools require unpredictable sequences of numbers. Solely computational means of generating truly random numbers do not exist; however, sufficiently unpredictable numerical sequences can be produced by mathematical algorithms called pseudorandom number generators.[100]

Through the careful use of cryptographic tools, one can improve system security in the face of any of the attacks defined in a given threat model.

The primary legal issue connected with encryption is export controls. Industrialized nations restrict the export of encryption algorithms that are of such strength they are considered "dual use" (for military and commercial purposes). For these encryption technologies, special export licenses must be obtained. A few countries, such as the United Kingdom, have adopted laws that require those with encryption keys to assist with the decryption of data or, in some cases, to actually hand the encryption keys over to enable law enforcement to decrypt the evidence itself.[101] Most countries (with the exception of some authoritarian regimes), however, have adopted a hands-off approach, deciding the benefits of encryption to good actors outweighed the challenges to law enforcement.[102] Ultimately, however, the time, effort, and expense of tracing digital communications—and securing, where necessary, international legal assistance—may be wasted if the data are encrypted and the agency lacks the technical or legal ability to decrypt it.

---

[100]A list of references about random number generators can be found at http://random.mat.sbg.ac.at/literature/.

[101]*See, e.g.,* the U.K.'s *Regulation of Investigatory Powers Act 2000,* 2000 Chapter 23 (in particular, Part III: Investigation of Electronic Data Protected by Encryption Etc.). "Great Britain passed legislation in 2000 that allows the government to track e-mails and seize encrypted Internet communications. It enables law enforcement authorities to demand records of Internet traffic and to view the content of encrypted messages. ISPs are required to set up secure channels to connect to the Government Technical Assistance Center. In turn, the government contributed $30 million to ISPs to cover the cost of installing the 'black box' link to the MI5 Technical Assistance Spy Center." *See also* Glaessner, Kellermann, and McNevin.

[102]*Cryptography and Liberty 2000: An International Survey of Encryption Policy,* Electronic Privacy Information Center, http://www2.epic.org/reports/crypto2000).

200   CHAPTER 4

2. AUTHORIZATION AND ACCESS CONTROL

The authorized use[103] of an organization's IT resources should be governed by institutional policy and controlled via security policies, practices, and implementation tools. Authorization technologies try to ensure that only persons authorized to access a digital resource may do so. According to the Monetary Authority of Singapore, authorization involves a combination of granting access rights to specific systems resources, conferring privileges as to what a user is allowed to do, and deciding what actions he can take with respect to data files or transactions."[104] For example, authorization[105] decisions govern which users may access which servers for what purposes and under what conditions. These decisions are reflected in and enforced by an access control policy.

Passwords

The first step in the access process is for the computer system to ask a potential user, in effect, "Who are you?" The user identification (user ID) or account name is a form of identification. The next step (authentication) is for the system to verify: "Are you who you claim to be?" At present, the most common procedure is for the system to verify the user's password. A primary weakness of passwords is that they may be guessed or "cracked." Computer software can easily try many millions of passwords. While a five-character password containing only letters has 11 million potential combinations, a ten-character, case-sensitive password containing alphanumerics plus punctuation signs has over 50 million trillion combinations (so-called high entropy). Users must be careful in choosing and protecting their passwords, and they should change them frequently. Even with careful and frequent choices of passwords, security is not ensured. The system may incorporate

---

[103]For a lengthy legal analysis of authorization and access misuse, *see* Orin Kerr, "Cybercrime's Scope: Interpreting 'Access' and 'Authorization Misuse' Statutes," *New York University Law Review*, Vol. 78, Nov. 2003 http://cyber.law.harvard.edu/digitalmedia/KERR-78_N_Y_U_L_Rev_1596-edit.htm.

[104]"Technology Risk Management Guidelines for Financial Institutions," Monetary Authority of Singapore, Draft Version 1.1, Feb. 28, 2003 at 10, http://www.worldbank.org/wbi/banking/finsecpolicy/globaldialogues/dl19/pdf/trm_singapore.pdf.

[105]"In a client-server architecture, the clients (on behalf of users) attempt to access resources that are controlled by servers. . . . access control decisions [are made] based on one set of digitally signed documents that represent the authorization instructions and another set that represent user attributes. Existing public-key infrastructure and secure message protocols provide confidentiality, message integrity, and user identity authentication, during and after the access decision process. " Abdelliah Essiari, Gary Hoo, Keith Jackson, William Johnston, Srilekha Mudumbai, and Mary R. Thompson, "Collaboratory Security Architecture and Services," http://www-itg.lbl.gov/security/Akenti/Security-FWP-5275.htm.

additional security measures. To guard against the capture of passwords by "packet sniffers"[106] as they pass across networks, passwords should be encrypted lest intruders gain access by seeming to be a legitimate user using a captured password. The CERT Coordinating Center notes:

> One-time password technologies address this problem. Remote users carry a device synchronized with software and hardware on the dial-up server. The device displays random passwords, each of which remains in effect for a limited time period (typically 60 seconds). These passwords are never repeated and are valid only for a specific user during the period that each is displayed. In addition, users are often limited to one successful use of any given password. . . .One-time password technologies significantly reduce unauthorized entry at gateways requiring an initial password.[107]

Smart Cards & Common Access Cards

The security of the password authentication process can be significantly increased through the use of an accompanying physical token with a built-in microprocessor. The most common such "smart card" is the size of a standard credit card bearing a small set of gold contacts.[108] The smart card reader powers the microprocessor, which can store and process data such as cryptographic keys and digital signature algorithms. The U.S. Department of Defense (DoD) has adopted the 32-kilobyte smart card through its Common Access Card[109] program; the card will serve as a photo-ID, permit entry to facilities, access DoD computers, and provide

---

[106]"A packet sniffer is a program that captures data from information packets as they travel over the network. That data may include user names, passwords, and proprietary information that travels over the network in clear text. With perhaps hundreds or thousands of passwords captured by the sniffer, intruders can launch widespread attacks on systems. Installing a packet sniffer does not necessarily require privileged access. For most multi-user systems, however, the presence of a packet sniffer implies there has been a root compromise." Thomas A. Longstaff, James T. Ellis, Shawn V. Hernan, Howard F. Lipson, Robert D. McMillan, Linda Hutz Pesante, and Derek Simmel, "Security of the Internet," *The Froehlich/Kent Encyclopedia of Telecommunications*, Vol. 15, Marcel Dekker, 1997, at 231-55, http://www.cert.org/encyc_article/ tocencyc.html (hereinafter "Security of the Internet").
[107]Security of the Internet, "Basic Security Concepts," http://www.cert.org/encyc_article/tocencyc.html#BasicSec.
[108]Standards for smart cards, such as physical size, position and size of contacts, electronic signals, and protocols, are provided in ISO 7816, EMV 963.11, and GSM/SIM. Nonetheless, smart cards from many vendors are not interoperable, requiring matching readers. NIST is working with governments and industry to develop interoperability standards. *See* "Smart Card: Standards and Research," National Institute of Standards and Technology, Information Technology Laboratory, http://smartcard.nist.gov.
[109]"How to obtain DoD PKI client certificates," Department of Defense, Public Key Enablement, https://www.dodpke.com/public/publicAccess.asp.

202   CHAPTER 4

digital signatures on purchase orders. Such cards are especially attractive authentication tools in server-thin client architectures.

Biometrics

As passwords and physical tokens are subject to theft, security may be enhanced by basing the authentication of identity on unique physiological characteristics (biometric identification)[110] of the user. "Biometrics goes from an enrollment or adaptation role—the initial stage where information is read or stored for future use—to recognition (verification) and to the identification stages. . . . Biometric products store a kind of digital hash of a fingerprint, iris scan or voice-print—not the actual image—in a database for later comparison."[111]

While biometrics-based identification can eliminate the need to remember a password or carry a token, another option is to use biometrics as part of two-factor authorization. Biometric data may be stored on a smart card itself to make the forgery of such tokens more difficult. The biometric hash may also serve as a password to be encrypted for transmission for remote login. Rapid biometric identification at a distance is the subject of considerable investigation, making it plausible that for ultrahigh security application all persons in a room with a computer could be verified as having access permission.[112] Obstacles to more rapid adoption of biometrics for access control include high costs, high "false authentication" rates,[113] the privacy of biometric data, and the lack of an industry standard.

---

[110]"The only way to be truly positive in authenticating identity for access is to base the authentication on the physical attributes of the persons themselves (i.e., biometric identification). Because most identity authentication requirements take place when persons are fully clothed (neck to feet and wrists), the parts of the body conveniently available for this purpose are the hands, face, and eyes." Micki Krause and Harold Tipton, "Change Management Controls," *Handbook of Information Security Management,* "Biometric Identification" Chapter 1-2-1 (written by Donald R. Richards), CRC Press LLC, 2001, http://www.cccure.org/Documents/HISM/033-037.html#Heading2.

[111]S. Zegiorgis, "Biometric Technology Stomps Identity Theft," The SANS Institute, Jan. 7, 2002, http://www.sans.org/rr/authentic/biometric_tech.php (hereinafter "Zegiorgis"). For the particulars and comparison of the different technical challenges of voice, fingerprint, face, iris, and retinal recognition, *see* Gregory Williams, "More Than a Pretty Face, Biometrics and SmartCard Tokens," The SANS Institute, Dec. 24, 2001, http://www.sans.org/rr/authentic/pretty_face.php.

[112]"Human ID at a Distance (HumanID)," www.darpa.mil/iao/HID.htm.

[113]"The error rate (1% to 3%) is high on the list of concerns. Physiological biometrics (palm, finger, iris scan, etc.) have higher 'false authentication rates (FAR).' This is the rate of wrongly identifying an imposter to be the real person. Behavioral biometrics, on the other hand, have higher 'false recognition rates (FRR).' This is the rate of failing to recognize the real person and wrongly saying the person is not who he purports to be. Some contact lenses, for instance, could throw off eye-scanning devices, and criminals can fake fingerprints using silicon imprints made from wax molds." Zegiorgis.

Implementation and Science & Technology 203

Among the many interesting amalgams of smart card and biometric authentication technologies is a system based on the use of mass-produced microchips, each of which responds in unique ways to random or pseudo-random challenges and generates one-time encryption keys. The technology protects digitized biometric data from being cloned or otherwise compromised. The goal of the system is to provide nonforgeable identification of individuals while ensuring user privacy.[114]

3. DIGITAL SIGNATURE AND AUTHENTICATION TECHNOLOGIES

Authentication protocols allow parties to distinguish between trusted and nontrusted entities. Digital signatures are technological tools that, among other things, use cryptography to authenticate the signer.

Digital signatures are created and verified by asymmetric cryptography, employing an algorithm using two different but mathematically related keys, one for creating a digital signature and another for verifying it. Digital signatures promise to provide a number of valuable benefits. In conjunction with a robust cryptosystem, they can provide a level of *confidentiality*, rendering a message unintelligible to all but its intended recipient. They can *authenticate* the sender, providing some level of assurance that the message came from its purported sender. This, in turn, within the context of an appropriate legal framework, can provide for *nonrepudiation,* meaning that it would be difficult for a sender to deny having sent a given message. Finally, they can *verify message integrity*, ensuring that the contents of the message have not been altered in transit.

The American Bar Association's Information Security Committee released an excellent treatment of digital signatures in its 1996 publication *Digital Signature Guidelines.*[115] Additionally, the Committee's PKI Assessment Guidelines,[116] currently publicly available in draft, explores public key cryptosystems, certification systems, and associated legal issues in depth.

4. DIGITAL TIME STAMPS AND AUDIT TECHNOLOGIES

Various data fields can be associated with a particular data record or set of data records in furtherance of establishing a reliable audit trail.

---

[114]*See, e.g.,* Cyonic, http://www.cyonic.com.

[115]*Digital Signature Guidelines,* American Bar Association, Section of Science & Technology Law, Information Security Committee, http://www.abanet.org/scitech/ec/isc/dsg.pdf.

[116]*PKI Assessment Guidelines*, American Bar Association, Section of Science & Technology Law, Information Security Committee, http://www.abanet.org/scitech/ec/isc/pag/pag.html.

204   CHAPTER 4

For example, a time and date stamp may be associated with an e-mail address at the time such an address is submitted to a company, for the purpose of establishing that that individual "opted in" to subsequent communication from the company. Additional data fields may further facilitate the audit process, such as the IP address reported by the data subject's client machine at the time the e-mail address was collected. Such fields could be cross-referenced against the privacy policy in effect at the time of data collection, to establish the permission status of the data record in question. This is a relatively simplistic example, which would take on several additional layers of complexity if the data record were to entail more sophisticated authentication requirements, or if the content of certain data fields were to be content-verified via some function involving a time or date stamp.

5. LOGS

A broad discussion of system logging is beyond the scope of this work. Generally, a privacy-sensitive program will require the implementation of a multifaceted logging and log analysis process. Applications, file systems, and network activity should typically be logged to ensure accurate data retention for effective auditing. Application audits should show what applications have been executed and who or what was responsible for their execution. File systems audits are a critical component of a data security/privacy compliance program. What files have been added or deleted? What files have been changed in either content or permissions? Network auditing should be able to establish what was happening on the network that allowed a breach or failure. Network auditing might also show events where security measures were in fact successful, or where preliminary probes and footprinting activities have been carried out in anticipation of an attack.[117]

The reporting and analysis of security incidents, as well as efforts to track attacks to their source, also require adequate logs of system activities. System administrators must identify the system components that warrant logging, determine the level of data logged for each component, and establish policies for securely handling and analyzing log files. The challenge in planning system administration is to record the correct information (events that need to be logged and their characteristics) without logging too much.[118] Firewall logs and other

---

[117]See, e.g., Paul J. Santos, "How to Make Linux System Auditing a Little Easier," Sept. 15, 2002, http://www.sans.org/rr/paper.php?id=81.
[118]For a detailed example, see Lance Spitzner, "Watching Your Logs," Oct. 16, 2002, http://secinf.net/unix_security/Watching_Your_Logs.html.

system components should be made into easily understandable reports that can be examined on a regular basis.

> Now the bad news. Many intruders modify, clean or completely destroy log files. If you haven't implemented a remote log server, there's often nothing left to inspect. The review process should not be overlooked though; it's very difficult to completely mask all traces of an exploit. Secondary logs, such as the application specific files, may catch stray events. The location of such files varies between systems, as opposed to default logs, so they're often left untouched.[119]

The automated log generation typical in most computing systems provides a valuable audit trail for promoting accountability and post-event forensics. However, the nature of computer-generated data is such that log data are often easily falsified and may require security controls of their own to preserve their audit value.

6. ANONYMIZING AND SANITIZING

Efficient management of information flows within the constraints of legal, regulatory, or self-imposed privacy policy restrictions may require the anonymization or sanitization of personally identifiable data. Within existing regulatory regimes, there are numerous contexts in which organizations must anonymize data records to share them freely with third parties. Anonymization and sanitization technologies and applications should be scrutinized closely to ensure persistent anonymity. Frequently, a veneer of anonymity can be stripped away through database cross-pollination or other techniques, and the rigor of anonymity should be commensurate with the sensitivity of the data at issue.

D. Conclusion

The FTC actions taken in *Lilly*, *Guess?*, and *Microsoft* clearly indicate that implementation is an important step in an enterprise-wide privacy program that cannot be left as an afterthought. Privacy is dependent upon security. The FTC will look at the security practices and standards employed in a privacy program in determining whether the company has used appropriate levels of protection. The *Microsoft* case demonstrates that even the possibility that private data may not be secure can trigger an FTC investigation. It will also scrutinize training

---

[119]Matthew Tanese, "Detecting and Removing Malicious Code," July 22, 2002, http://online.securityfocus.com/infocus/1610.

programs and whether policies and procedures were implemented as part of the business operations or were simply pieces of paper in a book. Even if a company trains its personnel, the FTC will also look to see if compliance with the policies and procedures was monitored and enforced.

The laws regarding employee monitoring vary significantly from one jurisdiction to another. The EU laws, for example, afford the employee a higher expectation of privacy in the European workplace than do laws in the United States. Internal and external audits are another avenue for determining compliance with the entire privacy program. Ideally, the external audits are conducted through counsel, with the intention they be privileged as attorney work product.

Numerous technological considerations affect privacy programs, and there are several useful technology tools that can assist in the implementation of and compliance with an organization's privacy program. The use of encryption, for example, can protect sensitive data but involves administrative overhead and performance considerations. Authorization and access controls (such as passwords, biometric technologies, and common access cards) are in a constant state of innovation but can inject new privacy considerations into an organization. Digital signatures, authentication technologies, and digital time stamps are useful for evidentiary, audit, and security purposes; however, administrative costs and interoperability between technologies must also be considered. System logs are crucial to tracking and tracing attacks and audits. Anonymizing and sanitization technologies also can be useful in protecting privacy.

Overall, privacy of information is dependent upon the effective implementation of the privacy program and the technology tools used to help automate the privacy plan and monitor the effectiveness of and compliance with policies and procedures.

BIBLIOGRAPHY

A. CASES

Caremark International Inc. Derivative Litigation, 698 A.2d 959 (Del. Ch. 1996).

Casualty & Surety Co. v. Superior Ct, 153 Cal. App. 3d 467, 478-479 (1984).

Chrysler Corp. v. Brown, 441 U.S. 281, 293 (1979).

Coastal States Gas Corp. v. Dept. of Energy, 199 U.S. App. D.C. 272; 617 F.2d 854, 864 (1980).

Connor v. Ortega, 480 U.S. 709 (1987).

Doe v. Chao, U.S., No. 02-1377, Feb. 24, 2004.

Eisenstadt v. Baird, 405 U.S. 438 (1972).

FTC v. 30 Minute Mortgage, Inc., Gregory P. Roth, Peter W. Stolz, Civil Action No. 03-60021 (SD FL 2003), http://www.ftc.gov/os/2003/03/30mincmp.pdf.

FTC v. Paula L. Garrett, d/b/a Discreet Data Systems, Civil Action No. H-01-1255 (SD TX 2002), http://www.ftc.gov/os/2002/03/index.htm#8.

FTC v. Victor L. Guzzetta, d/b/a Smart Data Systems, Civil Action No. 01-2335 (DGT) (ED NY 2002), http://www.ftc.gov/os/2002/03/index.htm#8.

FTC v. Information Search, Inc., and David Kacala, Civil Action No. AMD01-1121 (D MD 2002), http://www.ftc.gov/os/2002/03/index.htm#8.

FTC v. Rapp individually and dba Touch Tone Information, Inc., Civil Action No. 99-WM-783 (D CO 2000), http://www.ftc.gov/os/2000/06/index.htm#27.

Greidinger v. Davis, 988 F.2d 1344 (4th Cir. 1993).

Griswold v. Connecticut, 381 U.S. 479 (1985).

Harpers v. Kline, D. Kan., No. 03-42-9-RDR, Dec. 23, 2003.

Hickman v. Taylor, 329 U.S. 495 (1947) (codified as Federal Rules of Civil Proc. P 26(b)(3)).

In re Eli Lilly and Co., Agreement Containing Consent Order, FTC No. 0123214, Jan 18, 2002, http://www.ftc.gov/os/2002/01/lillyagree.pdf (consent order accorded final approval on May 10, 2002).

In the Matter of GeoCities, File No. 9823015, Docket No. C-3850, http://www.ftc.gov/os/1999/02/9823015cmp.htm.

In the Matter of Guess?, Inc. and Guess.com, File No. 022 3260, Docket No. 0223260, http://www.ftc.gov/os/2003/06/guesscmp.pdf.

In the Matter of Microsoft Corporation, File No. 012 3240, Docket No. C-4069, http://www.ftc.gov/os/2002/12/microsoftcomplaint.pdf.

In the Matter of The National Research Center for College and University Admissions, Inc., et. al., File No. 022 3005, Agreement Containing Consent Order as to NRCCUA and Munce, http://www.ftc.gov/os /2002/10/nrccuamunceagree.pdf.

Katz v. United States, 389 U.S. 347 (1967).

Kent Corp. v. NLRB, 530 F.2d 612 (1976).

Laird v. Tatum, 408 U.S. 1 (1972).

Lavigne v. Canada (Office of the Commissioner of Official Languages), 2002, SCC 53 at para. 23-24, http://www.lexum.umontreal.ca/csc-scc/en/pub/2002/vol2/html/2002scr2_0773.html.

McLaren v. Microsoft Corp., 1999 Tex. App. LEXIS 4103 (Tex. Ct. App., May 28, 1999).

NLRB v. Excelsior Underwear, Inc., 156 NLRB 1236 (1966).

NLRB v. Robbins Tire & Rubber Co., 437 U.S. 214, 242 (1978).

NLRB v. Wyman-Gordon Co., 394 U.S. 759 (1969).

O'Connor v. Ortega, 480 U.S. 709, 718 (1987).

Organizacion JD Ltd. v. Dept. of Justice, 124 F.3d 354 (2d Cir. 1997).

Paul v. Davis, 424 U.S. 693 (1976).

Roe v. Wade, 410 U.S. 113 (1973).

Rumac, Inc. v. Bottomley, 143 Cal. App. 3d 810, 815-16 (1983).

South Carolina Medical Assn. v. Thompson, 327 F.3d 346, 348 (4th Cir. Apr. 25, 2003).

Thomasson v. Bank of America, No. A061120 (Cal. Ct. App. 1994), app. den., 1995 Cal. LEXIS 1843 (1995).

Trans Union Corp. v. FTC, 81 F.3d 228, 234 (D.C. Cir. 1996).

United States v. Angevine, 281 F.3d 1130 (10th Cir. 2001).

United States v. Bonzi Software, Inc., Civ. Action No. CV-004-1048 RJK (Ex)

(C.D. Cal., 2004), http://www.ftc.gov/os/caselist/bonzi/040217comp bonzi.pdf.

United States v. Frank, Inc., Civ. Action No. 01-1516-A (E.D. Va., 2001), http://www. ftc.gov/os/2001/10/index.htm#2.

United States v. Hershey Foods Corp., Civ. Action No. 4CV:03-350 (M.D. Penn., 2003), http://www.ftc.gov/os/2003/02/index.htm#27.

United States v. Hsu, 40 F.Supp.2d 623, 630 (E.D.Pa. 1999).

United States v. Looksmart, Ltd., Civ. Action No. 01-606-A (E.D. Va., 2001), http://www.ftc.gov/os/2001/04/index.htm#19.

United States v. Martin, 228 F.3d 1, 13 (1st Cir. 2000).

United States v. Miller, 425 U.S. 435 (1976).

United States v. Mrs. Fields Famous Brands, Inc., et al., Civ. Action No. 2:03 CV205 JTG (Dist. of Utah, 2003), http://www.ftc.gov/os/2003/02/index.htm#27.

United States v. the Ohio Art Co., Civ. Action No. 3:02 CV 7203 (N.D. Ohio, 2002), http://www.ftc.gov/os/2002/04/index.htm#22.

United States v. Toysmart, Civil Action No. 00-11341-RGS, D.Mass. (2000), http:// www.ftc.gov/os/2000/07/toysmartcomplaint.htm.

United States v. UMG Recordings, Inc., Civ. Action No. CV-04-1050 JFW (EX) C.D. Cal., 2004), http://www.ftc.gov/os/caselist/umgrecordings/040217compumgrecording.pdf.

Upjohn Co. v. United States, 449 U.S 383 (1981).

Whalen v. Roe, 429 U.S. 589 (1977).

B. ORGANIZATIONS

American Institute of Certified Public Accountants, www.aicpa.org.

Council of Europe, http://www.coe.int.

Electronic Frontier Foundation, http:// www.eff.org/Legal/email_privacy.citations.

Electronic Privacy Information Center, http://www.epic.org/ privacy.

Federal Trade Commission, http://www.ftc.gov/privacy.

General Accounting Office, http://www.gao.gov.

Information Assurance Advisory Council, http://www.iaac.ac.uk.

Information Systems Audit and Control Association, http://www.isaca.org.

International Standards Organization, http://www.iso.org.

National Directorate for the Protection of Personal Data, http://www.jus.gov.ar/minjus/DPDP/.

Office of New York State Attorney General, http://www.oag.state.ny.us.

Office of the New South Wales Privacy Commissioner, http://www.lawlink.nsw.gov.au/pc.nsf/pages/index.

Organization for Economic Co-operation and Development, http://www.oecd.org.

Privacy International, http://www.privacyinternational.org.

United Nations, http://www.un.org.

United Nations Commission on International Trade Law, http://www.uncitral.org.

C. INTERNET SOURCES

A Matter of Policy: Model Privacy Statement," *CIO*, Apr. 1, 2000 at 198, http://www.cio.com/archive/040100/privacypol.html.

A. Guadamuz, "Habeas Data: The Latin-American Response to Data Protection," *The Journal of Information, Law and Technology*, 2000, http://elj.warwick.ac.uk/jilt/00-2/guadamuz.html.

A. Marshall Acuff, Jr., "Information Security Impacting Securities Valuations: Information Technology and the Internet Changing the Face of Business," Salomon Smith Barney, 2000, http://www.ciao.gov/industry/SummitLibrary/InformationSecurityImpactingSecurities Valuations.pdf.

Aaron Lukas, "Safe Harbor or Stormy Waters? Living with the EU Data Protection Directive," Cato Institute, Center for Trade Policy Studies, No. 16, Oct. 30, 2001 at 25-26, http://www.freetrade.org/pubs/pas/tpa-016.pdf.

Abdelliah Essiari, Gary Hoo, Keith Jackson , William Johnston, Srilekha Mudumbai, and Mary R. Thompson, "Collaboratory Security Architecture and Services," http://www-itg.lbl.gov/security/Akenti/Security-FWP-5275.htm.

Allan R. Paliotta, "A Personal View of a World Class IT Auditing Function," Information Systems Audit and Control Association, *InfoBytes*, June 1999, http://isaca.org/art11.htm.

"American Student List Complaint," http://www.ftc.gov/os/2003/01/aslcmp.htm.

Andrew Beckerman-Rodau, "Protection of Ideas, Trade Secret Law, Patent Law & Trademark Law," Section II.A.2, 1996, http://www.law.suffolk.edu/arodau/articles/ kiev-cle.html.

Andrew Orlowski, "Yahoo! Rips! Up! Privacy! Policy!" *The Register*, Mar. 4, 2002, http://www.theregister.co.uk/content/6/24683.html.

Andrew Rathmell, "Information Assurance: Protecting your Key Asset," http://www.iaac.ac.uk.

"Announcing Draft Federal Information Processing Standard (FIPS) 199 on Standards for Security Categorization of Federal Information and Information Systems; and Request for Comments," 68 *Federal Register* 26,573 (Dept. of Commerce 2003), http://csrc.nist.gov/publications/drafts/FIPS199-FRnotice.pdf.

Announcing the Advanced Encryption Standard (AES), Federal Information Processing Standards Publication 197, National Institute of Standards and Technology, Computer Security Division, http://csrc.nist.gov/publications/fips/fips197/fips-197.pdf .

"APEC Data Privacy Mapping Exercise—Submissions from Economies," APEC Electronic Commerce Steering Group, updated Mar. 19, 2003, http://www.export.gov/apececommerce/privacy/submissions_links.html.

APEC Privacy Principles (Version 9 Consultation Draft), Feb. 27, 2004, http://www.bakercyberlawcentre.org/appcc/apec_draft_v9.htm.

"Audit Documentation," *IS Auditing Guideline*, Information Systems Audit and Control Association, May 1, 1999, http://www.isaca.org/standard/guide12.pdf.

Barbara S. Wellbery and Miriam H. Wugmeister, "Privacy: The U.S., E.U., Compilation of State and Federal Privacy Laws," *Privacy Journal*, 2002, http://www.privacyjournal.net/work1.htm.

Ben Rothke, "Security Management Practices," http://www.cccure.org/Documents/Ben_Rothke/Sec_Mgmt_Practices.ppt.

California Financial Privacy Initiative, http://www.californiaprivacy.org/.

Carol A. Siegel, Ty R. Sagalow, and Paul Serritella, "Cyber-Risk Management: Technical and Insurance Controls for Enterprise-Level Security," CRC Press, Mar. 2002, http://www.aignetadvantage.com/content/netad/CyberRisk_Article_043002.pdf.

Charles J. Muhl, "Workplace e-mail and Internet Use: Employees and Employers Beware," *Monthly Labor Review*, Vol. 126, No. 2, Feb. 2003, http://www.bls.gov/opub/mlr/2003/02/art3abs.htm.

"Children's Online Privacy Protection Rule," Final Rule, Federal Trade Commission, *Federal Register*, Vol. 64, No. 212, Nov. 3, 1999 at 59,888 (codified at 16 C.F.R. Part 312), http://www.ftc.gov/os/1999/10/64fr59888.pdf.

"Children's Privacy: Education and Guidance," http://www.ftc.gov/privacy/privacyinitiatives/ childrens_educ.html.

"Children's Privacy: Enforcement," Federal Trade Commission, http://www.ftc.gov/privacy/privacyinitiatives/childrens_enf.html.

"Children's Privacy: Laws & Rules," Federal Trade Commission, http://www.ftc.gov/privacy/privacyinitiatives/childrens_lr.html.

"Children's Privacy: The Children's Online Privacy Protection Act," Federal Trade Commission, http://www.ftc.gov/privacy/privacyinitiatives/childrens.html.

Christopher Kuner, *European Data Privacy Law and Online Business*, Oxford University Press, 2003, http://www.iccwbo.org/home/e_business/word_documents/Final%20version%20July%202002%20Model%20contract%20clauses.pdf.

Circular No. A-130 (Revised), Management of Federal Information Resources, Office of Management and Budget, Feb. 9, 1996, http://www.whitehouse.gov/omb/circulars/a130/a130.html.

CobiT, *Control Objectives*, 3rd ed., July 2000, http://www.usmd.edu//leadership/USMOffice/AdminFinance/IAO/is/Cobit-Control-guidelines.pdf.

CobiT, *Management Guidelines*, 3rd ed., July 2000, http://www.isaca.org/cobit.htm.

Code on Access to Information, http://www.info.gov.hk/access/code.htm.

"Comments Regarding the President's Critical Infrastructure Protection Board's Exposure Draft of The National Strategy to Secure Cyberspace," Letter to Richard A. Clarke, President's Critical Infrastructure Board, from Barbara Hafer, President, National Association of State Auditors, Comptrollers and Treasurers, Nov. 18, 2002, http://www.nasact.org/techupdates/downloads/CRC/LOC/11_02-Cyberspace.pdf.

"Commission decisions on the adequacy of the protection of personal data in third countries," http://europa.eu.int/comm/internal_market/privacy/adequacy_en.htm.

Commission of the European Communities, *Report from the Commission: First report on the implementation of the Data Protection Directive* (95/46/EC), COM (2003) 265 final, May 15, 2003, para. 3.1 at 7, http://europa.eu.int/eur-lex/en/com/rpt/2003/com2003_0265en01.pdf.

"Committing to Security: A CompTIA Analysis of IT Security and the Workforce," Mar. 2003, http://www.comptia.org/research/files/summaries/securitysummary031703.pdf.

"Communications and Research," Council of Europe, http://www.coe.int/T/E/Communication_and_Research/Contacts_with_the_public/About_Council_of_Europe/An_overview/.

"Compilation of State and Federal Privacy Laws," *Privacy Journal*, 2002, http://www.privacyjournal.net/work1.htm.

Computer Crime and Intellectual Property Section (CCIPS). *VIII. Theft of Commercial Trade Secrets*, Apr. 23, 2001, http://www.cybercrime.gov/ipmanual/08ipma.htm.

"Computer Security Incident Response Teams (CSIRTs)," http://www.cert.org/csirts/more.html.

"COPPA FAQ," http://www.ftc.gov/privacy/coppafaqs.htm .

Cryptography and Liberty 2000: An International Survey of Encryption Policy, Electronic Privacy Information Center, http://www2.epic.org/reports/crypto2000).

Dale McNulty, "Management's Role in Information Security—The 7 Top Mistakes," Nov. 4, 2002, www.surrex.com/changing_it_landscape/2002_11_04.html.

Dan Verton, "Disaster recovery planning still lags," *Computerworld*, Apr. 1, 2002, http://www.computerworld.com/securitytopics/security/story/0,10801,69705,00.html.

Daniel J. Solove and Marc Rotenberg, *Information Privacy Law*, Aspen Publishers, 2003, http://www. epic.org/bookstore/epic_books.html.

"Data Retention," Electronic Privacy Information Center, http://www.epic.org/privacy/intl/data_retention.html.

David Banisar, "Data Protection Laws Around the World," Apr. 2003, http://www. privacy.org/pi/survey/dpmap.jpg.

David Holtzman, "The Privacy Imbroglio," *News.com*, Mar. 21, 2002, http://news.com.com/2010-1075-865409.html.

Deborah Radcliff, "The Annual Checkup," *ComputerWorld,* Sept. 9, 2002, http://www.computerworld.com/printthis/2002/0,4814,73993,00.html.

"Deceptive Mortgage Scam Halted," Federal Trade Commission, Mar. 20, 2003, http://www.ftc.gov/opa/2003/03/thirty6.htm.

Declan McCullagh, "US Twitchy on EU Data Privacy," Oct. 16, 1998, *Wired*, http://www.wired.com/news/business/0,1367,15671,00.html.

Declaratory Ruling and Notice of Proposed Rulemaking, GN Docket No. 00-185, CS Docket No. 02-52, FCC 02-77 (March 15, 2002), http://hraunfoss.fcc.gov/edocs_public/ attachmatch/FCC-02-77A1.pdf.

"Development of the Right to Privacy in Information," U.S. Congress, Office of Technology Assessment, Protecting Privacy in Computerized Medical Information, OTA-TCT-576, U.S. Government Printing Office, Sept. 1993, http://www.csu.edu.au/learning/ncgr/gpi/odyssey/privacy/orig_priv.html.

Dibya Sarkar, "Cybersecurity Laws Spread," *Federal Computer Week*, July 23, 2003, http://www.fcw.com/geb/articles/2003/0721/web-ncs-07-23-03.asp.

Digital Signature Guidelines, American Bar Association, Section of Science & Technology Law, Information Security Committee, http://www.abanet.org/scitech/ec/isc/dsg.pdf.

Douwe Korff, *EC Study on Implementation of Data Protection Directive: comparative summary of national laws*, Human Rights Centre, Colchester,

UK, Sept. 2002, http://europa.eu.int/comm/internal_market/privacy/docs/lawreport/ consultation/univessex-comparativestudy_en.pdf.

"Economic Espionage Act of 1996," http://rf-web.tamu.edu/security/SECGUIDE/T1threat/Legal.htm.

"Electronic Surveillance in the Workplace," *USA Today*, Oct. 18, 2001, http://www.usatoday.com/tech/columnist/2001/10/18/sinrod.htm.

"Employee Monitoring: Is There Privacy in the Workplace?" Privacy Rights Clearinghouse, Sept. 2002, http://www.privacyrights.org/fs/fs7-work.htm.

Employee Privacy: Computer-Use Monitoring Practices and Policies of Selected Companies, Report to the Ranking Minority Member, Subcommittee on 21st Century Competitiveness, Committee on Education and the Workforce, U.S. House of Representatives, GAO-020717, Sept. 2002, http://www.gao.gov/newitems/d02717.pdf.

"Enforcing Privacy Promises: Enforcement, Federal Trade Commission, http://www.ftc.gov/privacy/privacyinitiatives/promises_enf.html.

"Enforcing Privacy Promises: Reports & Testimony," Federal Trade Commission, Privacy Initiatives, http://www.ftc.gov/privacy/privacyinitiatives/promises_reptest.html.

"Enforcing Privacy Promises: Section 5 of the FTC Act," Federal Trade Commission, http://www.ftc.gov/privacy/privacyinitiatives/promises.html.

"EU Reservations on Australian Privacy Law," EU Working Party on Data Privacy, Apr. 23, 2001, http://www.qlinks.net/items/qlitem10338.htm.

"European Economic Area," http://europa.eu.int/comm/external_relations/eea/.

Fair Information Practices, Organisation for Economic Co-operation and Development, www.oecd.org/EN/document/o,EN-document-43-1-NO-24-10255-43,00.html.

"Financial Privacy: The Gramm-Leach Bliley Act," http://www.ftc.gov/privacy/glbact/.

Freedom of Information Act Guide, May 2002, "Introduction," U.S. Department of Justice, http://www. usdoj.gov/oip/introduc.htm.

Frequently Asked Questions about the Children's Online Privacy Protection Rule, Volume 1, Federal Trade Commission, http://www.ftc.gov/privacy/coppafaqs.htm.

FTC Policy Statement on Deception, appended to Cliffdale Associates, Inc., 103 FTC 110, 174 (1984), http:// www.ftc.gov/bcp/policystmt/ ad-decept.htm.

Gail Hillebrand, "After the FACT Act: What States Can Still Do to Prevent

Identity Theft," Consumers Union, Jan. 2004, http://www.consumers union.org/pub/core_financial_services/000756.html.

Gary Stoneburner, Alice Goguen, and Alexis Feringa, *Risk Management Guide for Information Technology Systems*, NIST Draft Special Publication 800-30, Rev A, June 21, 2001, http:csrc.nist.gov/publications/drafts.html.

George "Toby" Dilworth, "The Economic Espionage Act of 1996: An Overview," *U.S. Attorneys' Bulletin*, U.S. Dept. of Justice, May 2001 at 2, http://www.cybercrime. gov/usamay2001_6.htm.

Gregory Dalton, "Privacy Law Worries U.S. Businesses," October 26, 1998, *InformationWeek,* http://www.informationweek.com/706/06iulaw.htm.

Gregory Williams, "More Than a Pretty Face, Biometrics and SmartCard Tokens," The SANS Institute, Dec. 24, 2001, http://www.sans.org/rr/authentic/pretty_face.php

Guidelines for the Protection of Individuals with Regard to the Collection and Processing of Personal Data on Information Highways, Council of Europe, R(99)5, Feb. 23, 1999, http://cm.coe.int/ta/rec/1999/99r5.htm.

Guidelines for the Security of Information Systems, Organisation for Economic Co-operation and Development, Nov. 1992, http://www.oecd.org/document/19/0,2340,en_2649_34255_1815059_1_1_1_37409,00.html.

Guidelines on the Protection of Privacy and Transborder Flows of Personal Data, Organisation for Economic Co-operation and Development, Sept. 23, 1980, http://www.uhoh.org/oecd-privacy-personal-data.htm.

"Health Insurance Reform: Security Standards," 68 *Federal Register* 8333-81, Feb. 20, 2003 (codified at 45 C.F.R. Parts 160, 162, 164), http://www.wedi.org/snip/public/articles/HIPAA_Security_Final_Rule_official_version.pdf.

"Health Insurance Reform: Standards for Electronic Transactions, Final Rule and Notice," 65 *Federal Register* 50,311-72, Aug. 17, 2000 (codified at 45 C.F.R. Part 160, Subpart A and Part 162, Subpart I), http://a257.g.akamaitech.net/7/257/2422/14mar20010800/edocket.access.gpo.gov/2003/C3-3876.htm, amended by "Health Insurance Reform: Modifications to Electronic Data Transactions Standards and Code Sets," 68 *Federal Register* 8,381-99, Feb. 20, 2003 (codified at 45 C.F.R. pt. 162), http://a257.g.akamaitech.net/7/257/2422/14mar20010800/edocket.access.gpo.gov/2003/03-3876.htm, amended by "Health Insurance Reform: Modifications to Electronic Data Transaction Standards and Code Sets," 68 *Federal Register* 11,445, Mar. 10, 2003, (codified at 45 C.F.R. Part 162), http://a257.g.akamaitech.net/7/257/2422/14mar20010800/ edocket.access.gpo.gov/2003/C3-3876.htm.

"HIPAA," http://www.hipaadvisory.com/regs/index.htm.

How to Comply With The Children's Online Privacy Protection Rule: A Guide from the Federal Trade Commission, the Direct Marketing Association and the Internet Alliance, http://www.ftc.gov/bcp/conline/pubs/buspubs/coppa.pdf.

"How to obtain DoD PKI client certificates," Department of Defense, Public Key Enablement, https://www.dodPKE.com/public/publicAccess.asp.

"Human ID at a Distance (HumanID)," www.darpa.mil/iao/HID.htm

"Information Technology(Code of Practice for Information Security Management," ISO/IEC 17799:2000.

Internet Law and Business Handbook, Chapter II, "Standards," Ladera Press, 2001, http://www.laderapress.com/laderapress/tradesecretlaw.html.

"Internet Mortgage Scam Halted," Federal Trade Commission, Dec. 9, 2003, http://www.ftc.gov/opa/2003/12/30mm2.htm.

Inventory of Instruments and Mechanisms Contributing to the Implementation and Enforcement of the OECD Privacy Guidelines on Global Networks, Organisation for Economic Co-operation and Development, http://www.olis.oecd.org/olis/1998doc.nsf/linkto/dsti-iccp-reg(98)12-final.

Inventory of Privacy-Enhancing Technologies, Organisation for Economic Co-operation and Development, http://www.olis.oecd.org/olis/2001doc.nsf/linkto/dsti-iccp-reg(2001)1-final.

ISO/IEC 17799:2000, "Information Technology—Code of Practice for Information Security Management," Section 7, "Physical and Environmental Security," and Section 9, "Access Control."

IT Examination Handbook, Federal Financial Institutions Examination Council, Dec. 2002, http://wbln0018.worldbank.org/html/FinancialSectorWeb.nsf/SearchGeneral?openform&E-Security/E-Finance&Policies+&+Guidelines.

James H. A. Pooley, Mark A. Lemley, and Peter J. Toren, "Understanding the Economic Espionage Act of 1996," 1997 at 1, http://www.utexas.edu/law/journals/tiplj/volumes/vol5iss2/lemley2.htm.

Jim Hu, "Yahoo revises privacy policy," *News.com,* Mar. 28, 2003, http://news.com.com/2100-1023-870270.html.

Jody R. Westby, ed., *International Guide to Combating Cybercrime,* American Bar Association, Section of Science & Technology Law, Privacy & Computer Crime Committee, ABA Publishing, 2003, http://www.abanet.org/abapubs/books/cybercrime/.

Jody R. Westby, ed., *International Guide to Cyber Security,* American Bar Association, Section of Science & Technology Law, Privacy & Computer Crime Committee, ABA Publishing, 2004, http://www.abanet.org/abapubs/books/security/.

Keith Poulsen, "California disclosure law has national reach," *SecurityFocus Online*, Jan. 6, 2003, http://online.securityfocus.com/news/1984.

Lance Spitzner, "Watching Your Logs," Oct. 16, 2002, http://secinf.net/unix_security/Watching_Your_Logs.html.

"Legal Ideas, Trade Secret Protection," *Legal Ideas*, 1998, http://members.aol.com/cynthiabs/secret.html.

Letter from Privacy Commissioner George Radwanski to the Honourable David Coutts, Minister of Government Services, Government of Alberta, May 27, 2003, http://www.privcom.gc.ca/media/nr-c/2003/02_05_b_030527_e.asp.

Letter from Privacy Commissioner George Radwanski to the Honourable Sandy Santori, Minister of Management Services, Government of British Columbia, May 7, 2003, http://www.privcom.gc.ca/media/nr-c/2003/02_05_b_030508_e.asp.

Letter to David L. Roll and Warren L. Dennis from William E. Kovacic, General Counsel, Federal Trade Commission, June 30, 2003, http://www.abanet.org/poladv/glbfactsheet/amnestyletter.pdf.

M. Maureen Murphy, "Financial Privacy Laws Affecting Sharing of Customer Information Among Affiliated Institutions," *CRS Report for Congress,* RS21427, Feb. 27, 2003, http://www.epic.org/privacy/fcra/RS21427.pdf.

"Management of Federal Information Resources," Circular A-130 (Revised), Transmittal Memorandum No. 4, Office of Management and Budget, http://www.whitehouse.gov/omb/circulars/a130/a130trans4.pdf.

Marianne Swanson, *Security Self-Assessment Guide for Information Technology Systems*, National Institute of Standards and Technology, Special Publication 800-26, Nov. 2001, http://csrc.nist/gov/publications/nistpubs/.

Marilou King, "Lessons from the Eli Lilly Case," *Privacy Officers Advisor,* Vol. 2, No. 11, Aug. 2002, http://www.privacyassociation.org/docs/POA0802.pdf.

Matthew Tanese, "Detecting and Removing Malicious Code," July 22, 2002, http://online.securityfocus.com/infocus/1610.

"MB Guidance to Federal Agencies on Data Availability and Encryption," http://csrc.nist.gov/policies/ombencryption-guidance.pdf.

"Meet the Privacy Act, the Commissioner, & the Office," http://www.privacy.org.nz/recept/rectop.html.

Michael J. Miasek and Arlan Gates, "British Columbia and Alberta Introduce Private Sector Privacy Bills," *Baker & McKenzie—Canada*, June 2003, http://www.bmck.com/cnda_publ_bcab_030601.pdf.

Michael Rasmussen, "Common Mistakes in Information Security," June 14, 2002.

Michael Rasmussen, "Creating a Road Map for an Information Protection Program," June 25, 2002.

Michael Rasmussen, "Enterprise Security Architectures (Organizational Pressures on Information Protection)," Sept. 24, 2002.

Michael Rasmussen, "Information Protection: Assuring Stakeholder Value in a Digital Age," 2002.

Michelle Delio, "Yahoo's 'Opt-Out' Angers Users," *Wired.com*, Apr. 2, 2002, http://www.wired.com/news/privacy/0,1848,51461,00.html.

Micki Krause and Harold Tipton, "Change Management Controls" "Biometric Identification," *Handbook of Information Security Management*, Chapter 1-2-1, Donald R. Richards, ed., CRC Press LLC, 2001, http://www.cccure.org/Documents/HISM/033-037.html#Heading2.

Mike Chapple, Debra Shinder, & Ed Tittle, *TICSA Certification: Information Security Basics*, Que, 2003, http://www.examcram2.com/title/0789727838.

"Model Contracts for the Transfer of Personal Data to Third Countries," http://europa.eu.int/comm/internal_market/privacy/modelcontracts_en.htm.

OECD Guidelines for the Security of Information Systems and Networks: Towards a Culture of Security, July 25, 2002, http://www.oecd.org/document/42/0,2340,en_2649_34255_15582250_1_1_1_1,00.html.

Office of Management and Budget "Cookie" Policy, OMB Memorandum M-00-13, "Privacy Policies and Data Collection on Federal Web Sites," http://www.whitehouse.gov/ omb/memoranda/m00-13.html.

"Office of the New South Wales Privacy Commissioner," http://www.lawlink.nsw.gov.au/pc.nsf/pages/index.

"OMB Guidance for Implementing the Privacy Provisions of the E-Government Act of 2002," Memorandum M-03-22, Office of Management and Budget, Sept. 26, 2003, http://www.whitehouse.gov/omb/memoranda/m03-22.html.

"OMB Guidance to Federal Agencies on Data Availability and Encryption," http://csrc.nist.gov/policies/ombencryption-guidance.pdf.

Opinion 2/2001 on the Adequacy of the Canadian Personal Information and Electronic Documents Act, Article 29 Data Protection Working Party, 5109/00/EN, WP 39, Jan. 26, 2001, http://europa.eu.int/comm/internal_market/privacy/docs/wpdocs/2001/wp39en.pdf.

Organisation for Economic Co-operation and Development, Directorate for Science, Technology and Industry (Committee for Information,

Computer and Communications Policy, *Review of the 1992 Guidelines for the Security of Information Systems*, 1997.

"Origins of the EU Directive 2002/58/EC," Electronic Privacy Information Center, http://www.epic.org/privacy/intl/data_retention.html.

Orin Kerr, "Cybercrime's Scope: Interpreting 'Access' and 'Authorization Misuse' Statutes," *New University Law Review*, Vol. 78, Nov. 2003, http://papers.ssrn.com/sol3/papers.cfm?abstract_id=399740.

Overview of the Privacy Act of 1974, 2002 Edition, U.S. Department of Justice, http://www.usdoj.gov/04foia/04foia/04_7_1.html.

P. D. Squire, "Privacy of Health Information by way of the GLBA: The NIAC Model Act on Privacy of Consumer Financial Information," Jan. 1, 2001, http://www.ebglaw.com/article_389.htm.

Pablo A. Palazzi, "Data Protection in South America 2001."

Patricia Wilson, "Privacy Law in Canada," Jan. 15, 2003, http://www.osler.com/index.asp?menuid=86&layid=124&csid=7&csid1=1299.

Paul J. Santos, "How to Make Linux System Auditing a Little Easier," Sept. 15, 2002, http://www.sans.org/rr/paper.php?id=81.

"Personal Data Protection in Korea," Korea Information Security Agency, Secretariat of Personal Information Dispute Mediation Committee, Aug. 2002, www.cyberprivacy.or.kr/per01.doc.

Peter P. Swire, "The Great Wall of Europe," Feb. 15, 1998, CIO, http://www.cio.com/archive/enterprise/021598_intellectual.html.

Philip L. Gordon, "Federal Judge's Victory Just the First Shot in the Battle Over Workplace Monitoring," Sept. 20, 2001, http://www.privacyfoundation.org/workplace/law/law_show.asp?ed=75&action=0.

PKI Assessment Guidelines, American Bar Association, Section of Science & Technology Law, Information Security Committee, http://www.abanet.org/scitech/ec/isc/pag/pag.html.

Post 9/11 Anxiety Increases Substance Abuse—Legal Issues Surround Drug and Alcohol Testing," *HR Managers' Legal Reporter*, Issue 396 at 5, http://www.eapage.com/post911anxiety.doc.

Prepared Statement of the Federal Trade Commission on The Fair Credit Reporting Act, U.S. Senate Committee on Banking, Housing, and Urban Affairs, May 15, 2003 at 10, http://www.ftc.gov/os/2003/05/030515finalfcratestimony.pdf

"Privacy and Government," http://www.privacilla.org/government.html.

Privacy and Human Rights 2000: An International Survey of Privacy Laws and Developments, Electronic Privacy and Information Center (EPIC) and Privacy International, http://www.privacyinternational.org/survey/phr2000/.

Privacy and Human Rights 2000: An International Survey of Privacy Laws and Developments, "Country Reports," "Australia," http://www.privacy international.org/survey/phr2000/countriesag.html#Heading2.

Privacy and Human Rights 2000: An International Survey of Privacy Laws and Developments, "Country Reports," "Czech Republic," http://www. privacyinternational.org/survey/phr2000/countriesag.html#Heading11.

Privacy and Human Rights 2000: An International Survey of Privacy Laws and Developments, "Country Reports," "Republic of Estonia," http://www. privacyinternational.org/survey/phr2000/countriesag.html#Heading14.

Privacy and Human Rights 2000: An International Survey of Privacy Laws and Developments, "Country Reports," "Republic of Korea (South Korea)," http://www.privacyinternational.org/survey/phr2000/Heading8.

Privacy and Human Rights 2000: An International Survey of Privacy Laws and Developments, "Country Reports," "Republic of Lithuania," http://www. privacyinternational.org/survey/phr2000/countrieshp.html#Heading10.

Privacy and Human Rights 2000: An International Survey of Privacy Laws and Developments, "Country Reports," "Republic of Poland," http://www. privacyinternational.org/survey/phr2000/countriesru.html.

Privacy and Human Rights 2000: An International Survey of Privacy Laws and Developments, "Country Reports," "Republic of South Africa," http:// www.privacyinternational.org/survey/phr2000/countriesru.html# Heading7.

Privacy and Human Rights 2000: An International Survey of Privacy Laws and Developments, "Country Reports," "Republic of Turkey," http://www. privacyinternational.org/survey/phr2000/countriesru.html#Heading13.

Privacy and Human Rights 2000: An International Survey of Privacy Laws and Developments, "Country Reports," "State of Israel," http://www. privacyinternational.org/survey/phr2000/countrieshp.html#Heading5.

Privacy and Human Rights 2002: An International Survey of Privacy Laws and Developments, Electronic Privacy Information Center and Privacy International, 2002, http://www.privacyinternational.org/survey/ phr2002/phr2002-part1.pdf.

"Privacy Commissioner," http://www.privacy.org.nz/top.html.

Privacy Framework Exposure Draft, American Institute of Certified Public Accountants and Canadian Institute of Chartered Accountants, June 2003, www.aicpa.org/innovation/baas/ewp/2003_06_ed_execsumm .asp.

"Privacy Initiatives: Introduction," Federal Trade Commission, http:// www.ftc.gov/privacy/index.html.

"Privacy Laws by State," Electronic Privacy Information Center, http:// www. epic.org/privacy/consumer/states.html.

Bibliography   221

"Privacy of Consumer Financial Information," 65 *Federal Register* 33646-89, May 24, 2000 (codified at 16 C.F.R. Part 313), http://www.ftc.gov/os/2000/05/65fr33645.pdf.

Privacy Online: A Report to Congress, Federal Trade Commission, June, 1998, http://www.ftc.gov/reports/privacy3/priv-23a.pdf.

Privacy Online: Fair Information Practices in the Online Marketplace, Federal Trade Commission, May 2000, http://www.ftc.gov/reports/privacy2000/privacy2000.pdf.

Privacy Online: OECD Guidance on Policy and Practical Guidance, Organisation for Economic Co-operation and Development, DSTI/ICCP/REG(2002)3/FINAL, Jan. 21, 2003, http://www.olis.oecd.org/document/49/0,2340,en_2649_34255_19216241_119699_1_1_1,00.html.

"Privacy Policies and Data Collection on Federal Web Sites," OMB Memorandum M-00-13, June 22, 2000, http://www.whitehouse/gov/omb/memoranda/m00-13.html.

"Privacy Policies on Federal Web Sites," OMB Memorandum M-99-18, June 2, 1999, http://www.whitehouse.gov/omb/memoranda/m99-18.html.

"Privacy Rights Clearinghouse," Consumer//www.consumer-action.org/English/library/privacy_rights/1996_FS07_EmployeeMonitoring.php.

Protecting Children's Privacy Under COPPA: A Survey on Compliance, Staff Report, Apr. 2002, Federal Trade Commission, http://www.ftc.gov/os/2002/04/ coppasurvey.pdf.

"Ratification of the Convention on the OECD," Organisation for Economic Co-operation and Development, http://www.oecd.org/document/58/0,2340,en_2649_ 34483_1889402_1_1_1_1,00.html.

Regulatory Developments, Latvia Master Report, http://www.eu-esis.org/esis2reg/LVreg1.htm.

Rena Mears, Eileen MacNeil, and Kenneth DeJarnette, "A Matter of Trust: Vital Trust Requires a Delicate Balance between Security and Privacy," *Optimize,* March 2003 at 60, http://www.optimizemag.com/issue/017/ethics.htm.

Report to Parliament Concerning Substantially Similar Provincial Legislation, Privacy Commissioner of Canada, June 2003 at 2, http://www.privcom.gc.ca/legislation/leg-rp_030611_e.pdf.

Restatement of the Law Third, Unfair Competition, Chapter 2, "Trade Secret Law," American Law Institute, Jan. 1995, http://my.execpc.com/~mhallign/unfair.html.

Richard M. Peterson, "Protecting Your Secret Recipe: Trade Secrets, Espionage and Preserving Your Product in Associations," "Definitions

and Elements," *Forum Magazine*, May 2002, http://www.centerline.
org/knowledge/article.cfm?ID=2236&.

Roy Mark, "Feinstein Introduces Privacy Act of 2003," internetnews.com,
Apr. 3, 2003, http://dc.internet.com/news/article.php/2174701.

S. M. Entwisle, "E-mail and Privacy in the Workplace," http://www.
ucalgary.ca/~dabrent/380/ webproj/privacy.html.

S. Zegiorgis, "Biometric Technology Stomps Identity Theft," The SANS
Institute, Jan. 7, 2002, http://www.sans.org/rr/authentic/
biometric_tech.php.

"Safe Harbor FAQ No. 11: Dispute Resolution and Enforcement,"
http://www.ita.doc.gov/td/ecom/RedlinedFAQ11Enforc300.htm.

Safe Harbor Overview, U.S. Department of Commerce, Export Portal,
http://www.export.gov/safeharbor/sh_overview.html.

"Safe Harbor Principles," U.S. Department of Commerce, Export Portal,
http://www.export.gov/safeharbor/sh_documents.html.

Safe Harbor Workbook, U.S. Department of Commerce, Export Portal,
http://www.export.gov/safeharbor/sh_workbook.html

"Security Standards," 68 *Federal Register* 8,333-81, Feb. 20, 2003 (codified at
45 C.F.R. Parts 160, 162, 164), http://www.wedi.org/snip/public/
articles/HIPAA_Security_ Final_Rule_official_version.pdf.

"Senator Feinstein Seeks to Ensure Individuals are Notified when
Personal Information is Stolen from Databases," U.S. Senator Dianne
Feinstein, June 26, 2003, http://feinstein.senate.gov/03Releases/
datasecurityrelease.htm.

"Settlement with Internet Service Provider Ensures that Consumers
Receive Notice of Changes to Service Agreement," Office of New York
State Attorney General Eliot Spitzer, May 7, 2002, http://www.
oag.state.ny.us/press/2002/may/may07b_2.html.

"Smart Card: Standards and Research," National Institute of Standards
and Technology, Information Technology Laboratory, http://
smartcard.nist.gov.

"Standards for Safeguarding Customer Information," 67 *Federal Register*
36484-94, May 23, 2000 (codified at 16 C.F.R. Part 314), http://www.
ftc.gov/os/2002/05/67fr36585.pdf.

*Standards for Security Categorization of Federal Information and Information
Systems*, National Institute of Standards and Technology, Computer
Security Division, Federal Information Processing Standards
Publication FIPS PUB 199, Feb. 2004, http://csrc.nist.gov/
publications/fips/fips199/FIPS-PUB-199-final.pdf.

"State Settles Online Privacy Act Case," Office of New York State
Attorney General Eliot Spitzer, Jan. 14, 2003, http://www.
oag.state.ny.us/press/2003/ jan/jan14a_03.html.

Bibliography　223

"Status of implementation of Directive 95/45 on the Protection of
　Individuals with regard to the Processing of Personal Data,"
　http://europa.eu.int/comm/internal_market/privacy/law/
　implementation_en.htm.

Steven G. Schulman and U. Seth Ottensoser, "Duties and Liabilities of
　Outside Directors to Ensure That Adequate Information and Control
　Systems are in Place—A Study in Delaware Law and The Private
　Securities Litigation Reform Act of 1995," Professional Liability
　Underwriting Society, 2002 D&O Symposium, Feb. 6-7, 2002,
　http://www.plusweb.org/Events/Do/materials/2002/Source/Duties
　%20and%20Liabilities.pdf.

T. D. Wilson, "Information Management," University of Sheffield, United
　Kingdom, http://informationr.net/tdw/publ/papers/encyclopedia_
　entry.html.

Technology Risk Management Guidelines for Financial Institutions, Draft
　Version 1.1, Feb. 28, 2003 at 10, Monetary Authority of Singapore,
　http://www.worldbank.org/wbi/banking/finsecpolicy/
　globaldialogues/dL19/pdf/trm_singapore/pdf.

Technology Risk Management Guidelines for Financial Institutions, Draft,
　Monetary Authority of Singapore, Nov. 11, 2002, http://www.mas.
　gov.sg/display.cfm?id=94D063CD-5EB6-4636-82B5A725F9F6E9F5.

*The Basic Law of the Hong Kong Special Administrative Region of the People's
　Republic of China,* http://www.info.gov.hk/basic_law/fulltext/
　index.htm.

"The Children's Online Privacy Protection Act," Electronic Privacy
　Information Center, http://www.epic.org/privacy/kids/.

"The Elliptic Curve Cryptosystem," *Certicom,* July 2000, http://www.
　certicom.com/resources/download/EccWhite3.pdf.

"The European Union at a glance," http://europa.eu.int/abc/index_
　en.htm.

"The National Strategy to Secure Cyberspace," Feb. 14, 2003, http://www.
　dhs.gov/interweb/assetlibrary/National_Cyberspace_Strategy.pdf.

"The Next Generation of Cryptography: Public Key Sizes for AES," *Code
　& Cipher,* Certicom, http://www.certicom.com/resources/codeand
　cipher/volume1/issue1/template.php?article=1-nextgen.

"The Security-Privacy Paradox: Issues, Misconceptions, and Strategies," A
　Joint Report by the Information and Privacy Commissioner/Ontario
　and Deloitte & Toucher, August 2003, http://www.deloitte.com/dtt/
　cda/doc/content/dtt_financialservices_securityprivacyparadox_
　030829.pdf.

"The Selection and Evaluation of CPOs: A Guide to Companies," Privacy

& American Business, 2003 at 5, http://www.pandab.org/
conf2k3materials.pdf.

Theodor Meron, "The Implications of the Convention on the
Development of Public International Law," Ad Hoc Committee of
Legal Advisers on Public International Law, Contribution of the
CAHDI to the Celebration of the 50th Anniversary of the European
Convention on Human Rights, CAHDI (2000), 4 rev, Apr. 4, 2000, at 13,
http://www.legal.coe.int/international/docs/2000/CAHDI(2000)
4reve.pdf.

Theodore C. Ling, Michael J. Miasek, and Arlan Gates, "Canadian Privacy
Commissioner Sets High Standards for Handling of Customer Personal
Information: The Air Canada Case," *Baker & McKenzie (Canada)*, Apr.
2002, http://www. bmck.com/cnda_publ_airc_020401.pdf.

Theodore C. Ling, Michael J. Miasek, and Arlan Gates, "The European
Commission Ruling on Canadian Private Sector Privacy Legislation
and Its Impact on International Data Transfers," *Internet and E-
Commerce Law in Canada*, Vol. 3, No. 8, Oct. 2002 at 1-2, http://www.
bmck.com/cnda_publ_eubt_021001.pdf.

Thomas A. Longstaff, James T. Ellis, Shawn V. Hernan, Howard F.
Lipson, Robert D. McMillan, Linda Hutz Pesante, and Derek Simmel,
"Security of the Internet," *The Froehlich/Kent Encyclopedia of
Telecommunications*, Vol. 15, Marcel Dekker, 1997, pp. 231-55, http://
www.cert.org/encyc_article/tocencyc.html.

Thomas Glaessner, Tom Kellermann, and Valerie McNevin, *Electronic
Security: Risk Mitigation in Financial Transactions_Public Policy Issues*,
The World Bank, June 2002, http://wbln0018.worldbank.org/html/
FinancialSectorWeb.nsf/(attachmentweb)/E-security-RiskMitigation
version3/$FILE/E-security-Risk+Mitigation+version+3.pdf.

Tim Grance, Karen Kent, and Brian Kim, *Computer Security Incident
Handling Guide*, National Institute of Standards and Technology,
Special Publication 800-61, Jan. 2004, http://csrc.nist.gov/publication/
nistpubs/800-61/sp800-61.pdf.

Tom Karygiannis and Les Owens, *Wireless Network Security: 802.11,
Bluetooth and Handheld Devices*, NIST Special Publication 800-48, Nov.
2002, http://csrc.nist.gov/publications/nistpubs/.

"Trade Secret Protection," *Legal Ideas*, 1998, http://members.aol.com/
cynthiabs/secret.html.

United Nations guidelines concerning Computerized personal data files, United
Nations, General Assembly, Dec. 14, 1990, http://www.europa.eu.int/
comm/internal_market/ privacy/instruments/un_en.htm.

"What Is the OECD Privacy Statement Generator?" Organisation for

Economic Co-operation and Development, http://www.oecd.org/document/39/0,2340,en_2649_34255_28863271_119669_1_1_1,00.html.

"WHOIS," Electronic Privacy Information Center, http://www.epic.org/privacy/whois/.

William C. Barker, *Guide for Mapping Types of Information and Information Systems to Security Categories*, NIST Special Publication 800-60, Vol. I, Draft Version 2.0, http://csrc.nist.gov/publication/drafts/800-60V1f.pdf.

William C. Barker and Annabelle Lee, *Guide for Mapping Types of Information and Information Systems to Security Categories*, NIST Special Publication 800-60, Vol. II, Draft Version 2.0, http://csrc.nist.gov/publications/drafts/sp800-60V2f.pdf.

William J. Clinton, *Presidential Statement on the Signing of the Economic Espionage Act of 1996*, Oct. 11, 1996, http://www.opsec.org/opsnews/Dec96/protected/EEA96.html.

William J. Clinton and Albert Gore, Jr., *A Framework for Global Electronic Commerce*, 1997, http://www.open-technology.com/essay541.htm.

Working Document on Functioning of the Safe Harbor Agreement, Article 29 Data Protection Working Party, 11194/02/EN, WP 62, July 2, 2002, http://europa.eu.int/comm/internal_market/privacy/docs/wpdocs/2002/wp62_en.pdf.

"Workplace Privacy," Electronic Privacy Information Center, http://www.epic.org/ privacy/workplace/.

D. STATUTES AND LEGAL DOCUMENTS

15 U.S.C. Section 45(a), http://www4.law.cornell.edu/uscode/15/45.html.

15 U.S.C. Section 6801 *et seq.*, http://www4.law.cornell.edu/uscode/15/6801.html.

15 U.S.C. Section 6802(a)-(b), GLBA, http://www4.law.cornell.edu/uscode/15/6802.html.

15 U.S.C. Section 6802(d), GLBA, http://www4.law.cornell.edu/uscode/15/6802.html.

15 U.S.C. Section 6802(e)(1), GLBA, http://www4.law.cornell.edu/uscode/15/6802.html.

15 U.S.C. Section 6802(e)(1)(A)-(B), GLBA, http://www4.law.cornell.edu/uscode/15/6802.html.

15 U.S.C. Section 6802(e)(3)(A), GLBA, http://www4.law.cornell.edu/uscode/15/6802.html.

15 U.S.C. Section 6802(e)(3)(B), GLBA, http://www4.law.cornell.edu/uscode/15/6802.html.

226   BIBLIOGRAPHY

15 U.S.C. Section 6802(e)(6)(A)-(B), FCRA, http://www4.law.cornell.edu/uscode/15/6802.html.

15 U.S.C. Section 6802(e)(7), GLBA, http://www4.law.cornell.edu/uscode/15/6802.html.

15 U.S.C. Section 6802(e)(8), GLBA, http://www4.law.cornell.edu/uscode/15/6802.html.

15 U.S.C. Section 6806, FCRA, http://www4.law.cornell.edu/uscode/15/6806.html.

15 U.S.C. Section 6809(3)(B)-(D), GLBA, http://www4.law.cornell.edu/uscode/15/6809.html.

15 U.S.C. Section 6809(4)(A)(i)-(ii), GLBA, http://www4.law.cornell.edu/uscode/15/6809.html.

15 U.S.C. Section 6809(4)(B), GLBA, http://www4.law.cornell.edu/uscode/15/6809.html.

15 U.S.C. Section 6809(4)(C)(i), GLBA, http://www4.law.cornell.edu/uscode/15/6809.html.

15 U.S.C. Section 6809(6), GLBA, http://www4.law.cornell.edu/uscode/15/6809.html.

15 U.S.C. Section 6809(9), GLBA, http://www4.law.cornell.edu/uscode/15/6809.html.

16 C.F.R. Section 312.10.

16 C.F.R. Section 313.3(b)(1), .4(a), .5(a)(1), .7(a)(1), .8(a)(1).

16 C.F.R. Section 313.3(h),(i)(1).

16 C.F.R. Section 313.3(p)(1)(i)-(iii).

16 C.F.R. Section 313.3(p)(2)(i)-(ii).

16 C.F.R. Section 313.4(a)(1).

16 C.F.R. Section 313.4(a)(2).

16 C.F.R. Section 313.4(b)(1).

16 C.F.R. Section 313.4(c).

16 C.F.R. Section 313.4(e)(1)(i)-(ii).

16 C.F.R. Section 313.5(a)(1).

16 C.F.R. Section 313.5(b)(1).

16 C.F.R. Section 313.6(a)(1), (c)(1)(i)-(iv).

16 C.F.R. Section 313.6(a)(2), (c)(2)(i)-(ii).

16 C.F.R. Section 313.6(a)(3), (c)(3)(i)-(iii).

16 C.F.R. Section 313.6(a)(4).

16 C.F.R. Section 313.6(a)(5).

16 C.F.R. Section 313.6(a)(6).

16 C.F.R. Section 313.6(a)(7).

16 C.F.R. Section 313.6(a)(8), (c)(6)(i)-(ii).
16 C.F.R. Section 313.6(b).
16 C.F.R. Section 313.6(c)(5).
16 C.F.R. Section 313.6(d).
16 C.F.R. Section 313.7(a)(1)(i), (a)(2)(i)(A).
16 C.F.R. Section 313.7(a)(1)(ii), (a)(2)(i)(B).
16 C.F.R. Section 313.7(a)(1)(iii), (a)(2)(ii)(A)-(D).
16 C.F.R. Section 313.7(d).
16 C.F.R. Section 313.7(d)(2).
16 C.F.R. Section 313.7(d)(2)(i)-(ii), (3).
16 C.F.R. Section 313.7(e).
16 C.F.R. Section 313.7(f), (g)(1).
16 C.F.R. Section 313.8(a).
16 C.F.R. Section 313.9(a).
16 C.F.R. Section 313.9(f).
16 C.F.R. Section 313.9(g).
16 C.F.R. Section 313.10(a)(1)(iii).
16 C.F.R. Section 313.11(a)(1)(i)-(iii).
16 C.F.R. Section 313.11(b)(1)(i)-(iii).
16 C.F.R. Section 313.12(a)(1).
16 C.F.R. Section 313.12(b), (c).
16 C.F.R. Section 313.12(a)(1)(i)-(ii).
16 C.F.R. Section 313.12(b)(1).
16 C.F.R. Section 313.12(b)(2).
16 C.F.R. Section 313.12(c)(1).
16 C.F.R. Section 314.3(a).
16 C.F.R. Section 314.4(a).
16 C.F.R. Section 314.4(b).
16 C.F.R. Section 314.4(b)(1)-(3).
16 C.F.R. Section 314.4(c).
16 C.F.R. Section 314.4(d)(1).
16 C.F.R. Section 314.4(d)(2).
40 U.S.C. Section 11332.
42 U.S.C. Section 1177(b).
45 U.S.C. Section 1320d-1(c)(3)(B)(iii).
42 U.S.C. Section 1320d-2.
42 U.S.C. Section 1320d-2(a)(2).
42 U.S.C. Section 1320d-2(d)(2).

228   BIBLIOGRAPHY

42 U.S.C. Section 1320d-5, d-6.

42 U.S.C. Section 1320d-7.

45 C.F.R. Section 154.530(c).

45 C.F.R. Section 160.103 (definition).

45 C.F.R. Section 164.306(a).

45 C.F.R. Section 164.306(b).

45 C.F.R. Section 164.306(b)(2)(iii).

45 C.F.R. Section 164.306(b)(2)(i).

45 C.F.R. Section 164.504(e).

45 C.F.R. Section 164.520.

45 C.F.R. Section 164.530.

45 C.F.R. Section 164.530(c).

45 U.S.C. Section 1320d-1(c)(3)(B)(iii).

1917 Constitution of Mexico, English translation, http://www.ilstu.edu/ class/hist263/docs/1917const.html.

Access to Information Act (R.S. 1985, c. A-1), http://laws.justice.gc.ca/ en/A-1/text.html.

Act on Protection of Individuals with Regard to the Processing of Personal Data No. 77/2000, Republic of Ireland, http://www. mannvernd.is/english/laws/Act. DataProtection.html (English translation).

An Act Respecting the Protection of Personal Information in the Private Sector, 1994, Province of Quebec, R.S.Q., chapter P-39.1, http:// publicationsduquebec.gouv.qc.ca/dynamicSearch/telecharge .php?type=2&file=/ P_39_1/P39_1_A.html.

Additional Protocol to the Convention for the protection of individuals with regard to automatic processing of personal data regarding supervisory authorities and transborder data flows, Council of Europe, ETS No. 181, 8.XI.2001, Jan. 28, 1991, http://conventions.coe.int/Treaty/EN/ Treaties/Html/181.htm.

Agreement Containing Consent Order as to American Student List, http:// www.ftc.gov/os/2002/10/nrccuaagree.pdf (consent order accorded final approval on January 29, 2003).

Alaska Statutes Section 23.10.037.

Amendments to the Convention for the Protection of Individuals with regard to automatic processing of personal data (ETS No. 108) allowing the European communities to accede, Council of Europe, 28.I.1981, June 15, 1981, http://www.coe.int/T/E/Legal_affairs/Legal_co-operation/ Data_protection/Documents/International_legal_instruments/ Amendements%20to%20the%20Convention%20108.asp.

Arizona Revised Statutes Section 32.2701.

Bailiwick of Guernsey Data Protection Law 2001, http://www. dpcommission.gov.gg/2001%20Law/2001%20Law.htm.

Bank Holding Company Act, 12 U.S.C. Section 1843(k), http://www4. law.cornell.edu/uscode/12/1843.html.

Bermuda Electronic Transactions Act of 1999, Part VI, Para. 26, Aug. 5, 1999, http://www.fortknox.bm/NXT/gateway.dll?f=templates&fn =default.htm.

California Civ. Code Section 1798.82.

California Civ. Proc. Code 2018.

California Labor Code Section 432.2.

Canadian Charter of Rights and Freedoms, http://lois.justice.gc.ca/fr/ charte/ const_en.html.

CAN-SPAM Act, http://thomas.loc/gov/cgi-bin/bdquery/z?d108: s.00877.

Children's Online Privacy Protection Act, 1998, 15 U.S.C. Sections 6501-6506, http://www4.law.cornell.edu/uscode/15/6501.html.

Civil Code of Quebec, Articles 35-40, http://www.canlii.org/qc/sta/ csqc/20030530/c.c.q./part1.html.

CoE 1999 Amendments to Personal Data Convention at Article 1 (amending Article 3 of original CoE Personal Data Convention).

CoE 1999 Amendments to Personal Data Convention at Article 1 b.

CoE Additional Protocol to Personal Data Convention, Article 2.

CoE Personal Data Convention, Article 5, "Quality of data."

CoE Personal Data Convention, Article 2 c, "Definitions."

CoE Personal Data Convention, Article 7, "Data security."

CoE Personal Data Convention, Article 8, "Additional safeguards for the data subject."

CoE Personal Data Convention, Article 9, "Exceptions and restrictions."

CoE Personal Data Convention, Article 12, "Transborder flows of personal data and domestic law."

CoE Personal Data Convention, Article 13, "Co-operation between Parties."

Commission Decision of 15 June 2001 on standard contractual clauses for the transfer of personal data to third countries, under Directive 95/46/EC, Commission of the European Communities, (notified under document number C(2001) 1539), (2001/497/EC), http://europa. eu.int/eur-lex/ pri/en/oj/dat/2001/l_181/l_18120010704en00190031.pdf.

Commission Decision of 26 July 2000 pursuant to Directive 95/46/EC of the European Parliament and of the Council on the adequate protection of personal data provided in Hungary, Commission of the European Communities (notified under document number C(2000) 2305) (2000/519/EC), http://europa.eu.int/eur-lex/pri/en/oj/dat/ 2000/l_215/l_21520000825en00040006.pdf.

Commission Decision of 26 July 2000 pursuant to Directive 95/46/EC of the European Parliament and of the Council on the adequate protection of personal data provided in Switzerland, Commission of the European Communities (notified under document number C(2000) 2304) (2000/518/EC), http://www.edsb.ch/e/gesetz/eu/ adequacy.pdf.

Commission Decision of 20 December 2001 pursuant to Directive 95/46/EC of the European Parliament and of the Council on the adequate protection of personal data provided by the Canadian Personal Information Protection and Electronic Documents Act (notified under document number C(2001) 4539), Official Journal L 002, Apr. 1, 2002 at 13-16, http://europa.eu.int/ smartapi/cgi/sga_doc?smartapi!celexapi!prod!CELEXnumdoc&lg= en&numdoc=32002D0002&model=guichett.

Commission Decision of 27 December 2001 on standard contractual clauses for the transfer of personal data to processors established in third countries, under Directive 95/46/EC, Commission of the European Communities (notified under document number C(2001) 4540) (2002/16/EC), http://europa .eu.int/eur-lex/pri/en/oj/dat/2002/l_006/l_00620020110en00520062 .pdf.

Commission Decision of 30 June 2003 pursuant to Directive 95/46/EC of the European Parliament and of the Council on the adequate protection of personal data in Argentina, Commission of the European Communities, C(2003) 1731 final, http://europa.eu.int/comm/internal_market/ privacy/docs/adequacy/decision-c2003-1731/decision-argentine_en. pdf.

Communications Act, 47 U.S.C. Section 222, http://www4.law.cornell. edu/uscode/47/222.html.

Computer Matching and Privacy Protection Act of 1988, 5 U.S.C. Section 552a(a)(8)-(13), (e)(12), (o), (p), (q), (r), (u), http://www4.law. cornell.edu/uscode/5/552a.html.

Computer Matching and Privacy Protection Amendments, Pub. Law 101-508.

Computer Matching and Privacy Protection Amendments of 1990, 5 U.S.C. Section 552a(p), http://www4.law.cornell.edu/uscode/5/552a .html.

Computer Misuse Act, Cap. 50A, s. 15, http://statutes.agc.gov.sg.

Computer Security Act of 1987, Pub. Law 100-235, http://www.cio.gov/ Documents/computer_security_act_Jan_1998.html.

Connecticut General Statutes Annotated Section 31-48b (2003).

Connecticut General Statutes Section 31-48b(b).

Connecticut General Statutes Section 31-48d(3)(b)(1).

Connecticut General Statutes Section 31-51g.

Connecticut General Statutes Section 31-51t.

Constitution of Republic of Turkey, http://www.tbmm.gov.tr/anayasa/constitution.htm.

Consumer Privacy Protection Act of 2003, H.R. 1636, http://thomas.loc.gov/cgi-bin/query.

Convention for the Protection of Human Rights and Fundamental Freedoms as Amended by Protocol No. 11, with Protocol Nos. 1, 4, 6, 7, 12, and 13, Article 8, Feb. 2003, http://www.echr.coe.int/Convention/webConvenENG.pdf.

Convention for the Protection of Individuals with Regard to Automatic Processing of Personal Data, Council of Europe, ETS No. 108, 28.I.1981, 1981, http://conventions.coe.int/Treaty/EN/Treaties/Html/108.htm.

Customer Proprietary Network Information, 47 C.F.R. Section 64.2001 *et seq.*

Declaration on Transborder Data Flows, Organisation for Economic Co-operation and Development, Apr. 11, 1985, http://www.oecd.org/document/25/0,2340,en_2649_34255_1888153_199820_1_1_1,00.html.

Declaratory Ruling and Notice of Proposed Rulemaking, GN Docket No. 00-185, CS Docket No. 02-52, FCC 02-77 (March 15, 2002), http://hraunfoss.fcc.gov/edocs_public/ attachmatch/FCC-02-77A1.pdf.

Delaware Code Title 11, Section 1335(a)(2).

Delaware Code Title 19, Section 704.

Delaware Code Title 19, Section 705 (2003).

Directive 95/46/EC of the European Parliament and of the Council of 24 October 1995 on the protection of individuals with regard to the processing of personal data and on the free movement of such data, Official Journal L 281/31, Nov. 23, 1995, http://europa.eu.int/smartapi/cgi/sga_doc?smartapi!celexapi!prod!CELEXnumdoc&lg=EN&numdoc=31995L0046&model=guichett.

Directive 2002/58/EC of the European Parliament and of the Council of 12 July 2002 concerning the processing of personal data and the protection of privacy in the electronic communications sector (Directive on privacy and electronic communications), Official Journal L 201/37, July 31, 2002 (replacing EU Directive 97/66/EC), http://europa.eu.int/smartapi/cgi/sga_doc?smartapi!celexapi!prod!CELEXnumdoc&lg=en&numdoc=32002L0058&model=guichett.

Disclosure of Customer Information, N.D. Cent. Code, Ch. 6-08.1-03 (2003), http://www.state.nd.us/lr/cencode/T06C081.pdf.

District of Columbia Code Section 36-801.

232   BIBLIOGRAPHY

Do Not Call Implementation Act, Pub. Law 108-10 (2003), http://www.mbaa.org/industry/docs/03/h_395_0213.pdf.

Economic Espionage Act of 1996, 18 U.S.C. Sections 1831-1839, http://www4.law.cornell.edu/uscode/18/1831.html.

Electronic Communications Privacy Act, 18 U.S.C. Sections 2701-2712, http://www4.law.cornell.edu/uscode/18/2701.html.

Fair and Accurate Credit Transaction Act of 2003, Section 624, Pub. Law 108-159, Dec. 4, 2003.

Fair Credit Reporting Act, 15 U.S.C. Section 1681 *et seq.*, http://www4.law.cornell. edu/uscode/15/1681.html.

Federal Author Rights Act, http://www.cddhcu.gob.mx/leyinfo/pdf/122.pdf (Spanish).

Federal Consumer Protection Act, *Mexican Official Gazette*, Aug. 27, 1997, http://www.profeco.gob.mx/new/html/mjuridic/lfpc.htm (Spanish).

Federal Criminal Code of Mexico, http://www.cddhcu.gob.mx/leyinfo/pdf/9.pdf.

Federal Electoral Institutions and Proceedings Code of Mexico, http://www.cddhcu.gob.mx/leyinfo/pdf/5.pdf.

Federal Employment Act, http://www.cddhcu.gob.mx/leyinfo/pdf/125.pdf (Spanish).

Federal Information Security Management Act, Pub. Law 107-347, Title III of E-Government Act of 2002, http://csrc.nist.gov/policies/FISMA-final.pdf.

Federal Reserve Board Regulation Y, 12 C.F.R. Section 225.28.

Federal Telecommunications Act (Mexico), http://www.cddhcu.gob.mx/leyinfo/pdf/118.pdf (Spanish).

Federal Trade Commission Act,15 U.S.C. Section 45.

Federal Transparency and Public Governmental Information Access Act, June 11, 2002, http://www.ifai.org.mx/textos/gobiernofederal/marconormativo/LFAIPG/LEYFEDTR.pdf (Spanish).

Financial Services Modernization Act of 1999, Pub. Law 106-102, Nov. 12, 1999.

Financial Services Modernization Act of 1999, Nov. 12, 1999, "Gramm-Leach-Bliley Act," 15 U.S.C. Section 6801 *et seq.*, http://thomas.loc.gov/cgi-bin/bdquery/z?d106:SN00900.

Florida Statutes Section 760.40.

Freedom of Information Act, 5 U.S.C. Section 552 (2003), http://www4.law. cornell.edu/uscode/5/552.html.

FTC Act, 15 U.S.C. Section 45(n), http://www4.law.cornell.edu/uscode/15/45.html.

Geographic and Statistics Information Law, *Mexican Official Gazette,* Dec. 30, 1980, amended on Dec. 12, 1983, http://www.inegi.gob.mx/ difusion/espanol/fdimj.html (Spanish).

Georgia Code Section 43-36-1.

Gramm-Leach-Bliley Act, 15 U.S.C. Section 6807, http://www4. law .cornell.edu/uscode/15/6807.html.

Hawaii Revised Statutes Section 378.1.

Health Information Act, http://www. qp.gov.ab.ca/documents/acts/ H05.cfm.

Health Insurance Portability and Accountability Act of 1996, Pub. Law 104-191, http://aspe.hhs.gov/admnsimp/pl104191.htm.

HIPPA, 47 U.S.C. Section 1320d-1(a).

Idaho Code Section 44-903.

Identity Theft and Financial Privacy Protection Act of 2003, H.R. 2035, http://thomas.loc.gov/cgi-bin/query.

Industrial Property Act (Mexico), http://www.cddhcu.gob.mx/ leyinfo/ pdf/50.pdf (Spanish).

Interagency Guidelines Establishing Standards for Safeguarding Customer Information and Rescission of Year 2000 Standards for Safety and Soundness, Final Rule, 12 C.F.R. Part 30 *et seq.*

International Covenant on Civil and Political Rights, General Assembly Resolution 2200A (XXI), Dec. 16, 1966 (adopted), Mar. 23, 1976 (entry into force), http://193.194.138.190/html/menu3/b/a_ccpr.htm.

Iowa Code Section 730.4.

Isle of Man Data Protection Act 2002, http://www.gov.im/odps/ legislation/dpact2002.xml.

Jersey Data Protection Law 1987, http://www.dataprotection.gov.je/.

Law for Regulating Credit Information Companies, Jan. 15, 2002, http://www. cddhcu.gob.mx/leyinfo/pdf/237.pdf (Spanish).

Law No. 1682 that Regulates the Private Character Information, http:// ulpiano.com/habeasdaata_paraguay_Ley.htm.

Louisiana Statutes Section 36-A:2848.

Maine Revised Statutes Title 32, Section 7166.

Maryland Code of Labor and Employment, Section 3-702.

Massachusetts General Laws ch. 149, Section 19B.

Medical Independence, Privacy, and Innovation Act, H.R. 2196 and H.R. 2544, http://thomas.loc.gov/cgi-bin/query.

Michigan Compiled Laws Section 37.201.

Ministerial Declaration on the Protection of Privacy on Global Networks, Organisation for Economic Co-operation and Development,

DSTI/ICCP/REG(98)10/FINAL, Oct. 7-9, 1998, http://www.oecd
.org/dataoecd/39/13/1840065.pdf.

Minnesota Statutes Section 181.75.

Montana Code Section 39.2-304.

Montana Code Section 50-16-1009.

National Uniform Privacy Standards Act of 2003, H.R. 1766, http://
thomas.loc.gov/cgi-bin/query.

Nebraska Revised Statutes Section 81-1932.

Nevada Revised Statutes Section 613.480.

New Mexico Statutes Annotated Section 28-10A-1.

New York Labor Law Section 733.

Norwegian Data Protection Law, http://www.lovdata.no/all/ hl-
20000414-031.html.

Ohio Revised Code Annotated 1349.17.

Online Privacy Protection Act of 2003, H.R. 69, http://thomas.loc.gov/
cgi-bin/query.

*Opinion 2/2001 on the Adequacy of the Canadian Personal Information and
Electronic Documents Act,* Article 29 Data Protection Working Party,
5109/00/EN, WP 39, Jan. 26, 2001, http://europa.eu.int/comm/
internal_market/privacy/docs/wpdocs/2001/wp39en.pdf.

Oregon Revised Statutes Section 659.225.

Pennsylvania Statutes Title 18, Section 7321.

Personal Data (Privacy) Ordinance, Chapter 486, http://www.pco.org.
hk/english/ordinance/ordfull.html.

Personal Data Protection Act, No. 25.326, Oct. 4, 2000, http://www.aaba.
org.ar/ln25326.htm (Spanish).

Personal Information Privacy Act of 2003, H.R. 1931, http://thomas.loc.
gov/cgi-bin/query.

Personal Information Protection Act, Province of Alberta, Bill 44, http://
www.assembly.ab.ca/pro/bills/ba-bill.asp?SelectBill=044.

Personal Information Protection Act, Province of British Columbia, Bill
38-2003, http://www.legis.gov.bc.ca/37th4th/1st_read/gov38-1.htm.

Privacy Act of 1974, 5 U.S.C. Section 552a, http://www4.law.cornell.edu/
uscode/5/552a.html.

Privacy Act, 1980-81-82-83, c. 111, Sch. li "1," http://www.privcom.gc.ca/
legislation/02_07_01_e.asp.

Privacy Act 1988, http://www.austlii.edu.au/au/legis/cth/consol_act/
pa1988108/ index.html#longtitle.

Privacy Act of 2003, S. 745, Mar. 31, 2003, http://thomas.loc.gov/cgi-bin/
query/D?c108:11:./temp/~c108QJ74pW::.

Quebec Charter of Human Rights and Freedoms, Articles 4 and 5, http://www.cdpdj.qc.ca/en/commun/docs/charter.pdf.

Restrictions on Telephone Solicitation, 47 C.F.R. Section 64.1200.

Rhode Island General Laws 6-13-17.

Rhode Island General Laws Section 28-6.1-1.

Sarbanes-Oxley Act of 2002, Pub. Law 107-204 Sections 302, 404, http://news.findlaw.com/hdocs/docs/gwbush/sarbanesoxley072302.pdf.

Security Breach Information Act (SB 1386), Feb. 12, 2002, http://info.sen.ca.gov/pub/01-02/bill/sen/sb_1351-1400/sb_1386_bill_20020926_chaptered.html.

South Korean Constitution, Article 17, July 17, 1948, http://www.oefre.unibe.ch/law/ icl/ks00000_.html.

Standards for Privacy of Individually Identifiable Health Information, 45 C.F.R. Parts 160, 164, http://www.hhs.gov/ocr/hipaa/finalreg.html.

Stop Taking Our Health Privacy Act of 2003, H.R. 1709, http://thomas.loc.gov/cgi-bin/query.

Student Privacy Protection Act of 2003, H.R. 1848, http://thomas. loc.gov/cgi-bin/query.

Telemarketing Sales Rule, 16 C.F.R. Part 310.

Telephone Consumer Protection Act, 47 U.S.C. Section 227, http://www4.law.cornell.edu/uscode/47/227.html.

Tennessee Code Section 62-27-123.

Third Report and Order and Third Further Notice of Proposed Rulemaking, CC Docket Nos. 96-115, 96-149, 00-257, FCC 02-214 (July 25, 2002), http://hraunfoss.fcc.gov/ edocs_public/attachmatch/FCC-02-214A1.pdf.

Uniform Trade Secrets Act, Drafted by the National Conference of Commissioners on Uniform State Laws, as amended 1985, Section 1(4)(i), http://nsi.org/Library/ Espionage/usta.htm.

Universal Declaration of Human Rights, United Nations, General Assembly, Resolution 217 A (III), Dec. 10, 1948, http://www.un.org/Overview/rights.html.

USTA Sections 1-4, http://nsi.org/Library/Espionage/usta.htm.

Utah Code Section 34-37-16.

Vermont Statutes Title 21, Section 5a.

Vermont Statutes Title 21, Section 495(6).

Vermont Statutes Title 21, Section 511.

Virginia Code Section 2.1-385.

Washington Revised Code Section 49.44.120.

Washington Revised Code Section 49.60.172.

West Virginia Code Section 21-5-5a.

Wireless Privacy Protection Act of 2003, H.R. 71, http://thomas.loc.gov/cgi-bin/query.

E. BOOKS AND ARTICLES

U.S. LEGAL FRAMEWORK

Allison R. Michael and Scott M. Lidman, "Monitoring of employees still growing: Employers seek greater productivity and avoidance of harassment liability; most workers have lost on privacy claims," *The National Law Journal*, Jan. 29, 2001.

Annual Report to Congress on Foreign Economic Collection and Industrial Espionage, June 1997, National Counterintelligence Center.

Barbara S. Wellbery and Miriam H. Wugmeister, "Privacy: The U.S., E.U., Latin America, and Asia."

Cheryl Blackwell Bryson and Michelle Day, "Workplace Surveillance Poses Legal, Ethical Issues," *The National Law Journal*, Jan. 11, 1999.

"Computer Use Policy, Widespread Monitoring Doom Claim of Privacy in Company Computer," *Electronic Commerce & Law Report*, Bureau of National Affairs, Vol. 7, No. 10, Mar. 6, 2002.

Devon Hewitt, "New California privacy law has nationwide ripple," *Washington Technology*, July 7, 2003.

"High Court Says 'Actual Damages' Needed to Win $1,000 for DOL's Privacy Act Breach," *Privacy & Security Law Report*, vol. 3, no. 9, Mar. 1, 2004 at 235–36.

"HIPAA Privacy Rule Compliance to Enter Enforcement Phase in 2004," *Privacy & Security Law Report*, Bureau of National Affairs, Vol. 3, No. 4, Jan. 26, 2004 at 106–107.

Jody R. Westby, "Protection of Trade Secrets and Confidential Information: How to Guard Against Security Breaches and Economic Espionage," *Intellectual Property Counselor*, Jan. 2000.

Joel R. Reidenberg and Paul M. Schwartz, *Data Privacy Law: A Study of United States Data Protection*, Michie, 1996.

Kathleen M. Porter, David Wilson , and Jacqueline Scheib, "Work Station or purgatory? Steps Toward a Company Policy on E-Mail and Using the Net," *Business Law Today*, July/Aug. 2002.

Linda A. Malek and Brian R. Krex, "HIPAA's Security Rule Becomes Effective 2005," *The National Law Journal*, Mar. 31, 2003.

Patti Waldmeir, "US Employees Find No Right to Privacy in Cyberspace," *The Financial Times*, Aug. 13, 2001.

Randy Gainer, Michael van Eckhardt, Rebecca Williams, and Richard D. Marks, "WiFi Devices in Hospitals Pose Major HIPAA Challenges," *Privacy & Security Law Report*, Bureau of National Affairs, Vol. 2, No. 21, May 26, 2003.

Richard D. Marks, "Implementing HIPAA: Guidelines for Initiating HIPAA Systems Implementation Projects," *Electronic Commerce & Law Report*, Bureau of National Affairs, Vol. 5, No. 18, May 3, 2000.

Richard D. Marks, "Surviving Standard Transactions: A HIPAA Roadmap," *Privacy & Security Law Report*, Bureau of National Affairs, Vol. 2, No. 24 , June 16, 2003.

The Economic Espionage Act of 1996: A Brief Guide, National Counter Intelligence Center.

Thomas Cooley, *Law of Torts*, 2nd ed., Vol. 29, 1888.

"True Scope of HIPAA's Privacy Protection to Be Defined Through Lawsuits, Lawyers Say," *Privacy & Security law Report*, Bureau of National Affairs, Vol. 3, No. 11, Mar. 15, 2004 at 305–06.

Vanessa A. Nelson, "Use of UCE: An Overview of State Laws Regarding Unsolicited Commercial Electronic Mail Advertisements," Privacy Regulation, American Bar Association, Summer 2002.

INTERNATIONAL LEGAL FRAMEWORK

Alan Charles Raul, Edward R. McNicholas, and Julie Dwyer, "European Court of Justice's Landmark Decision on EU Data Protection Directive Accords Broad Scope to EU Privacy Regime, Addresses Applicability to Internet," *Privacy & Security Law Report*, Bureau of National Affairs, Vol. 2, No. 48, Dec. 8, 2003 at 1387–89.

"As Data Privacy Laws Evolve Globally Many Nations Consider European Model," *Privacy & Security Law Report*, Bureau of National Affairs, Vol. 2, No. 16, Apr. 21, 2003 at 425-28.

Christopher Kuner, *European Data Privacy Law and Online Business*, Oxford University Press, 2003.

David E. Case, "The New Japanese Personal Information Protection Law," *Privacy & Security Law Report*, Vol. 2, No. 23, June 9, 2003 at 633-35.

Don McGowan, "New and Upcoming Developments in Canadian Privacy Law," *Internet and E-Commerce Law in Canada*, Butterworths, Vol. 4, No. 4, June 2003 at 29.

"European Data Protection Law Seen as Spilling into Latin America," *Privacy & Security Law Report*, Bureau of National Affairs, Vol. 2, No. 16, Apr. 21, 2003 at 428-30.

238   BIBLIOGRAPHY

Harbaksh Singh Nanda, "India Drafting EU-Style Data Privacy Bill: Seeks to Attract Business From Europe," *Privacy & Security Law Report,* Bureau of National Affairs, Vol. 2, No. 22, June 2, 2003 at 584.

International Strategy for Cyberspace Security, American Bar Association, Section of Science & Technology Law, Privacy & Computer Crime Committee, ABA Publishing, 2003.

James Lim, "South Korea Slates June Introduction of Sweeping Data Privacy Legislation," *Privacy & Security Law Report,* Bureau of National Affairs, Vol. 3, No. 11, Mar. 15, 2004.

"Japanese Parliament Enacts Bills on Personal Information Protection," *Privacy & Security Law Report,* Vol. 2, No. 22, June 2, 2003 at 584.

Murray Griffin, "APEC Privacy Policy Task Force Wrestles With U.S. Text on Preserving Data Flows," *Privacy & Security Law Report,* Bureau of National Affairs, Vol. 3, No. 12, Mar. 22, 2004 at 337.

"Nine EU Nations Get EC Challenge Over Failure to Adopt Privacy Directive," *Privacy & Security Law Report,* Bureau of National Affairs, Vol. 2, No. 48, Dec. 8, 2003 at 1368–69.

PRIVACY PROGRAMS: PLANS, POLICIES, & PROCEDURES

Ann Cavoukian and Tyler J. Hamilton, *The Privacy Payoff: How Successful Business Build Customer Trusts,* McGraw-Hill Ryerson Inc., Toronto, 2002 at xx.

Christian F. Byrnes and Dale Kutnick, *Securing Business Information: Strategies to Protect the Enterprise and Its Network,* Intel Press.

Christopher M. King, Curtis E. Dalton, and T. Ertem Osmanoglu, *Security Architecture Design, Deployment & Operations,* McGraw-Hill, 2001.

Daniel J. Solove and Marc Rotenberg, *Information Privacy Law,* Aspen Publishers, 2003 at 721-24.

Harold F. Tipton and Micki Krause, editors, *The Information Security Handbook,* 4th ed., Vol. 2, CRC Press LLC, 2001.

Jody R. Westby, "Digital Corporate Governance," May 5, 2003.

Jody R. Westby, "Protection of Trade Secrets and Confidential Information: How to Guard Against Security Breaches and Economic Espionage," *Intellectual Property Counselor,* Jan. 2000.

Roberta Bragg, "CISSP Security Management and Practices," Dec. 20, 2002.

Pat Carbine, "Questions for Board Members to Ask About Information Security," Presentation at the White House, Apr. 18, 2000.

Mastering the Ten Domains of Computer Security, John Wiley & Sons, Inc., 2001.

Michael Erbschloe and John Vacca, *Net Privacy*, McGraw-Hill, 2001 at xvii.

Michael Rasmussen, "Creating a Road Map for an Information Protection Program," RPA-062002-00026, Giga Information Group, June 25, 2002. Ronald L. Krutz and Russell Dean Vines, *The CISSP Prep Guide:*

Michael Rasmussen, "Four Responses to Risk," RIB-092002-00209, Sept. 26, 2002.

Michael Rasmussen, "The Difference Between Information Security Policy, Guidelines, Procedures and Standards, *Ideabyte*, Sept. 3, 2001.

"Yahoo Web Portal Changes Privacy Policy, Opt-In Policy for Unsolicited Advertisements," *Privacy & Security Law Report*, Bureau of National Affairs, Vol. 1, No. 14, Apr. 8, 2002.

IMPLEMENTATION AND SCIENCE & TECHNOLOGY

Alan Charles Raul, Frank R. Volpe, and Edward R. McNicholas, "Eli Lilly-FTC Consent Order Is a Good Road Map for Corporate Data Protection," *Electronic Commerce & Law Report*, Bureau of National Affairs, Vol. 7, No. 6, Feb. 6, 2002.

Allison R. Michael and Scott M. Lidman, "Monitoring of Employees Still Growing: Employers Seek Greater Productivity and Avoidance of Harassment Liability; Most Workers Have Lost on Privacy Claims," *The National Law Journal*, Jan. 29, 2001 at B9, B15, B17-18.

"As Data Privacy Laws Evolve Globally Many Nations Consider European Model," *Privacy & Security Law Report*, Bureau of National Affairs, Vol. 2, No. 16, Apr. 21, 2003 at 425-28.

Bruce Schneier, *Secrets and Lies: Digital Security in a Networked World*, John Wiley and Sons, Inc., 2000.

Cheryl Blackwell Bryson and Michelle Day, "Workplace Surveillance Poses Legal, Ethical Issues, *The National Law Journal*, Jan. 11, 1999 at B8.

"Computer Policy Did Not Dispel Employee's Expectation of Privacy in State Employment," *Privacy & Security Law Report*, Bureau of National Affairs, Vol. 3, No. 6, Feb. 9, 2004 at 144 45.

"Computer Use Policy, Widespread Monitoring Doom Claim of Privacy in Company Computer," *Electronic Commerce & Law Report*, Bureau of National Affairs, Vol. 7, No. 10, Mar. 6, 2002 at 217.

Devon Hewitt, "New California privacy law has nationwide ripple," *Washington Technology*, July 7, 2003 at 12.

"Eli Lilly's Unintentional Online Disclosure of Consumer Data Leads to FTC Settlement," *Electronic Commerce & Law Report*, Bureau of National Affairs, Vol. 7, No. 4, Jan. 23, 2002.

Ellen Temperton and Ana-Marie Norbury, "Workplace Monitoring Standards in Europe," *Privacy & Security Law Report,* Bureau of National Affairs, Vol. 3, No. 7, Feb. 16, 2004 at 190–91.

"European Data Protection Law Seen as Spilling into Latin America," *Privacy & Security Law Report,* Bureau of National Affairs, Vol. 2, No. 16, Apr. 21, 2003.

Kathleen M. Porter, David Wilson, and Jacqueline Scheib, "Work Station or purgatory? Steps Toward a Company Policy on E-Mail and Using the Net," *Business Law Today,* July/Aug. 2002 at 59-62.

Michael Rasmussen, "Adopted But Not Implemented Security Policies May Be Your Liability," *Ideabyte,* Apr. 9, 2002.

Michael Rasmussen, "Common Mistakes in Information Security," June 14, 2002.

Michael Rasmussen, "Creating a Road Map for an Information Protection Program," RPA-062002-00026, Giga Information Group, June 25, 2002.

Michael Rasmussen, "Enterprise Security Architectures—Organizational Pressures on Information Protection," Sept. 24, 2002 at 5.

Michael Rasmussen, "Information Protection: Assuring Stakeholder Value in a Digital Age," Special Report 2002, Giga Information Group, Inc.

Patti Waldmeir, "US Employees Find No Right to Privacy in Cyberspace," *The Financial Times,* Aug. 13, 2001 at 12.

R. L. Rivest, A. Shamir, and L. M. Adleman, "A method for obtaining digital signatures and public-key c ryptosystems," *Communications of the ACM,* Vol. 21, Feb. 1978 at 120-26.

Whitfield Diffie and M. E. Hellman, "New Directions in Cryptography," *IEEE Transactions on Information Theory,* Vol. IT-22, Nov. 1976 at 644-54.

INDEX

accountability principle, OECD
  Privacy Guidelines, 85
*Act Respecting the Protection of
  Personal Information in the
  Private Sector,* Quebec, 108,
  109
annual audit, 186–188
anonymizing and sanitizing, 205
APEC's Electronic Commerce
  Coordination forum, Asia,
  118
application audit, 190
Application of English Law,
  Singapore, 125
Argentina, privacy laws, 114–117
Asia
  countries with little privacy
    protection, 118–119
  privacy laws, 118–127
associational privacy, 12
asymmetric (public/private) key
  encryption, 198
attorney-client privilege audits,
  193
audit, reporting requirements for,
  190
audit technologies, 203–204
Australia
  privacy laws, 125–127

state/territory legislation,
  126–127
authentication technologies and
  digital signatures, 203
authorization and access control,
  200–203

Bank Holding Company Act of
  1956, 19
Basic Law, Hong Kong, 119
BBBONLINE Privacy Program, 72
Bill of Rights, 11–12
biometrics, 202
Boards and senior-level
  management, training for
  privacy plans, 177
Brandeis, Louis, 12

cable and satellite television, state
  regulations, 76
Canada
  privacy laws, 106–109
  provincial legislation, 109
Canada's Personal Information
  Protection and Electronic
  Documents Act, 11
Canadian Charter of Rights and
  Freedoms, 106
CAN-SPAM Act of 2003, 62–63

241

Caremark International, Inc. Derivative Litigation, 143–144

change management, privacy policy, 166

Children's Online Privacy Protection Act (COPPA), 46–50, 129

Coastal States Gas Corporation, 193–194

Code on Access to Information, Hong Kong, 120

collection limitation principle, OECD Privacy Guidelines, 84

common access cards, 201

company property, limit to business purposes only, 184

Computer Matching and Privacy Protection Act of 1988, 17

confidential information, 158, 159

Constitutional right to privacy, 11–15

consumer, definition, 21

consumer report, definition, 34–35

contracts and nondisclosure agreements, privacy plans and, 155

Convention for the Protection of Human Rights and Fundamental Freedoms (CoE), 87

Convention for the Protection of Individuals with regard to Automatic Processing of Personal data (CoE), 88–89

Council of Europe (CoE), 87–89

Crimes Act 1914, Australia, 126

critical success factors (CSFs), privacy plans, 179

cross-organizational privacy team, 148–149

customer, definition, 21

Customer Proprietary Network Information (CPNI), 69–70

data classification, in privacy plans, 157–161

Data-matching Program (Assistance and Tax) Act 1990, Australia, 126

Data Protection Directive, EU, 89–102

international data transfer restrictions, 93–94

key principles, 91–92

model clauses and other contractual solutions, 97–100

non-EU European countries and associated territories, 100–102

role of data protection authorities, 93

U.S./EU Safe Harbor Agreement, 94–97

data quality principle, OECD Privacy Guidelines, 84

digital signatures, 199, 203

digital time stamps, 203–204

directors and senior management, role in enterprise privacy plan, 142–148

Do Not Call List, 71

Economic Espionage Act of 1996 (EEA), 54–58

conspiracies, 58

misappropriation and knowledge, 57

penalties, 58

protection of trade secrets, 59

protective orders and confidentiality, 58

two-part prohibition, 56–57

Eisenstadt v. Baird, 12

Electronic Communications Directive (EU), 102–105

privacy protections, 102–103

privacy risks through data retention, 104–105

Electronic Communications Privacy Act (ECPA), 50–54, 152, 155

electronic surveillance, state regulations, 73–74
Electronic Transactions Act, Singapore, 125
employee communications, right to review and monitor, 183–184
employee e-mail monitoring, state regulations, 79
employee privacy awareness and ethics training, 175–176
employment testing, state regulations, 74–76
encryption, 197–199
European Economic Area (EEA), 100
European Free Trade Agreement, 100
European Union (EU), 89–106, 152
    Privacy in Electronic Communications, 102–105
European Union's Data Protection Directive, 11, 152, 155
external audit, 188–189
external privacy policies, 162–164
extraterritorial application of law, 128–130

Fair and Accurate Credit Transactions Act of 2003 (FACTA), 38
Fair Credit Reporting Act (FCRA), 34–38
fair information practices, 15
Federal Communications Commission (FCC), 69–71
    Customer Proprietary Network Information (CPNI), 69–70
    subscriber privacy rules for cable network operations, 70
    telemarketing and junk fax rulemaking, 70–71
Federal Consumer Protection Act, Mexico, 110
Federal legal landscape, 11–71

Federal Trade Commission Act (FTC Act), 64
    Unfair Methods of Competition section, 64–65
Federal Trade Commission (FTC), 63–69
    enforcement of GLBA, 31–33
Federal Transparency and Public Governmental Information Access Act, Mexico, 110, 112
financial institutions
    definition, 19–20
    state regulations, 77
Financial Services Modernization Act of 1999 (Gramm-Leach-Bliley Act), 18–33
    disclosure of NPI, 22–23
    enforcement, 31–33
    entities covered, 19–20
    extraterritorial application, 33
    interpretation of requirements, 20–21
    marketing activities, 28–29
    notice requirements, 23–27
    opt-out procedures, 27–28
    privacy and safeguard component, 136–137
    relation to state law, 33
    safeguarding information, 29–31
Foreign instrumentality, definition, 57
Fourteenth Amendment, 13
Fourth amendment, 12–14
Freedom of Information Act (FOIA), 16–18
Freedom of Information Law, Israel, 128
FTC v. Toysmart, 65

General Principles of Civil Law, China, 119
Geographic and Statistics Information Law, Mexico, 110
Gramm-Leach-Bliley Act. *see* Financial Services Modernization Act of 1999

Greidinger v. Davis, 13
Griswold v. Connecticut, 12
Guidelines concerning Computerized personal data files (UN Computerized Guidelines), 82
Guidelines for the Protection of Individuals with Regard to the Collection and Processing of Personal Data on Information Highways (CoE), 88–89
Guidelines for the Security of Information Systems (OECD), 82
Guidelines on the Protection of Privacy and Transborder Flows of Personal Data (OECD Privacy Guidelines), 82

habeas data (Argentina), 114–117
Handbook of Information Security Management, 166
Health Information Act, Alberta, Canada, 108
Health Insurance Portability and Accountability Act (HIPAA), 38–46
compliance requirements, 154
criminal and civil penalties, 45–46
interrelation between Security and Privacy Rules, 44–45
privacy and security rule, 136–137
Privacy Rule, 40–41
Security Rule, 41–44
Standard Transactions Rule, 40
Hickman v. Taylor, 193

India, privacy laws, 120–121
individual participation principle, OECD Privacy Guidelines, 85
Information Systems Audit and Control Association (ISACA), 190

In re Eli Lilly & Co., 65–68, 137, 139–141, 172–174
Insurance companies, state regulations, 77
internal audit, 189–190
internal information, 159
internal privacy policies, 161–162
International Covenant on Civil and Political Rights, UN text, 82
International Guide to Cyber Security (OECD), 83, 174
International legal framework, 81–127
internet advertising, state regulations, 77–78
Internet service providers (ISPs), 50–54
In the Matter of GeoCities, 64
In the Matter of Guess?, Inc. and Guess.com, 66, 173
In the Matter of Microsoft Corporation, 67–68
In the Matter of The National Research Center for College and University Admissions, Inc., et al, 65
Israel, privacy laws, 127–128

Japan, privacy laws, 121–123
jurisdictional differences, privacy plans, 154–155

Katz v. United States, 12
Kent Corp. v. NLRB, 193
key performance indicators (KPI), privacy plans, 179

Law for Regulating Credit Information Companies (LRCIC), Mexico, 110, 112

managers, line and middle-level, training for privacy plans, 177
message authentication codes (MACs), 199
Mexican E-commerce Law, 110–112

Mexico, privacy laws, 110–114
Microsoft Passport case, 173
Middle East and Africa, privacy laws, 127–128
multinational laws, treaties, and agreements, 82–105

National Association of State Auditors, Controllers and Treasurers (NASACT), 187–190
National Strategy to Secure Cyberspace, 187
New Zealand, privacy laws, 127
Nonpublic personal information (NPI), 20–23
notice and consent language, privacy plans, 184

O'Connoe v. Ortega, 14
OECD Guidelines for the Security of Information Systems and Networks: Towards a Culture of Security, 83
one-way hash functions, 198
openness principle, OECD Privacy Guidelines, 85
operational personnel, training for privacy plans, 177
Organisation for Economic Co-operation and Development (OECD), 82–87
  privacy guidelines
    basic principles of international application, 85–86
    basic principles of national application, 84–85
    international cooperation, 86
    national implementation, 86

packet sniffer, 201
Paraguay, privacy laws, 117
passwords, 200
People's Republic of China and Hong Kong, privacy laws, 119–120

Personal Data (Privacy) Ordinance, Hong Kong, 119–120
Personal Data Protection Act, Argentina, 115–117
Personal Information Protection and Electronic Documents Act (PIPEDA), 107–109
Personal Information Protection (PIP), India, 121–123
personally identifiable information (PII), 133
political and cultural expectations, privacy, 156
political privacy, 12
polygraphs, state regulations, 74–76
pretexting, GLBA enforcement, 31–32
privacy
  comprehensive enterprise-wide approach, 139–141
  impact of laws, regulations, principles, standards, and guidelines, 138–139
  interrelation with security, 136–137
  legal considerations and risks, 152–156
  risk assessment and gap analysis, 149–152
Privacy Act, Australia, 125–127
Privacy Act, Canada, 106
Privacy Act, New Zealand, 127
Privacy Act of 1974, 11, 15–17
Privacy Commissioner, 81
privacy plan
  assessment by senior officers and directors, 145–146
  compliance, 147
  compliance and audits, 184–194
  compliance requirements with laws, regulations, and standards, 152–154
  confidential and proprietary information and due diligence, 155–156
  contracts and nondisclosure agreements, 155

data classification, 157–161
development of, 141–160
enforcement and reporting, 194–196
governance structure, 142–149
implementation, 147
implementation and science & technology, 171–205
internal controls, 146
jurisdictional differences, 154–155
main policy elements, 161–165
monitoring policy, 180–184
personnel involved in, 149
policies and procedures, 160–161
political and cultural expectations, 156
practical tips, 164–165
procedures, 165
reviewing and updating, 165–168
technological considerations, 196–205
training, 175–179
privacy policies, state regulations on, 78–79
privacy programs, plan, policies and procedures, 133–168
Privacy Rule, GLBA enforcement, 31
Protection of Privacy Laws, Israel, 127–128
public information, 159
publicly available information, 21
purpose specification principle, OECD Privacy Guidelines

random number generators, 199
reporting, state regulations on, 78
reporting requirements for audits, 190
Republic of Korea (South Korea), privacy laws, 123–124
Republic of South Africa, privacy laws, 128
Republic of Turkey, privacy laws, 128

restricted information, 159
right to anonymity in public expression, 12
right to be alone, 12
risk-based privacy plans, 135
Roe v. Wade, 12

Safeguards Rule, GLBA enforcement, 31
Safe Harbor Agreement, U.S./EU, 94–97, 157
  Privacy Principles, 95–96
Seal Programs, 71–72
secret information, 158
security, interrelation with privacy, 136–137
Security Breach Information Act, 78
Security Breach Information Act (SB 1386), California, 195
security safeguards principle, OECD Privacy Guidelines, 85
Singapore, privacy laws, 124–125
smart cards, 201
Social Security numbers, state regulations, 74
specific industries, state regulations, 76–78
State attorneys general actions and case rulings, 78–79
State legal landscape, 72–79
symmetric key encryption, 197–198
system administrators and computer security incident response teams, training for privacy plans, 176–177
system logging, 204

technical employees, training in software and equipment for privacy plan, 176
Telecommunications Act 1997, Australia, 126
telemarketing, state regulations, 77
Telemarketing Sales Rule (TSR), 71

Telephone Consumer Protection
Act (TCPA), 70–71
top secret information, 158
trade secrets, 54–58, 59–62
TRUSTePRIVACY Program, 72

U. S. laws and regulations, 15–63
U. S. legal framework, 11–80
U. S. Regulatory action, 63–76
Federal Trade Commission
(FTC), 63–69
unclassified information, 159
Uniform Trade Secrets Act
(UTSA), 59–62
determination of trade secrets,
60
reasonable efforts and
misappropriation, 60–61

remedies, 61–62
United Nations (UN), 82
*Universal Declaration of Human
Rights*, UN text, 82
Upjohn Co. v. United States, 193
USA PATRIOT Act, 167–168
use limitation principle, OECD
Privacy Guidelines

video rentals and sales, state
regulations, 76

Warren, Samuel, 12
Whalen v. Roe, 13
workplace privacy, 13–15
work product privilege audits,
193